James

Oliver

Curwood

JAMES OLIVER CURWOOD

God's Country and the Man

Judith A. Eldridge

Bowling Green State University Popular Press
Bowling Green, OH 43403

Library of Congress Catalogue Card No.: 92-74542

ISBN: 0-87972-604-0 Clothbound
        0-87972-605-9 Paperback

Cover design by Laura Darnell-Dumm

To James Oliver Curwood

and to lovers of nature the world over

Acknowledgements

I wish to express my appreciation to those who have helped make this book possible. First and foremost are my family who have listened to me expound about James Oliver Curwood for many years, and have been patient with me during all my research and writing. My sister and brother-in-law, Ruth and David Whaley, provided me a quiet place to begin putting my material into book form. Ivan Conger, a real Curwood afficionado and collector of Curwood memorabilia, gave me invaluable help. Then there are the librarians—at the Bentley Historical Library in Ann Arbor, and at libraries across the country and in Canada, and especially Irene Schechter at the Library of Michigan who guided me in my research, and Owosso Public Library, where I was allowed to lug home those huge volumes of the old Owosso Evening Argus to read late into the night. There are the friends and acquaintances of Curwood who granted me interviews—and even those who refused to talk about Curwood, for they gave me insight into the complexity of Curwood's character. People from all over the country responded to my letters seeking information.

And a posthumous thank you to the late Carlotta Curwood Tate, who opened her home and her heart and memories to me. I hope she will be pleased with what I have written about her father.

Contents

Foreword

Where does it all begin, this urge to write? Is it in the genes? Does it begin there in the womb, this need to tell stories, to communicate, to reveal our thoughts, our dreams or imaginings?

Or is it all acquired? Does it come with the influences around us—family, friends, the place or places we live, how we're brought up, the events that occur to shape our lives? If so, why us?

Another thing, if it is in the genes, why is one child born a writer and not his or her siblings? Are we all born with this same ability that develops in some and not in others?

If it is genes, why did James Oliver Curwood, fourth of four children, become famous and rich, while his brother ineptly failed in one business after another, and his two sisters lived ordinary lives?

And if it is environment, still why Jim and not the others? Other than being the last child, and therefore doted on, Jim Curwood had the same upbringing his brother and sisters had. He experienced the same degree of genteel poverty, the same rural and semi-rural life, the same circle of family.

Yet Jim daydreamed and, more importantly, began writing down his daydreams on paper almost as soon as he knew how to write the words. His older sister, Amy, was his mentor, his encouragement, but there is no indication that she ever attempted to write anything herself. His brother Ed remains, in the history of this family, a rather nondescript entity, remembered mainly as being "very homely." His sister Cora was slow-witted.

Curwood's parents, too, were ordinary people; that is, Abby was fun-loving, plump, poor in health, her youngest son's ideal of saintly womanhood, but noted mainly as being a good friend and neighbor. His father, a stern-visaged little Englishman, was revered, though not quite as warmly as his wife, honest but hardly a success.

Jim was born in the last quarter of the 19th century in a small Midwestern city, more a town than a city, and on the wrong side of the tracks. Nevertheless, he said of his hometown later, when he could afford to choose anywhere he wanted to live, that it was the nicest place he knew. "I was born here and I want to die here," he wrote in the forward of one of his books. He did die there, though in between there were many sojournings to various places, including the wilds of then little explored parts of northern and western Canada, and towards the last, Europe.

Certainly wives and children had no influence on his choice of career for he was already headed down the pathway of authorship when he married Cora Leon Johnson, and had become rather well established by the time he married

1

Ethel Greenwood. Neither could have deterred him in the slightest from his writing and, indeed, it was his dedication to his craft that caused the divorce from Leon—he admitted this later—and many of the storms in his life with Ethel (though difference of temperaments, it must be admitted, figured strongly in both marriages).

No, James Oliver Curwood was born to write. It was the only goal he ever had in life. It *was* his life. It mattered not what his fellow townsmen thought of it, writing was the only thing he wanted to do.

And he was ambitious. He wanted to succeed, to make money, to be known. He did all that.

When he died at age forty-nine, he was considered the highest paid—per word—writer in the world. His stories and books were published in the best magazines of the day and by the finest publishing houses, and were eagerly awaited and devoured by the multitudes. They were printed in many languages, and in Braille, of which he was extremely proud. His stories flashed across the silver screen with his name always in large letters.

His last illness and death were front page news across the country, and noted with sadness around the world. Men high up in the literary and movie worlds, businessmen, lonely trappers near the Arctic Circle, the governor of his state, lovers of nature and readers of his stories everywhere all paused to remember him as their friend.

No one else in his family rated anything of similar nature. They were known and endeared only by and to their neighbors, or as Jim Curwood's family, their deaths duly recorded no further than the county line.

Most of them lie side by side in the family plot. Jim lies there with them.

Chapter 1

On a late summer day in 1914, two horsemen crested a ridge and looked down into a small cup of a valley encircled by hills, with the snow-capped peaks of the Canadian Rockies beyond.

Each man viewed the scene with a common goal but differing thoughts.

Jack Otto, long, lean and muscled, with a huge handlebar mustache and keen searching eyes, sat hunched over in his saddle, a mountaineer born and raised in the splendor of these mountains. He scanned the valley and the surrounding slopes and tested the wind, seeking some sight or sound of the wounded grizzly he and his companion were trailing.

"We'll find him in there," he said, pointing to the aspens along the creek that ran through the center of the valley.

His companion was a "city" man, but he was no stranger to the wilderness. Smaller than Otto and slight of build, his brown hair was marked by a white streak over his right temple, and his newly-grown neat beard was tinged with red.

James Oliver Curwood sat upright in his saddle, thrilled, as always, by the beauty and ruggedness of any wild place. He, too, scanned the valley below, but his thoughts were of more than the bear. His writer's senses took note of the rainbow of wildflowers across the green meadow—purples and blues, pinks and yellows, blended with the cream of mountainspray and strewn amid the green grass as though painted with abandon by some surrealistic painter. He sniffed the air, sweet with the scent of wild roses and tangy wild onion drifting up from the banks of the stream. A soft breeze brushed his cheeks, and he marveled at the diamond drops left sparkling on the meadow grass by an early morning rain.

Near his ear a bee droned. The leaves on a nearby bush rustled, and a raven called harshly from a tree ahead. He could hear the little grunts and whistles of gophers or tiny rock rabbits making their way over the rocks, and the faint trill of the rapids in the stream below.

A mountain bird sweetened the air with its morning song, and overhead, against the backdrop of snowcapped mountains and craggy peaks, an eagle circled and dipped, looking for its breakfast.

Jim thought of the bear, too, of course, a record-breaker, if he was any judge of grizzlies—and he had hunted many of them—and of the stories he might write of this latest of his adventures in the wild.

It was a glorious day.

Before dawn that morning a sudden mountain storm, gone almost as

3

quickly as it had come, had left everything in their camp drenched and had given Jim a chance for some good-natured ribbing of his guide.

"Fine day tomorrow," Jack had said as they'd yawned before the supper fire the evening before. "Look how white the snow is on the peaks." Jim had laughed.

Drying out around their pre-dawn fire this morning, Jim had grumbled in mock irritation, "Yeah, fine day." But now, because of that shower, the music of the mountain stream seemed louder, the landscape more green and lush, the wildflowers taller and richer even than the day before.

Jack and his brothers had guided Jim before; three times, in fact. Only two years before Bruce Otto and Jim had hunted in a mountain valley where Jim had shot three huge black bears within a half hour.

This time, though, they were deeper into unknown country than ever before. They might be the first men other than Indians to gaze at this valley, Jim thought. The idea heightened his enjoyment of the day.

The hunting camp they had left behind lay in a valley much like the one they looked down into now. Besides Jim and Jack, there were two camp men, a dozen or so bear dogs, and more than a dozen horses, their tents and the various accoutrements of camping in a wilderness.

And there was Jim's beautiful wife, Ethel, almost as good a woodsman as her husband.

The tents had been set up and armfuls of balsam boughs cut for beds, the pack horses unloaded of the provisions necessary for weeks of travel beyond the reach of supplies, and a wild sheep shot for camp meat.

"Bighorn Camp," they'd named it, and cut into the bark of a tree that it was "100 miles on way to Heaven."

Jack and Jim had then sat down side by side to glass the slopes around them, Jack with his Civil War telescope and Jim with his imported French binoculars. They were watching several mountain goats clamber about the steep slopes when Jack nudged Jim and pointed out a huge bear digging out gophers above a rock slide.

They had set out immediately with the wind in their favor, Jack stopping at a coulee while Jim climbed down one side and up the other to get within range of the bear. Jim had shot but he was at a disadvantage. He knew, though, that he'd wounded the bear at least once, but it had been too late in the day to start tracking it. Better to wait until morning.

So they'd risen early—earlier than they'd intended, due to that early morning storm. Jim had baked the bannock and fried the sheep steaks while Jack saddled the horses and put several days' provisions on one pack horse. They'd left the dogs behind with the two camp men and Ethel.

Then they had set out through the wet grass on horseback, Jack in the lead, the pack horse trailing behind Jim, determined to stay on the trail until they got the bear. Jim left behind instructions that if he and Jack weren't back in two days, one of the men should follow with the dogs.

It was up to Jack, as guide, to do the tracking, and to figure out what the bear might do and where it might go. Jim was free to look around, to take note of the country and study the trail, and to ask questions. The Otto brothers were an unlimited source of information about the mountains, the way of wild things, of camping and hunting, and Jim had an untiring curiosity and thirst for knowledge.

Now Jim's blood was warm with the thrill of the hunt for the huge grizzly. He listened, storing it away for later when he would be at his typewriter, as Jack pointed out where the bear had first waded in deep pools of cold water and then lay all night in a clay wallow to soothe the pain of his wound, and where he'd eaten a mixture of kinnikinnic, soap berries and spruce and balsam needles, and licked fresh pitch from a jackpine as a tonic for the wound beginning to fester inside him.

The bear was not in the valley before them, and the two men went on over the next ridge. For days they trailed it, and twice more Jim wounded it, but again the shots were not fatal. The dogs were brought up, and twice they closed with the bear who fought them off and left a trail of dead and broken dogs behind him as he escaped. Finally, Jim ordered the dogs tied up.

Jim was still confident. He'd been hunting since he was a boy. The walls of his home were hung with the heads of moose, deer, bear and wild sheep. After all, wasn't he the superior of any four-legged animal, even this giant grizzly?

The chase led them, sometimes on horseback and sometimes afoot, over crags and along goat paths, and down into beautiful little valleys, across wild jumbles of rock slides, and through thickets and streams.

Once they came across the mangled body of a black bear lying in blood-soaked grass. "Killed in a fight with another bear," Jack said, "maybe your grizzly." The ground was trampled and torn up around the body, branches and bushes snapped off. Strips of hide and pieces of flesh and red splotches of blood left signs of the struggle that were easy to read. Jim got out his notebook and began writing, asking questions of Jack and picturing in his mind what must have happened as the two giants of the mountains fought. He wrote long after Jack grew restless, eager to get on with the hunt.

They mounted at last and rode on, Jim still marveling at the might of the grizzly. It had stopped to fight the black bear—over a kill of a caribou, Jack had surmised—but never once had the bear become the aggressor in his struggle to elude his hunters, except, of course, when the dogs had tried to corner him. Always he ran before them in an effort to escape.

The question began to seep into Jim's mind—who was really the greater, man who pursued so relentlessly with murder in his heart, or the bear, wounded and sick, who labored to avoid the fight?

Walking along a ledge one day, beneath an overhanging cliff, he'd come across a bone, "heavy as iron." It looked like part of the vertebrae of some giant animal, a whale perhaps, left here when this part of the world had been an ocean long before the mountains were formed. How long had it lain there, he wondered. How many centuries, how many millenia had come and gone since the ocean had dried up, leaving this bone beached and forgotten? Generations, even civilizations, had passed. Am I so significant after all, he had wondered. How important is one single person in the greater scheme of things?

This trip had brought many new thoughts into Jim's mind. A waster, a spoiler, a wanton killer, that's what he'd been all of his life. Those three bears he'd killed two years before, for instance. He'd snuffed out how many years of life—a hundred or more?—in a matter of minutes. A flicker of shame shot through him whenever he thought of it.

Then one morning Jim climbed alone up the side of a slope to look over into the valley on the other side, hoping to spot the bear, but what he saw was the splendor of the Canadian Rockies. Breathing in the perfume of the August day, he felt the soft cool breeze on his face and gloried in the magnificance of the scene, his gun held forgotten in his hands.

He felt all-powerful, that he should have come to this point on earth with all that God had created spread out for his enjoyment, and at the same time insignificant, a tiny speck in the universe.

Climbing higher, he came to a sheer wall with a ledge running along its side, and followed the ledge until he came to a jumble of rock from a recent slide. The rock was rough and he slipped and fell. Reaching out to catch himself, his gun struck a sharp rock. Jim rubbed his knee, injured in a fall two years before and twisted now in this near fall, and surveyed the damage to his gun. It was shattered, useless, but he counted himself lucky that it was only his gun that had been damaged.

Sitting there on a rock, Jim surveyed the scene spread out before him, and again, for a moment, the hunt was forgotten, his senses alive only to the glory of the day and the scene before him. He took out his pipe and lit it, settling down to enjoy the moment. How many years had the valley lain there peacefully, roused only by the drama of nature, peopled only by the creatures of the wild?

Lost in thought, the clicking sound coming along the ledge behind him came slowly into his consciousness, but then he knew instantly what it was— the click of a bear's toenails on hard rock.

He turned, and found himself looking at a great grizzly, barring the ledge and the way to safety.

Jim's heart seemed to stop. A low moan, almost soundless, escaped him. He could see wounds in the bear's shoulder and foreleg, a crease through the hair along its back that could only have been made by a bullet. It was his bear, it had to be; they were the only hunters in these mountains. Then the realization of his danger drove all else from his mind.

"Oh, God," he cried in a low moan, "Please, God, no!"

The bear rose on its hind legs, staring down from its enormous height for a few seconds at the man below him, seeming to recognize him as the creature that had brought such pain, and finding him insignificant after all. Even in his fright Jim marveled at the magnificence of the animal, its coat glistening in the sunlight, its massive bulk towering over him.

Dropping down on all fours again, the bear's great head swung slowly from side to side, its breath stirring the dust at Jim's feet. There was no escape except over the side of the ledge, a drop of at least a hundred feet. Death was surely inevitable.

And then—the bear turned! With bared lips it gave a last look over its shoulder, a low growl rumbling from deep in its wounded chest, and disappeared back the way it had come, the click of its claws ringing clear on the hard rock, growing fainter as it made its way down the ledge.

It had all taken less than a minute. Death had come—and gone!

Still trembling, Jim gazed uncomprehendingly at the empty ledge. The bear had not attacked. Why? It had no way of knowing the gun at his side was useless, that it was no longer in danger from this thing which had already brought it great pain. Still shaken, hardly able to believe his escape from death, Jim made his way back to where he'd left his horse, a different man than the one who had set out that morning.

"We're going back," he told Jack when they met back at their temporary camp. "We'll move north in the morning, go on up into the Yukon as we'd planned."

"The bear...?" Jack asked in puzzlement.

"Let him go," Jim said.

* * *

The story of the bear was an exciting tale, but this account of it may be no nearer the truth than James Oliver Curwood's final version that appeared as *The Grizzly King*.

Certainly his wife Ethel did not appear in his story, even though she was with him on the trip to British Columbia. A bear cub captured on an earlier trip and kept as a camp pet became instead a companion of the wounded grizzly. Jim would weave into the story the bear's mating with a female, though it hardly seems reasonable a wounded bear would have time for that with two men trailing it. The fight of the black bear may have happened— sometime—but more likely on another trip. He may have only heard about such bear fights, but his account of it, like all of his writings about Canadian scenes and wildlife, is too vivid to have come entirely from hearsay.

8 James Oliver Curwood

James Oliver Curwood was a storyteller, a writer with a gargantuan imagination. Like many writers, he took incidents in his own life and others' and turned them into stories. Certainly he traveled a great deal in Canada, particularly in the more remote places. He saw and heard much that was to him greatly interesting.

The basic incident of the bear seems to have been true. Jim Curwood came back from this hunt a changed man, not violently so, but with some quite different views about wildlife. He came back pledged to its conservation rather than its destruction.

In the meantime, however, he had a career to pursue. When Ray Long, editor of *The Red Book Magazine*, and his wife Pearl came up from Chicago to visit the Curwoods in December, Jim told the story to his friend. Ray's trip to Owosso was a mix of business and pleasure. He had come primarily to talk about Jim's latest novel, soon to be serialized in *Red Book*. The fact that an editor came to Jim, rather than the other way around, was a sign of Jim's growing stature as a writer. The visit was also one of pleasure, for Jim and Ray and their wives had become close friends.

Ray was enthused over the story of the bear, so much so that when he returned to Chicago he had several conferences with the editors of *Red Book* and its companion magazines, *The Blue Book* and *The Green Book*.

"We are all so enthusiastic over that bear story that we are going to agree to your suggestion that you send the new novel to the East and let us count on the bear story," he wrote Jim the next day. The new novel, which Jim had just completed, was *The Hunted Woman*, a story set amidst the building of the Yellowhead Highway in British Columbia, where Jim and Ethel had spent three weeks two years before.

"I am giving it up with a pang," Ray wrote, "but I believe the *Red Book* is going to gain a better story in the bear story."

"The Grizzly King" ran January through June 1916 in *Red Book*, adding to Jim's fame as a writer of nature stories but without quite the success of his earlier story of a dog, "Kazan." The story was published in book form later that year by Doubleday, Page & Co.

In the meantime, Jim's transformation from killer to savior of wildlife was well underway.

Chapter 2

James Oliver Curwood was 36 when he met the wounded bear on the mountain ledge. Had he died there, his death would have been reported across the United States and Canada, in all of Europe and in Australia, all places where his books were eagerly read. The news would have been met with sadness, but there would have been a few people who believed it a hoax, a publicity stunt, until proven otherwise. After all, a report of his death in the wilds ten years before had been in error, and, like Jack London and Mark Twain before him, considered a ploy to gain attention.

James Oliver Curwood did not die that day; he had, in fact, 13 years yet to live and 19 more books to write.

In order to understand James Oliver Curwood, and what brought him to this mountain on the trail of the bear, and the depth of change this incident with a bear made in him, and its significance, and, in fact, in order to understand James Oliver Curwood at all, it is necessary to understand the time and the places in which he grew up and the people in his life.

He was born June 12, 1878, in Owosso, Michigan.

The small city of Owosso lies 80 miles northwest of Detroit, along the banks of the Shiawassee River. Shiawassee is an Indian name, given it by the Chippewas who roamed along its banks and through its forests before the settlers came. The name means, variously, "sparkling waters," which is, or was, apt, or the "straight-ahead river," more readily accepted but less accurate since the river winds like a snake from its beginnings in lower Michigan to where it empties into Saginaw Bay and thus into Lake Huron, one of the five Great Lakes.

In the spring the river is lusty and brawling, full of ice floes and swollen with the runoff of melted snow from the land along its banks. Come summer, the river becomes lethargic, shrinking in width and depth, hardly moving in the summer heat. Autumn's splash of color and heavy rains give the river new life; red and yellow leaves, dropped from the maples and oaks and birches along its banks, swirl and eddy in the current. Winter locks the river under a coat of ice. In some places, the banks are sloping and grassy; in others, they are high and graveled.

The river was an important part of Jim Curwood's life.

The land through which the Shiawassee flows is mainly farmland, flat fertile fields with white houses and red barns and shade trees in the yards and gardens out back, and pastures dotted with cows and horses, sheep and pigs.

There are many small towns along the river's banks, most with a dam or two, the water slack above and quick below.

The river was there long before the towns, of course, or the cows or sheep or barns or houses or farmers on their plows, or even the Chippewa Indians. It was carved out by the great glacier that crept down over the American continent and then crept back again into oblivion, leaving gouges and scratches that seeped full of water.

Owosso's first settler arrived in 1836, the year before Michigan Territory became a state, and built a log cabin along the riverbank. Others followed, and the settlement quickly grew, with the usual small shops and businesses along Main Street and up and down Washington Street. From the main corners, Washington Street led north to the finer homes of the city and south to the mineral springs that became, for a time, the city's claim to fame, as far as tourism went. The springs had the usual bathhouses and hotels and doctors to serve those who came for treatments. If the springs didn't do the trick, it was at least "on the way to the cemetery," as one writer of the day put it, a very fine cemetery indeed, at the top of the hill out of which the springs flowed.

There were many small Michigan towns with mineral springs and doctors and bathhouses, and the proliferation of them soon diluted this business so that the city fell back on its original purpose as a business center for the farmers and small villages around it.

By 1878, when James Oliver Curwood was born, all this juggling for position, the tug and pull of original inhabitants and newcomers, the quick rise and fall as a resort had already taken place, and the city had settled down to what it still is today, a pleasant spot along a sparkling river.

There was only one dam then, but it held back a sufficient amount of water to allow pretty little sailboats and a small sturdy steamboat and numerous skiffs to ply up and down its waters. There was already the division of old inhabitants who lived in the big houses north of Main Street, most of whom were merchants, doctors, lawyers and the town fathers, from the rest of the town—respectable tradesmen and merchants' employees down to the usual rubble and rabble of any town.

Owosso is a place of wide, regular streets, shaded by huge elms and maples, hickory and walnut trees. The streets then were mires of mud in the springtime, dusty avenues in the summer, white with snow in winter, and, in autumn, drowned in scarlet and gold leaves.

In 1878, there were hotels and restaurants, an opera house, churches of nearly every denomination, and schools, livery stables, blacksmith and cobbler shops, millinery shops, boarding houses, a boot factory and emporiums where almost anything could be purchased from overalls to face cream and sugar, pickles out of a barrel, cheese, chicken feed and wash tubs. There was a coal mine along the river at the end of Shiawassee Street, fairgrounds on the east between Williams and Exchange streets and a tannery down on Comstock Street. A mill race served the woolen and flour mills and other industries downtown.

Owosso had a volunteer fire department, and two newspapers.

There were also saloons, of course, quite a few of them, a town drunk or two, and a few ladies of the night. There was an orphanage in town and a poor farm out of town.

In other words, Owosso was a typical Midwestern town approaching the last quarter of the 19th century.

The river split the city in two from southeast to northwest, and two bridges held the city together. Several railroads ran through the city, linking it to the rest of the world.

The population, in 1878, was about 3,000 people.

Owosso also had a sort of second town, aptly called "West Town," out towards the city's western limits where Main Street was bisected by the Jackson, Lansing and Saginaw Rail Way tracks.

Unlike bustling downtown, West Town was almost rural, and except for the comings and goings of the trains, life was slow and simple. There were a few small businesses, a handle factory, a few houses and a grove of trees over by the river. A row of hickory trees ran down the center of Main Street. There was even the smell of country—dust and barnyards, newly sawn wood and oozing pitch from the handle factory, trees and horses.

Cocks crowed in the morning, chickens clucked contentedly as they scratched in the yards, cows lowed from backyard pens at milking time, and horses whinnied and stamped in the barns. Saws and shapers whined and whirred at the handle factory. Men called across the street to each other, women gossiped over their clotheslines and children whooped and hollered at play. Barking dogs were everywhere.

In summer, the clip-clop of horses' hooves, the creak of wagon wheels, and the sing-song whir of buggy wheels sounded up and down Main Street. Dust rose up in little swirls behind horses' hooves and hung in trails behind the buggies and drays.

In winter, everything was muffled by snow.

Winter or summer, after sundown everything was quiet. Except for the trains, of course.

The heart of West Town was the railroad junction, two blocks south of Main Street, on the very edge of town, where the tracks of the Michigan Central and the Detroit, Grand Haven and Milwaukee railroads, running east and west, crossed those of the J, L & S, running north and south. Trains came in at all hours, smelly and noisy. They whistled as they came in, belching smoke and ashes, with brakes squealing, steam gushing and swirling around the wheels, fireman and engineer waving and calling out to the crowd at the station. The trains whistled their departures, straining to get up speed, wheels clacking in slow rhythm and then turning faster, steam spurting, fireman and engineer too busy now to wave and call out.

The trains came in filled with boxes and trunks, with visitors and drummers and townspeople returning to glad cries of welcome, and went away with more boxes and trunks, and with tears and waving handkerchiefs and filled order books.

The junction was a place of excitement for small boys.

In between trains, the river, only a couple of blocks away, drew boys like a magnet. They fished in it and swam in it, paddled their boats and canoes on its shimmering surface, sat along its banks to dream during lazy summer days, camped out on its small island, pretending to be pioneers or Indians or explorers, and skated on its winter ice.

West Town was a busy, bustling, yet unhurried kind of place.

That was the kind of place and the kind of time in which James Oliver Curwood's life began.

He was born on a Wednesday in June in the family living quarters in back of his father's cobbler shop on Main Street in West Town, the fourth and last child of Abigail Griffin Curwood, a plump little woman with a sense of humor, and James Moran Curwood, a small, neat, reserved Englishman. Abby was 32, James 40 or 41. Amy, their oldest child, was 14, Cora ten and Ed nearly nine.

The family called the new baby Jimmy. They doted on him.

The Curwoods were a close family and this closeness extended beyond mother and father, brothers and sisters to aunts, uncles and cousins. Actually, it was the Griffins who made up Jimmy's large family, extending over him like an umbrella. Eventually it was Jim who held the umbrella over most of them, financially anyway.

The reason it was the Griffins and not the Curwoods was that James Moran Curwood was the only one of his family in America. His past was somewhat of a mystery. He said he had a family back in England—brothers and sisters who were looked after in the nursery by a nanny. There was the story that he had set out from home with a trunkful of white linen suits, twelve dollars in his pocket, headed for an uncle in Australia, and for some mysterious reason disembarked in New York, but whether this was true, or how much of it was true, no one seemed to know.

Two other facts about the Curwoods were known. James's mother was named Jane Shakespeare and was reportedly related to William Shakespeare, the famous playwright, and his uncle was Captain Frederick Marryat, a noted English writer of the mid-1800s. Not much else was known about the Curwoods.

There was enough family on Abby's side to make up for any scarcity of Curwoods.

Abigail Elizabeth Griffin was born September 12, 1845 (or perhaps 1846, records weren't very well kept in those days), in Penn Yan, New York. Her name has been spelled numerous ways. Her marriage certificate lists her as Abbey and in some places her name appears as Abbie, but she signed herself as Abigaile when applying for a widow's pension in 1919. Mostly she was known as Abby. She was the second of ten children.

The Griffins were a large, boisterous and sometimes cantankerous family. They moved from New York to northern Ohio in 1850, and eventually on to Michigan, all but John, a year or so older than Abby, who stayed on in Ohio.

After Abby came Lydia Jane, called Jane; these sisters were very close. Next came Ellen, or Helen, then Adelbert, known as Delbert or Del, and then Charles and Frances. Frances became known as Aunt Frankie, the "hot shot" of the family. She, too, was close to Abby.

Next came Amy for whom buying a pair of shoes led to romance and marriage for Abby.

The last of the Griffens were Sidney and Lila. Lila's was the fatal romance story in the Griffin family, and it was probably the part her family played in her tragedy that helped them earn some notoriety as a "mean bunch."

Add to these the relatives by marriage, and the ensuing cousins, and it adds up to a large family. They all visited back and forth, went on picnics, hunted and fished together, were a source of news both good and bad, and of gossip, and, oftentimes, of exasperation.

Abby's great-great-grandmother was said to have been a full-blooded Mohawk princess and very beautiful. She was wed by a Dutch adventurer, this fact in itself more or less attesting to her beauty and virtue since such adventurers usually overlooked marriage in their romantic liaisons. By the time it reached Jim the strain of Indian blood was pretty well diluted, but he was fascinated by this bit of Indian heritage. The streak of white that developed in his hair was said to be inherited from this Indian grandmother.

The Griffens settled in the small town of Wakeman in northern Ohio where Abby's grandfather had a cooperage. Abby and James met when Abby took her small sister Amy to the new cobbler in Wakeman, James Curwood, for a pair of shoes. Romance flowered and Abby and James were married December 12, 1862 in nearby Norwalk, Ohio, by Justice of the Peace E. A. Pray, Jr.

Amy Moran Curwood—there were a lot of Amys in the family, which sometimes becomes very confusing—was born January 5, 1864. Abby's little sister Amy, she whose new shoes had brought Abby and James together, died that year. In March 1865, with the Civil War on, James enlisted in Company B, 5th Ohio Volunteer Cavalry, but he became ill and was soon discharged.

Cora Alice was born April 10, 1868.

Charles Edward was born August 12, 1869.

By this time Abby's family had moved to Michigan and settled in the small village of Chesaning. Abby and James soon followed as far as Owosso, thirteen miles to the south, where James set up his cobbler's shop in West Town.

James was a good cobbler but a poor businessman. He made new shoes to order, put new heels and lasts on old boots and shoes, sold a few related goods, and spent quiet hours. There was never very much money in the Curwood household, but they were a happy and contented family.

The family settled down in the rooms behind the cobbler shop. The nearby train took them north to Chesaning to visit Abby's folks now and then, or a few miles further to the small village of St. Charles where they went fishing and camping.

When Jimmy was born in 1878, the little family was complete. Abby had grown a bit plump. This last birth had not been easy and she was often in poor health from then on, but she was a jolly person, taking ill health in stride. She and James were much of a size—short. James was only five foot four, Abby a little less than that. Both had light brown hair and blue eyes. James was a neat and spare man and, in later life anyway, sported a small goatee.

James was apparently never called "Jim," and for purposes of clarity, "James" is James Moran, the father, and "Jim" is James Oliver, the son.

Amy was much like her mother, brown-haired, blue-eyed and comely. She was rounded; this bit of plumpness would stay with her. She, too, liked to have a good time. Amy was intelligent, also like her mother, and she would later channel her energies into encouraging her youngest brother's talents.

Cora was different. She was slow-witted, it was true, but perhaps smarter than most people gave her credit for. Cora was dependable, and likeable, with her twinkling eyes, and untidy, which aggrieved her younger brother after he'd become fastidious in his own clothes.

Ed was homely. There was no other way to put it. He was thin and gangly, awkward and shy. He tried, but he seldom succeeded in doing things well.

Jimmy was the baby, a handsome blond little boy, doted on by his parents and his big sister Amy, who acted as a second mother to him. He was quick and intelligent and loving. He didn't like teasing, especially when he was the one being teased. He looked up to his big brother Ed and loved his sister Cora in spite of her different ways. The family spoiled him dreadfully.

There was apparently little or no rivalry between these disparate siblings, for they left behind no slightest hint of anything other than fondness and goodwill.

In the first years after Jimmy Curwood was born, West Town and the river and his family were his world. What more could a small boy want?

Chapter 3

Milton "Jack" Gaylord arrived in Owosso in 1880. He was employed by the Michigan Central Railroad, transferred up from Jackson near where he'd grown up. Jack—no one ever called him Milton—was a handsome man and a spiffy dresser. Eventually he came into James' shop for shoes and met Amy, who was helping her father in his shop. It was almost like James and Abby all over again.

Amy and Jack were married by the Rev. T. S. Leonard, a Baptist minister, on December 5, 1883, a month before Amy's twentieth birthday. Jack was 27.

Jack's background, like James', was another mystery. He was brought up in Eaton Rapids, a small town south of Lansing, Michigan, by Augustus Gaylord, postmaster, strict temperance man and abolitionist, and his wife, Mary. There were a number of children in the Gaylord family; Jack was a sort of adopted son. About the time Jack and Amy were married, a woman named Virginia Smith came to live with them. This was Jack's real mother who, it was said, had run away from her well-to-do West Virginia family to marry—or maybe she didn't marry—a sailor, and then Jack had been born. She had somehow given him over to the Gaylords to raise. Now she was a "widow" and had come to live with her son. Granny Smith soon became a favorite, especially of the children, ready with cookies and other treats.

As for Jack, his upbringing in a strict household didn't dull his sense of humor or his love of fun. He found in Abby a kindred spirit, fond of pranks and jokes.

Jack and Amy's son, Ralph, was born in September of 1884. Jim was six. The two boys seemed more like cousins than uncle and nephew.

Jimmy had a friend his own age down at the junction at Miller House where the traveling men stayed. Charlie Miller was the son of the young proprietors, William and Julia. The boys watched the trains arrive and depart, teased Kate Russell, the Miller's handsome waitress, and played boyish pranks.

That same fall, in 1884, the Griffin family scandal broke. Abby's young sister Lila, then 18, ran off with a tall, blonde, handsome railroad man, a Catholic, of whom her family disapproved. The Griffins went after her and brought her home. The next May, Lila gave birth to a daughter, Golda Cecilia. Shortly afterward, the young husband was killed in a railroad accident. Lila took sick, and in July she died. The local newspaper, still calling her Lila Griffin, said she died of "quick consumption" but some folks claimed it was from grief. It was whispered, too, that the husband's family, well-to-do folks from Owosso named Clarke, wanted to take the baby, but Grandma Griffin would never let her go.

In the meantime, the little cobbler shop in West Town was not prospering. James and Abby decided to move back to Ohio. James and 15-year-old Ed went down to Ohio that winter to look for a farm in their old home area near Wakeman. The one they found, a few miles from Ceylon, was along a tree-lined, winding road, with a big white house, apple trees and a barn. Down the road at the corner was the red brick schoolhouse. They were close enough to Lake Erie to almost smell the lake from home.

It was a pleasant place with 40 acres of snow-covered fields. But in the spring, when the snow had melted, they discovered what lay beneath that concealing blanket of white—stones. When the great glaciers several millenia before had come down over the North American continent, and then receded, scooping out the Great Lakes and forming the hills and hollows of Michigan and the northern edges of its neighboring states, they had left behind along their trailing edges billions of small stones. Just before the last glacier dipped to form Lake Erie, it had dumped an especially generous portion of them on the land just below the lake. The Curwoods and their neighbors were reaping the harvest of this legacy.

For the next seven years, one of Jimmy's principal tasks was to pick up stones. He and Ed and their father picked them up and built fences. They put them in piles. They even managed to sell a few. And every turn of the plow or disk brought up more.

It was hot, dirty and stultifying work, picking up stones, and one of the best things that could have happened to Jim. It gave him time to think, and to dream. Many years later, in advising young people about what it takes to become a successful writer, Jim Curwood remembered the dreary task of picking up stones and said it built "character." Writing was like picking up stones, he said, putting words down one at a time and keeping at it, like picking up stones one at a time and building a fence.

During a youngster's seventh summer, though, it was merely hot, dusty, boring work.

In the spring of 1885, however, Abby, Jim and Cora were as yet unaware of what lay ahead as they boarded the train in West Town for their new home. James met them at the small station at Ceylon. Unlike Owosso, or even West Town, Ceylon was only a village—two stores, two saloons, a hotel, sawmill, post office, the small train station and a few houses. The slightly rolling countryside stretched away towards Lake Erie which they'd been able to see from the train windows now and then ever since Toledo. For Abby it was coming home, to six-year-old Jimmy it was a new adventure. The dirt roads, muddy and rutted from the springtime thaw, curved past fields and woodlots, farmhouses and barns. They came to Ogontz School where Jimmy would soon be spending his days, and at last drove up peaceful, curving Church Road to their own house.

The house was two-storied, painted white, with a porch on the front and apple trees along the west side. This was to be home for the Curwoods for most of the next six years.

Almost at once Jimmy found a new friend, a girl, older than himself. Jeanne Fisher from across the road took Jimmy under her wing from the very beginning. Blue-eyed Jeanne had a sprinkling of freckles across her nose, but most entrancing to Jimmy was her gold-brown hair. It would have a lasting effect upon the impressionable boy. His mother and sisters had long hair, pinned up or fastened in knots at the back of their heads. Jeanne, eleven when the Curwoods moved to Ohio, still let her hair hang loose and wavy or in a long braid that hung down her back.

Jim would scatter traces of Jeanne throughout the stories he wrote long after they had parted, especially in his heroines, all of whom had long, flowing tresses.

The two new friends spent hours together. He could talk to Jeanne, tell her his childish fantasies and his dreams. She listened and didn't laugh.

Clarence Hill, Jeanne's cousin, lived further up Church Road. The two boys quickly became pals. Clarence was "Skinny" and Jimmy was "Slip," short for "Slippery," because he was good at getting away with pranks.

And there was Jack, Jimmy's mongrel dog of indiscriminate heritage, who was a constant companion.

Those first summer days were spent playing with Skinny, talking to Jeanne, doing chores for his mother and, of course, picking up stones.

Golden, idyllic days, the years in Ohio, a prelude to growing up, days to treasure and remember fondly. Slip and Skinny scuffed down the road, lost in their boys' world, dust rising in little puffs about their bare feet and settling on their worn overalls. Jack trailed at their heels or ranged into the brush alongside the road, smelling out rabbits and gophers. Nearby Black's Woods held secret places where the boys could give their imaginations full rein, playing scouts and Indians or other games of adventure.

In the fall grapes hung in purple clusters and the trees everywhere were ablaze with color. Green-hulled black walnuts and hard-shelled hickory nuts dropped from branches overhead, and the boys picked them up by the basketsful and took them home to be shucked and later cracked for their mothers' winter baking.

When winter blanketed the countryside with snow, they coasted down the road, swerving out around the occasional cutter whose occupants, bundled up in robes with heated soapstones at their feet, waved and called out to them.

In spring they went barefoot as soon as the first dandelion had peeked up through the grass, the soft mud of the road squishing up between their bare toes.

"Happiness," Jim fondly recalled many years later, "meant merely to eat regularly and to keep warm." A trip to town, new clothes, a wedding or a new baby in the neighborhood were all exciting topics of conversation for days or even weeks.

James gave Jimmy a gun and he shot with abandon at birds and squirrels and rabbits. He and Ed roamed the woods, hunting. One day he shot at a squirrel and got two. It was just by chance, of course, but the local correspondent got hold of the story and wrote it up for the Sandusky paper. Sandusky was a big town, as big as Owosso, about twenty miles away along the Lake Erie shore. It was Jim's first hunting success, and his entry into the world of newspapers and fame.

On another day he shot a bluebird. It was not yet dead and he held it in the palm of his hand and watched the life pulse out of the tiny creature. Pride seeped away to be replaced by shame.

In the 1880s, itinerant preachers still roamed the country roads, traveling about by horse and buggy, setting up their tents and holding camp meetings, delivering their hell and brimstone religion. The Curwoods, like most of their neighbors, usually attended the meetings. At one of these tent meetings, not long after the Curwoods moved to Ohio, Jimmy was moved to "come forward" and declare his salvation. His religious fever was brief, and he soon reverted to a normal mischievous boy.

Jim Curwood's real religion, believed in nebulously as a child, and solidly and unequivocably as an adult, was nature. He came to believe that everything—trees, birds and animals, and even every blade of grass—has a soul.

As Slip and Skinny grew a little older they roamed further from home. Soon they knew every woods, every tree, every rock of the surrounding countryside. They fished in nearby Old Woman's Creek, which emptied into Lake Erie a few miles away. They built a raft of scraps of lumber salvaged from here and there and stored it in an abandoned barn along the creek, ready for the day they'd be brave enough to set sail. In the meantime, they pretended adventures and sometimes slept overnight in the barn.

Upstairs in his bedroom in the old farmhouse, Jimmy stored his treasures and read the boys' magazines of the day. His imagination was fired by the magazine stories and the play with Skinny. The long hours in the field, while his hands were busy picking up stones, his mind was free to dream his own adventures. When he was about nine, he took pencil in hand, and laboriously, on large squares cut from rough paper, and with many misspellings and much hard work, he wrote down these tales, not of the boyish happenings in his ordinary life, but of pirates and swashbuckling heroes.

He became a writer.

Later when he read his stories to his parents, James would nod his head and say, "Fine, Jimmy, fine," Abby smiling fondly at his side.

Adventures, real adventures more fascinating than his youthful mind could imagine, would come later.

Chapter 4

The teacher at Ogontz School, also called Four Corners School, was a nice portly lady of about 50 named Mrs. Bacon. Jimmy was an ordinary student, as well-behaved as can be expected of a boy with an active imagination and a normal amount of energy. He was neither one of the good children nor one of the bad ones—most of the time.

As in most country schools, Four Corners had a bully and one of his followers was Jimmy Curwood.

"I dare ya'," the bully whispered to Jimmy one day, and Jimmy proceeded to get into a fight with Mrs. Bacon. He "licked" her. Mrs. Bacon sat down on the floor and cried. Jimmy puffed up with pride but his elation lasted only until a member of the school board called on James and Abby.

One lesson was not enough. It hardly ever is. The second proved to be nearly disastrous. Abby had a small pistol, kept from the days when James had been away at war. One day Jimmy swiped it and took it to school. Raising his hand to be excused to go to the outhouse, his plan was to fire the gun behind the schoolhouse and scare Mrs. Bacon and his classmates. A better plan appeared.

Out of the schoolhouse came three giggling girls, also on their way to the outhouse. These girls were teacher's pets, and Jimmy didn't like them.

Each of us at some time or other is prompted by devilish impulse to do something daring. This was one of those times for Jim; he fired not in the air but at the outhouse where the three girls were ensconced.

The air erupted with screams, the outhouse door flew open and out ran the three girls in disarray. About the same time the schoolhouse door flew open and out poured Mrs. Bacon and the rest of the students. Mrs. Bacon, upset, frightened and angry, but with one hand firmly gripping Jimmy by the collar, sent Skinny running down the road to Dr. Benschoter's house for help. Appalled at the turn events were taking, Jimmy wrenched free from Mrs. Bacon's grip and headed across the fields for home.

There was no one there but Cora. "Mama's at Mrs. Vincent's," she told Jimmy. James and Ed were in the fields. Jimmy wasted no time putting together a few items of necessity— bread and butter, some fishing tackle and a homemade knife, but neither dog nor gun—and lit out for the barn along Old Woman's Creek. He spent the night in the barn, waiting for morning when he would take his and Skinny's raft and escape to Lake Erie.

Jimmy and Skinny had often slept overnight in the barn, but then they had been together. At eleven, especially when you are expecting retribution for some misdeed at any moment, everything takes on a magnitude out of all proportion. Probably no night was ever blacker in Jim Curwood's life, nor its sounds more menacing, nor punishment for misdeeds more feared.

Morning finally came, as it always does, and Jimmy set off on the homemade raft, down the creek and out into the lake. The water was shallow along the shore and he poled his raft along the edge toward Ruggles Grove, a popular picnic and swimming spot.

Fate—how often it takes a hand and sweeps us away. He found himself over a deep hole, his pole no longer touched bottom, and a brisk breeze began blowing him away from shore. Suddenly he was out on the big lake, and without a paddle, as it were. He sat upon his raft and watched with alarm as the shore receded.

He was rescued, of course. Floating helplessly on his runaway raft, Jimmy was soon sighted by a group of young people on a small sailboat. They hauled Jimmy aboard and asked how he came to be on Lake Erie on such a flimsy craft. His tale, told seriously, was met with laughter. Nevertheless, they carried him away with them to Sandusky and sent a message to his father to come and get him.

The city of Sandusky lies along the Lake Erie shore on the southern side of the mouth of Sandusky Bay, about fifteen miles west of Ceylon. While waiting for James to come, Jimmy's rescuers showed him around the city. They took him to their school, vaster than any he'd ever imagined, two stories high, and peopled with the most wonderful-looking, well-dressed, sophisticated boys and girls he'd ever seen, studying things he'd never heard of before.

Jimmy drank it all in like a thirsty shipwrecked sailor landed on a foreign shore.

When he got home again at last, all he could think about was what it would be like to go to a school like that. Four Corners School seemed so small and dull after his glimpse of a big city school. There was a school at Wakeman, about eight miles to the south of the Curwoods, not nearly as big as Sandusky, of course, but certainly bigger than Four Corners. He made up his mind that he would go there the next year.

Abby and James did their best to talk Jimmy out of any such idea. It would mean moving to town and that took money and money was always in short supply at the Curwoods. Someone would have to stay on the farm and look after the livestock and the house. Jimmy persevered and finally wore James and Abby down.

All fall and winter Jimmy worked to help earn the money necessary for the move. He hunted and trapped rabbits which he sold to a man in nearby Florence. In the spring—this was now 1891 and Jimmy was nearly 13—he cleared brush for a neighboring farmer.

Ed solved the problem of who would stay behind. He was now 22, shy and quiet, and didn't want to move into town.

The day finally came. Part of the family's furniture was piled onto the wagon and they set off down the dusty road, past the schoolhouse and south towards Wakeman, Jimmy and his dog Jack walking alongside. Wakeman was not as big as Owosso but it was certainly bigger than any other town nearby. Wakeman was where they went to do their shopping, when a need arose for something store boughten, and it was where Abby had lived as a girl and where she'd met James.

James set up a cobbler's shop, of course. Abby was happy to be "home" again. And Jimmy reveled in this new adventure.

The universe literally expanded before his eyes. A lecturer on astronomy visited the school, letting the students look at the planets through his long brass telescope. They even came back at night to look at the stars. The universe is endless, Jimmy thought. And more, he realized that there was a guiding hand controlling it all.

God's not far away, Jimmy realized. He's someone friendly, even chummy, someone who knows about boys. "He became not only romantically interesting to me, but intensely admirable," Jim recalled many years later. Rather than an austere being of wrath and vengeance, "God was a great fellow and worth having as a pal."

The boys and girls at Wakeman were different from his old classmates at Four Corners. They had dances and other refined activities. They had manners and they were better dressed.

Up until now Jimmy hadn't cared how he looked. What did it matter if his overalls were raggedy and dirty? His mother minded, but not Jimmy. His hair, bleached out in the sun, was uncombed and his face often smudged, unless his mother took him in hand, examined his ears and ordered him to change his clothes.

Here in Wakeman, girls were different, too. He began to notice them, but was mortified one day when one of them told him to "Go home and wash your neck." He stood before the mirror and took stock of himself. From then on, how he looked began to matter to him.

These were great changes in Jim's life. He was growing up, taking an interest in how others saw him, broadening his outlook and his knowledge, but most important during his year at school in Wakeman was the time he spent in a small store where magazines were sold. The woman who owned the store let Jimmy read the magazines cover to cover without buying them, knowing he didn't have the money. He read the stories, and began to take note of the names of the authors.

By the end of winter Jimmy's own stories had grown from a few hundred words to thousands, exciting tales like "The Red Sagamore's Hidden Treasure" and "The Captain of the Renegades." He began to think about how it would be to have one of his stories printed in a magazine. He sought out the names of editors of the magazines he read and wrote to some of them. Several of them replied.

Someday, he vowed, one of the stories in one of those magazines would be his, his name printed there for all the world to see.

"Gee, Slip, you've changed," Skinny said when Jim got home again at the end of the school year, wistfulness beneath the gladness in his voice. And Jim *had* changed. If he'd looked closely, he could have seen the changes in himself. Jeanne had changed, too, grown up, become more womanly. He was glad to be home, but it was different. He had a lot of new material to think and write about.

If he'd known how many years it would take, how many hundreds of thousands of words he would have to write before he would see one of his stories in print, and how many years more before he would actually be paid for his stories, he might have thrown away his pencils and his wrapping paper notebooks.

But Jim had developed a singleness of purpose now, nothing and no one would keep him from his destiny.

James and Abby were as encouraging as ever, listening to him read his stories to them in the evenings. But when he tried to tell them of his need to expand his horizons even more, that he was beyond the little one-room school on the corner, they didn't understand why he couldn't be content to stay at home.

There had been a lot of visiting back and forth between Ohio and Michigan. Abby had gone to Owosso in the fall of 1885, and Amy had come to Ohio two or three times. She had listened patiently to Jimmy's stories, and encouraged him to keep on writing.

Now Amy and Ralph, not quite eight, came for a visit in August, 1892. Amy listened to Jimmy's latest stories, and he sensed an ally in his sister and begged her to talk to their parents about his going back to Owosso with her. It took another year, and another visit from Amy, but finally James and Abby agreed because they had decided to go back to Owosso again themselves and leave Ed on the farm in Ohio.

On a hot July day in 1893, Jim, Amy and Ralph set out for the little train station in Ceylon and the trip to Owosso. Jim was fifteen.

Skinny followed down the dusty road. "Gee, I'll never see you again," he called out to Jim as the buggy rounded the corner by the schoolhouse.

Jim waved to his chum standing still and forlorn in the middle of the road, growing smaller and smaller as the buggy drew away, the dog Jack at his side.

As the small train chugged out of the station, though, Jim was looking forward, not back, to a future not even his vivid imagination could foresee.

Chapter 5

Jim listened to the click of typewriter keys coming from behind the closed door. Beyond that door was a real, published author, someone whose stories appeared in magazines, with his name printed there, too. He'd read the latest one in *Golden Days Magazine* about the 1871 forest fire in Michigan and a serial story called "Roland Ankney."

Fred Janette had still been in high school when he'd had his first story published. Now he'd been away to the University of Michigan and was home for the summer. The Janettes and the Curwoods had been friends since Abby and James first moved to Owosso. Amy lived right around the corner from the Janettes now, and she had brought Jim to meet this local author. Fred was going to talk to Jim about writing.

The sound of the typewriter keys stopped, the door opened, and a tall, slim young man appeared.

"So this is our young author," Fred said. In his early twenties, Fred Janette seemed much older to the fifteen-year-old youth. He invited Jim into his study and showed him the story he was writing for *Golden Days*, "Twenty Rebels: A Story of Cadet Life," and his play, *Martino*, to be performed at Salisbury's Opera House, and maybe, if it went over well, at other theaters as well.

Jim was excited and enthralled that a real author would take time to talk to him about writing. It was an excitement he never quite forgot; dozens of young writers over the next thirty-four years owed Jim Curwood thanks for the encouragement and help he gave them.

Fred even showed him the check *Golden Days* had sent him for his last serial, a check for three hundred dollars—half a cent a word! Three hundred dollars! Jim's head fairly reeled at the thought of being paid all that money for just words that came out of one's head.

Jim's goal in life was firmly established from here on: To have his words published, with his name on the page, and to get paid for them.

West Town had changed. There were now more than a dozen stores and two hotels, a wheat elevator, coal yard and several manufacturing plants. Some of the old familiar faces were still there, like Mace Wood and his handle factory and his neat, white house with the picket fence. Kate Russell, whose old-fashioned bustle Jimmy and Charlie had once vowed to ride upon, still waited tables at Miller House, but Charlie Miller was gone. His father had died and Charlie and his mother had moved away, no one knew where.

The line of hickory trees down the center of the street was gone, too.

James' shoe shop and their home at the back were now Green's Hotel, enlarged and changed and taking in overnight guests. Andrew Green, a baby when Jim had gone away, had grown into a boy already deserving of the nickname "Bull." Jim resented his appropriation of the old haunts, but Bull Green would become the best indoor baseball umpire in the state, and a favorite with Jim and the Curwood Veterans who played in the 1920s.

The river was still the same, singing of freedom and adventure as it tumbled over the little dam, whispering secrets around the island in the bend. Jim got out his fishing pole and made plans to get reacquainted.

"I have always had an unvoiced hope that when I drift through the soft and velvety twilight of death it may be the spirit of this stream which is bearing me on," Jim wrote of the Shiawassee many years later in his autobiography.

Jim's life began to expand again. Certainly it was more exciting in Owosso than in the sleepy little countryside around the old house on Church Road in Ohio. There were horse races at the fairgrounds at the end of Exchange Street. Fred Peterson's "White Frank," actually a gray, beat out Fred Wildermuth's sorrel, "Yankee." There was a lot of friendly wagering going on.

W A. Connors, the ice cream man, made a hit with the race fans with his new "Hoky Poky Ice Cream," blocks of ice cream wrapped in paper. They sold like hotcakes for a nickle.

Excursion trains took folks to Island Lake on Sundays, espcially in August when Company G of the National Guard was there.

A circus came to town. Jim went, as wide-eyed as when he'd seen his first circus as a five-year-old. Circuses in those days traveled by train, of course, and, while often as dusty and tawdry as most traveling shows, they were usually family affairs, like the Wixom circus from nearby Bancroft which traveled southern Michigan every summer. Jim loved circuses and fairs. Many years later he bought the Owosso Fair when it fell on hard times and was in danger of folding.

Some people, of course, couldn't afford excursions or circuses or horse races. At the Estey factory, workmen making more than $1.25 a day agreed to take a ten percent cut in wages in order to keep the factory running; for ten weeks only, they were promised. Then things got even worse and they took a fifty percent cut, this time for 90 days, though.

Still, the *Weekly Press* reported that people in Owosso hardly knew there were hard times.

There were five newspapers in Owosso now, all eager to report everything that went on in town.

The Detroit newspapers were brought up daily by the train eighty miles from Detroit, and the Tribune made its own news one day by being a day late.

White Frank beat Yankee again.

There were bicycle races at the park every Friday, and Professor Kennedy held mesmeric entertainments at Salisbury's Opera House.

People were still talking about the attempted lynching of William Sullivan last New Year's Day. They were dissatisfied with the sheriff's handling of the affair, and there was talk of an investigation. The sheriff had arrested Sullivan in Detroit and brought him back to the county jail over at Corunna on a charge of murder—Sullivan had been romancing another man's wife, but it was the husband who ended up shot to death—when a mob smashed in the jail doors and forced its way past the sheriff and eight armed deputies. Sullivan, hearing the ruckus, slashed his own throat and died before they could reach him, saving the lynchers, and the sheriff, a lot of trouble.

Frank Topping, the sewing machine agent who lived down the street from Jack and Amy, was attacked in a robbery attempt over in Byron one Saturday night. What was the world coming to? Such violence soon followed closer to home.

"Jack Gaylord of West Owosso has a local reputation as being a slugger and the boys are all afraid of him," the *Evening Argus* stated in reporting that Jack had been bested in a tussle with a stranger Labor Day night. Jack and Amy had been walking along Main Street when a man "laboring under a beastly jag" brushed against Amy. "Biff! and the stranger felt the force of a blow from Gaylord's fist," the Argus went on. "It sobered him up and he pounced onto Gaylord, giving him one of the most complete pummelings he ever had."

The next day, the *Argus* retracted its exciting story. Jack said he'd merely pushed aside one of a bunch of drunken loafers who failed to make room for him and his wife. The man pounced on Jack and "was going to do him up but Jack warded off every blow until the man gave up."

In September, Jim was put into the ninth grade.

For $5.85 that summer you could take the train round trip to Chicago to attend the World's Fair. Jack and Amy went in September, and Jack gave Jim his choice, a trip to the Fair with them or a gun. Jim chose the gun.

The next month, James, Abby and Cora came back to Owosso, leaving Ed on the farm. They stayed with Amy on River Street, where the Shiawassee flowed smoothly by the edge of the back yard, then briefly to another house, then to Bradley Street behind the Catholic Church. James went to work for E.L. Brewer, a downtown shoe dealer.

Of course, all summer long Jim had been writing, and now his stories grew longer and more vivid, like "Firelock of the Range" and other tales of hunting, adventure and the lakes, still written in pencil on wrapping paper pages.

School was dull, especially with the outdoors calling, drowning out the voices of his teachers. He was a "helpless horror" in algebra, and when he maintained that a skipper was a bug in cheese (it is) rather than the master of a vessel (as it also is), his teacher thought him dumb.

A little girl died of diptheria and two others in her family were sick; there were 29 cases in all that summer in Owosso, and six deaths. Dr. Baker of the state board of health arrived to look over the problem of contaminated water in Owosso and said there should be sewers and city water up on Oliver Street instead of private wells, as most people had. Two people died of typhoid fever, but all six cases of scarlet fever recovered. Owosso claimed it wasn't so bad, other cities were lots worse off.

In November the city announced it would pay a bounty of three cents each for sparrows, to be brought in whole, not just the heads, and in lots of ten. Enterprising boys—Jim may have been one of them—made money shooting sparrows, at least for the first ten days or so, until the city clerk refused to handle any more of the gruesome things and the bounty was abandoned.

Owosso's population was now 11,000. There was talk of paving some of the streets.

The holidays meant a lot of family visiting for the Curwoods. Ed was married now, and he and his new wife, Stella, came up from Ohio. Other Ohio relatives came visiting, too, and James, Abby and Cora visited the Griffins in Chesaning.

There were always a lot of family get-togethers. The Curwoods were a close family. Jack was a joker and there was always fun, playing pranks on one another—Jim didn't like being the object of a joke but the others didn't mind. Abby was in on some of the pranks, too.

Jim trapped along the river that winter, running his trapline in the cold, early morning darkness before he went to school. Late to class one morning, Professor Austin ended the morning prayer by giving thanks for the return of "Nimrod," and Nimrod he became to his classmates and teacher.

Sledding, "catching on bobs," which was hitching a ride on a bobsled, a dangerous thing children got warned about but did anyway, skating, boxing matches held in Bigelow's barn, the Boy's Brigade at the Baptist Church; there was a lot for young people to do in the wintertime.

At school, Jim took part in a debate, the question being, "Resolved, that taxation without representation is unjust, therefore, women holding taxable property should have the privilege of voting." Jim and Lizzie Todd argued the positive side against Nellie Carpenter and Homer Palmer on the negative.

"Women who are taxed should vote," Jim said, because, he explained, if women had a vote it would make it easier for them in their fight against liquor. "Is there a person who has a child's welfare more at heart than the mother?" Jim asked. Yet they had to raise their children in a country controlled by the "saloon element," he said. "One-eighth of all the money collected for taxes in the United States is paid by women," Jim concluded, "yet they have nothing to say about the disposition to be made of this money."

Nellie argued that women's nerves were too weak to stand the excitement around the polls. "A true American woman does not want to vote," she said.

Jim and Lizzie won the debate.

Jim's attitude toward women and liquor remained pretty much the same the rest of his life. He seldom drank, and then only moderately, and although he would be reviled by some as a womanizer, "womanhood" was to him just short of sainthood.

Social life for Jim that winter budded, and withered before it had hardly bloomed. He asked Nellie to a party at Vera Haskell's but she turned him down. Vera, the city's violin virtuoso, would always figure in Jim's life in one way or another. She was, perhaps, even a romantic notion for a time, at least on Jim's part—he later wrote a story entitled "Veronica Haskelle." But Vera was mostly a friend and, later on, pianist at the local theatre where some of Jim's movies were shown, and then a neighbor.

Fred Janette's play, *Martino*, opened to a full house in March. Mumby, the Corunna cigarmaker, put out a new cigar called Martino. Even the *New York Dramatic Mirror* ran a review. Fred was at work on his fifth serial for *Golden Days*, a story of life on an island in Lake Erie based on material he'd gathered during the summer.

Abby fell dangerously ill in March with inflammation of the lungs, and her worried family gathered around her bedside. From then on, Abby's health would be a cause of concern for the entire family.

Grandma Griffin, Abby's mother, died in May and the Clarkes again asked to have Golda, but the Griffins refused.

Jim was 16 that June. His parents gave him a second-hand Caligraph typewriter. James fixed up a writing table from an old sewing machine base and covered the top with yellow oilcloth. The clicking of the typewriter keys sounded now from Jim's room, and in the evenings, Jim read his stories to his parents. "Fine, Jimmy, fine," his father would say, nodding his head.

Jack supplied fresh strawberries, picked no doubt from Granny Smith's strawberry patch, to the railroad dining cars that summer. Connor's Hoky Poky ice cream was popular again, and the carpet sewers on the third floor of Christian's store on Main Street had some hauled up to them by a line through the window.

James also bought Jim a bicycle. Jim and Jack rode to Chesaning so that Jim could gather material for a story about an Indian battle waged there before the village existed.

Then on Friday, August 17, Abby was alone in the house. James was at the shoe shop, Cora probably at Amy's. Jim had gone to the school yard, though Abby thought he was still in his room upstairs. She decided to lie down in the downstairs bedroom.

The back screen door slammed and a strange man appeared in the bedroom doorway. He was a good-looking man with a dark mustache, of medium height and well-dressed in dark clothes. He wore a summer straw hat.

"What do you want?" Abby asked in a frightened voice.

"I want to transact some business," the man replied in a pleasant voice. He sprang at Abby and grabbed her around the waist. She wrenched free and ran up the stairs to Jim's room. Finding he was not there, she grabbed up Jim's shotgun but the man was right behind her and grabbed the gun away. They struggled again and Abby picked up a slat of wood and struck the man, cutting a gash in his forehead that bled, but Abby was by now too distraught to notice, only recalling it later.

"I don't remember if I screamed or not," she told Marshall Barrisford, weeping, when he came to investigate. Anyway, if she did, no one heard. Still polite, the stranger threw her, half fainting, onto Jim's bed, she said, and he raped her. He raped her again. She thought later that he raped her a third time and maybe a fourth; by then she hardly knew what was happening. He may have stayed in the house two hours, she told the officer. Before he left he dragged her down the stairs and tied her hands behind her back. "Sorry," he said, still polite, but he didn't want her to raise an alarm too soon, not until he'd had time to get away.

Abby, near exhaustion and only semi-conscious, finally roused herself enough to attract the neighbors with her cries. None of them had seen the man come or go.

A reporter came for the story and, still crying, she described her assailant. He had a mole on the left side of his face, she said. "I've never seen him before."

Police and townsmen searched the city. Rumors flew that a man of that description was seen crossing the fairgrounds, and boarding a train, and Jim said that a man like that was lounging around the school yard earlier in the afternoon. Officer Barrisford arrested a tramp and brought him to the house. "No," Abby said, still in tears, "he's not the one."

Abby lay in bed for days while James offered a $200 reward for her assailant's capture. Recriminations flew about whether the police were doing a good job or not. The man's description was sent to all parts of the county, but Prosecuting Attorney Watson thought the man lived right there in the city because he seemed to know the house and when Abby might be alone. The incident was reported in numerous papers. Prosecutor Watson said he'd authorize any reward the sheriff might want to put up. Sheriff Jacobs declined, but a few days later he matched James's reward offer with another $200.

The Curwoods didn't have a known enemy and the whole case was very puzzling. By Monday, no trace of him had yet been found and Sheriff Jacobs now complained that he hadn't been "duly notified" and came over to get some facts. But Abby was still very sick, sometimes hysterical. Dr. Arnold was attending her.

It was the end of August before Abby was able to be up and about again. Detective Van Hoten, in September, reportedly following a clue, was confident he was on the right trail but reluctant to say more. Her attacker was never found.

What effect the rape had on Jim is hard to say. He loved his mother dearly, adored his sister Amy and had great respect for the other women around him. At 16, he probably didn't understand all the aspects of rape, but he surely realized his mother had been grievously hurt, as a woman as well as physically.

In October, James took Abby on a healing trip to Buffalo and Niagara Falls.

For Jim, pounding away at his typewriter, new and exciting events lay just ahead, and a kind of fame which reached all the way to New York.

Chapter 6

Jim's first published story was awful. It hopped around incomplete and was filled with inconsistencies and with dialect, which never would go over well. But already he had the vigor and the descriptive writing which would make him famous. He created an excitement that readers were hungry for.

"The Terror of Athabasca" was published in the *Owosso Evening Argus* on October 21, 1894, a Saturday.

It was a tale told by an old guide in Canada about how he got a scar on his cheek. There is much about filling and smoking a pipe; many of Jim's characters would smoke pipes, as he would himself later on. The story was weak and the dialect distracting, but there were also passages such as "The sun had just reached the tops of the trees on the farther side of the lake and its bright warm beams cast a golden glory over the glassy surface of Athabasca." This was at least ten years before he saw the Athabasca River himself.

There is nothing so elative to a writer than seeing your name in print the first time, unless it is holding in your hands your first check for something you've written. Jim did not get paid for this story, nor until many published stories later, but his name—J. Curwood—was there for everyone to see. The story apparently brought no response. His next story did.

"The Fall of Shako" was published in two parts, the first on November 24, 1894, and the second a week later, on December 1. This time the byline read "Jas. O. Curwood." Jim's fictionalized tale of the Indian battle at Chesaning brought a little flurry of criticism followed by defense of the author.

A local "critic"—he was never named by the Argus but it was Dr. William Jopling, the local veterinarian—took exception to Jim's changes of weather in a letter to the editor. The day had begun "bright and beautiful; not the shadow of a cloud marred the sky," but shortly a "fierce wind was blowing from the north, the sky was overcast and a deep gloom hung over the valley." The bad weather continued until night, when a calm fell "and the stars came out bright and clear." Michigan weather is changeable, of course, but this was too much for Dr. Jopling who thought anyway that he was dealing with James Curwood, the shoe dealer, and he didn't like James.

Jim was hurt and told the editor so, and sent a copy of his story and of the critical comments to his friend and mentor, Fred Janette, now literary editor for the *New York Dramatic Mirror*.

Fred's answer, published two days after the second installment of Jim's story and without knowing the name of Jim's critic, noted the "splutter of idiocy, self-sufficiency and conceit which some censor of art and letters in Owosso has foisted upon the public through the medium of the *Argus*." A "bumptious ass," he called the critic.

Without comment on the story itself, Fred said that such condemnation of it by its critic was neither criticism nor manly. "A man and a gentleman, if he cannot treat a story fairly, pointing out its merits as well as its defects, will keep his mouth shut, and his pen dry," Fred said. Jim would meet a lot of ungentlemanly critics before he was through.

"Mr. Curwood has suffered the experience that every aspirant after literary honors has to suffer, if he tries to gain an audience among his own townspeople before having established himself in a wider field," Fred wrote. He had himself not been the object of criticism by his fellow townsmen, Janette admitted, but he knew the type. Jim took his comments to heart and began to send his stories to the *Detroit Journal*.

"Criticism Makes Men," Tuesday's editorial was headlined. Editor John Klock, or maybe it was Roland Eisley—they were co-owners of the paper— pointed out that exception was taken to the story's critic only because he made the criticisms, and to the *Argus* because it printed them. Friends and family had sent letters in defense of the young author, but neither for nor against his story, but he ought rather to have "rejoiced that he was considered of enough importance to awaken a criticism." It was a "compliment to his story" and should be to his benefit.

"He has talent," the editorial said, "but unless he can brave criticism, it will never do him any good."

One more response marked the end of the affair. Dr. Jopling, now on the defensive from Fred's criticism, was vitriolic and abusive, derisive of Fred, and still did not sign his name. In an editor's note at the bottom, the paper defended Jopling and said readers were "sick of this controversy and this ends it as far as the *Argus* is concerned." In February, George T. Campbell, secretary of the YMCA for three years, bought the *Argus*. He took a liking to the young writer, and eventually he printed almost anything Jim wanted.

Also in February, the first three chapters of Fred Janette's newest serial appeared in *Golden Days*, a story of Michigan's Upper Peninsula copper country where Fred had done a brief stint as a newspaper editor. He was just finishing a new story based on his brother Pierre's adventures as an actor. Jim surely read these stories avidly, searching for what might be missing in his own writing and noting that Fred's successful writing was based on his own experiences.

D.R. Salisbury opened his shoe factory in rooms over his shoe store, and with four machines and four workmen, began manufacturing farm and railroad shoes at the rate of 175 per month. Automation had come to Owosso's shoe industry. Nevertheless, in September James left Brewer's employ to open his own shop again, this time downtown on East Main Street between city hall and his old friend Merrick Blair's gun shop.

In spite of the six-year difference in their ages, Jim and Ralph were pals. One day that spring the boys were racing, Jim on his bicycle and Ralph afoot. Ralph veered too close to Jim and was knocked down and unconscious. He was carried home and a doctor summoned, then two, then three. They determined Ralph had a concusion, and, shaking their heads, concluded that he might not live. The next day he was getting around nicely.

Bicyles and bicycle clubs were the rage that summer. Owosso ladies were now wearing bloomers and members of the Aurora Club voted to wear black or dark blue short skirts—to their shoe tops—and matching leggings. The ladies over in Corunna, however, voted down bloomers or short skirts of any kind.

Jim had been writing furiously all winter and sending his stories out to magazines, getting a few replies but none favorable. Still stung by the criticism from "The Fall of Shako" but undaunted, he was desperate to have something published again. He copied a poem out of one magazine and sent it to another. Shortly a check came for fifty cents. Then he was ashamed, and confessed to Mrs. Janette, that good lady having already recognized both the poem and his crime but kindly not accusing Jim. The poem he had chosen to copy was Lord Byron's "A Fragment"; he had changed the name to "A Prayer."

In April, Jack and Jim rode their bicycles over to "Indian Town" near Durand, about a dozen miles southeast of Owosso, to see Jim Fisher, a chief of the Chippewa Indians. "The Boy Spies" was published in the *Argus* on June 8, 1895. This time his byline was James O. Curwood. There was still no pay.

A fire wiped out an entire block in Corunna. Two houses of ill repute were raided in Owosso, and a sick girl shamefully left behind, but a family took her in. "Captain" George Gute launched his 35-foot steam yacht, "Islander," at Corunna, planning to run it between there and the little park upstream he was developing. But he'd built the yacht with his wife's money and she sued him for divorce, ending that project.

On June 12, Jim was seventeen. He was sick that month, probably with some type of virus. Many maladies floated around town, carried by those impure wells, by flies, by mosquitoes from the swamp south of town and by the city's generally unsanitary conditions.

By late June, though, he was up and well again, and ready for adventure. It came in the form of a bicycle trip. And as would become his way, he announced his intentions to the press before he began.

Abby's sister, Frankie Van Ostran, had a son, Bert, a bit older than Jim. The two boys were friends, though Frankie and her son lived down by Williamston, about thirty miles south of Owosso. Thirty miles was a good day's drive by buggy, half a day by train, and a long ride on a bike. At the end of June, Aunt Frankie came up to see Abby, Bert with her, and the two boys

plotted an adventure, a bicycle trip to Kentucky and other parts south.
Mammoth Cave, where Floyd Collins was entombed, was to be their primary
destination but they planned on visiting a long list of cities and sights in Ohio
and Kentucky and maybe even into Tennesee.

Alright, James and Abby said, thinking he might go to Bert's and back,
and that would be enough.

With the shoebox lunch Abby had packed him firmly stowed among his
dunnage strapped to the bicycle, and the 50 cents James had given him secure in
his pocket, Jim set out on a July afternoon and rode to Williamston to meet
Bert. They did not come back until August 24, Jim full of their adventures: the
broken pedal that delayed them in Wakeman where they'd gone to see Ed and
Stella, their boat trip down the Ohio, their foraging for food along the way. He
added fanciful touches when he recounted this trip in his autobiography, but
nowhere did he admit to the greatest adventure of all, their near drowning when
they put out onto Lake Erie in a leaky boat. Bert told this story much later, after
Jim was dead.

At any rate, they had a wonderful time.

Sometime in 1895, the *Detroit Journal* published "The Girl With the
Rareripe Lips and Raven Hair," a mishmash of improbability fancifully set in
India. Nevertheless, three years later he would submit this, verbatim—the only
change was that the heroine's hair was now golden—to *Four O'Clock
Magazine* where it was published under the title "The Poison of Heredity."

Jim was in the tenth grade that fall. He and a school chum, Hugh Conklin,
concocted a "corn salve" which they peddled door to door, pedalling their
bicycles around the countryside on Saturdays. It was the first of two medicine
sales ventures for Jim. Hugh would continue in medicine and by the 1920s head
a large sanitorium, though it's doubtful his patients or colleagues ever knew of
his early foray into medicine.

Fred Janette was now in Chicago, after a summer home again, this time as
telegraph editor on the *Chicago News*. The *Argus* published his picture,
showing a serious young man with a shock of dark hair, big ears, pince-nez
glasses and a mustache. He didn't look an especially venturesome fellow.

Jim went hunting at Matthias Swamp on the south side of Owosso on
Thanksgiving Day, making news again with his hunting skills. He was out for
rabbits when he came face to face with a huge "wildcat," four feet long tail to
nose, and shot it. He had the animal, a bobcat, skinned for a rug for his room. It
was probably his first hunting trophy.

Winter again was filled with family events, sledding and skating and
tobogganing and school. There were horse races on the river when the ice got
thick enough. Again, Jim took tentative steps towards entering the social scene,
without much success.

In December one of the downtown stores had a window display of one of the new electric cars. There was more talk of paving the streets in the spring. The city got electric lights in time for Christmas and the council discussed making day current a permanent thing.

Amy, to be known as "Queen," was born December 30, 1895 to Jack and Amy. Ralph was eleven.

Jim trapped again that winter. He got 15 cents for muskrat pelts, 75 cents to a dollar for mink. There were more muskrat than mink but he was making quite a bit of money and putting it away.

And he wrote. Words poured out of his head and seemed to flow down his arms through his fingertips and onto the paper via the keys of his typewriter. The click of the keys sounded from his little slant-ceilinged upstairs bedroom almost night and day.

He wasn't selling stories but he was getting encouragement. R.H. Titherington of Munsey's chain of magazines wrote him, "Almost, but not quite what we want. Send us a good adventure yarn for *Argosy*," adding not to get discouraged, that the first story was "hardest of all to get accepted," but that after his name appeared "*once* in a magazine, the game will be largely won."

"Keep at it, kid!" Bob Davis of *Munsey*'s scrawled on a rejection slip, "you're bound to win!" John Sleicher of *Leslie*'s wrote that someday he would publish everything Jim sent him, a prophesy that was to come true.

Without the encouragement and help of such editors, then and always, Jim's career might have faltered. Perhaps it would never have blossomed at all. Men like those early editors above, and Hewlett Hanson Howland of Bobbs-Merrill, Russell Doubleday, Harold Kinsey of *Cosmopolitan*, and, most of all, his friend Ray Long enthused over his writing, bolstered his courage when he faltered, gave him advice and editorial assistance and special treatment, welcomed his stories and corresponded as friends, seeing the spark of talent even in those early days of exaggerated and flowery prose and implausible plots.

James filed for a veteran's pension but kept his little shop.

The sportsmen of Owosso met that winter in John Brooks & Sons office in West Town to form the Owosso Hunting and Outing Club. Mace Wood, the Izaak Walton of Owosso, was president.

"Pontiac's Last Blow," another Indian saga, was published April 7, 1896, in the *Detroit Journal*. In it, Jim took the facts of the siege of Detroit and the ensuing Battle of Bloody Run and brought them to life for his readers in a spirited tale that took them into the minds of the protagonists and into the battle with his descriptive account of the scene. He was learning how to write of nature—"the elm with its graceful and weeping top"— which would become the one thing in his writing his critics would seldom, if ever, attack. The byline read James O. Curwood.

It was a glorious spring. The sap was running in the maples, and the robins were back, chirruping and hopping about the lawns and flying into the trees with bits of twigs in their beaks. There were pools and rivulets from melting snow everywhere. The creek broke free of winter's embrace and went tumbling merrily down to the river which promptly overflowed its banks. Basements flooded, including the Curwoods', and rafts of strange driftage roared and danced down the river past their back door. The streets, still waiting to be paved, were impassable bogs of mud.

How could school hold a boy on days like this?

"Come with me," he wrote Skinny down in Ohio, and waited impatiently for him to answer. But Skinny couldn't come, and Jim packed his gear, bid his parents good-bye and set off alone for the St. Charles Flats where he and his family had spent many happy days fishing and boating.

It was a 22 mile train ride to St. Charles, a small village with thousands of acres of wild land just beyond.

The Flats is a maze of bayous, channels and marshes where the Shiawassee is joined by the Bad River and numerous small creeks. That spring there were still remnants of the recent lumbering days—a few stands of white pine, rafts of logs cut for the mills, shanty houses and old houseboats, rotting booms and rows of spiles. Perch, bass and pike, partridge and pheasants, geese and ducks, white-tailed deer and other creatures peopled this area. And a few Indians.

Jim rented a boat for 50 cents a week, piled in his dunnage and set out into this wilderness. The air was loud with the cries of Canada geese, the skies darkened overhead at times with hundreds of ducks, of more kinds than he knew. Frogs boomed in the reeds and fish leaped before his paddles. What was a classroom compared to this? How could girls and dances and even bicycle riding interest him when there was all this to be had for the taking? Yet those other things were what his friends found important. No wonder they couldn't understand him.

His boat skimmed through the water, taking him deeper into the swamp. He turned down a branch into a place called Kimberly's Bayou and set up camp at an old shack on an island. Jim stayed in the Flats for three weeks, hunting, fishing and listening to a new-found friend, an ancient Indian known as Muskrat Joe. From Joe he learned more of the river and woods than he could have learned from a thousand books. When he got home he wrote another story, "The Mystery Man of Kim's Bayou," about Muskrat Joe, of course.

The new illuminated electric cars of the Owosso and Corunna Traction Company were operating nicely between the two towns —Corunna, the county seat, was three miles to the east—running smoothly compared to the old ones. The Ann Arbor Railroad put on two new night trains; it took just 13 hours for the run between Toledo and Frankfurt, up on Michigan's "Little Finger," with Owosso half-way between.

Mat Wixom's circus came to town, as it did every summer, and the Chicago Marine Band played at the opening of Caledonia Park in Corunna. The post office decided to close in the afternoon on Decoration Day.

"Senor Valentino, A Romance of the Cuban Revolution" appeared June 30, 1896 in the *Detroit Journal* under the byline James Oliver Curwood. In this story—and he had never been to Cuba, of course—he wove, as the title said, "romance." It was a story of two rebels fighting for a cause, one with a sweetheart with "a pale sweet face with the soft dark curls clinging about it like a veil." He still received no pay.

He had just turned 18. His blond hair had darkened to medium brown, a white streak just beginning to show faintly above his right eye, an inheritance from that Mohawk great-grandmother. He had reached his full height of five feet, eight inches, and his slim build was hardened by his outdoor life. He was opinionated, dedicated and strong-willed, eager and outgoing yet sometimes oblivious of others, even family. He was no longer a boy and not quite yet a man.

He got a job. His typewriter was busy, too, but there were no more stories published that year. He began to wonder what he was doing wrong.

Chapter 7

"You should go to college, Jimmy," Mrs. Janette told the despairing writer. Fred Janette was married now and living in Southwestern Michigan, but Jim still sought Mrs. Janette's advice on his work.

Go to college? He hadn't finished high school and it didn't look as though he ever would. But, swallowing his pride, he went back to class and told Professor Austin that he wanted to go to college. "How are you going to get into college without a diploma, James, break in with a set of burglar's tools?" Austin asked him. "He's going to college," his classmates snickered. Miss Boice, however, invited him to her house after classes to help him catch up on his work.

"You *can* get in without a diploma," Mrs. Janette told him. "All you have to do is pass an entrance examination."

In February of 1897 the *Detroit Journal* accepted "Angel of Heaven," another tale of heroism and romance set in Cuba, and in April printed "Hades, A Tale of the Invisible Worlds," a wild, weird tale of a journey by three men and a dog in a strange craft through the center of the earth. His byline this time was J. Oliver Curwood.

There was a measles epidemic in the spring. The streets were mires of mud, no paving had yet even been started, but the new sewers were in and there was talk of extending them all the way to West Town. That ageless writer, Anon., asked why the city didn't do something about the streets. Bicyclists were everywhere now, and the wheelmen used the sidewalks "which are supposed to be for footmen, because there's not a street in town fit for wheels."

Decoration Day, May 30, was on Monday in 1897. A soldiers' monument, assured by last minute donations, was dedicated during services at the cemetery on the hill. Grand Army of the Republic veterans, bands, lodge members, children carrying flowers, about a thousand people in all, paraded up the hill to the cemetery.

Two days after Jim's nineteenth birthday he set out on a second medicine-selling trip.

Jim and a schoolmate, Leslie Hanes, concocted a sure-fire cure-all of cinchona, hot cayenne and a lot of calomel. Bottled and nicely labeled "Infallible Blood Purifier," the concoction was guaranteed to cure boils, pimples and carbuncles, goitre, cancer and corns, "every ailment known to the human flesh." The two youths rented a horse and rig for two dollars a week and headed south.

The mixture sold for 39 cents a bottle or three bottles for a dollar. When they ran out, they stopped at a pump and mixed up more. They even sold it to druggists. Sometimes the bottles exploded from the summer heat coupled with the jouncing of the buggy.

Infallible Blood Purifier was an unqualified success, but it worked almost while they waited and they soon learned to keep moving well ahead of their customers.

Jim and Leslie made their way leisurely down through Ohio and back up to Jim's old territory, the scene of his "barefoot days," but everything seemed so different. Skinny was dead, so were Dr. Benschoter and Hiram Fisher, and Jeanne was married and living in a house so poor they'd passed it by as no hope for a sale.

They stopped at Ed's, of course, and found Ralph was waiting to go home with them, having come down earlier with Jack who'd gone home again on the train.

Jim and Leslie had traveled a thousand miles in the buggy and made a nice profit. Jim put his share of the money aside and went to work. He had another story, "Glenville of the Lone Peak," printed in the *Detroit Journal.* He was still determined to go to college, especially now that he knew a way to get in without finishing high school.

Ethel Greenwood was fourteen that year. An Indiana farm girl with aspirations of bettering her life by becoming a teacher, she worked for her room and board at the home of Dr. and Mrs. J D. Crum in Owosso because her family was too poor to send her to school. Why did she come to Owosso? Who put her in touch with the Crums? It is hard to say now, but Mrs. Crum taught her how to act like a lady, and Ethel always gave her credit for that. She stayed with the Crums only one school year. The next summer she went to live with Bert and Louise Sullivan where she found a more congenial atmosphere and a friend in Bert's sister, Minnie, who was a teacher.

In the fall—this was still 1897—Ed and Stella came to visit through the holidays. Ed and Jim went out shooting, and came home with two and a half dozen rabbits, enough to make the papers with another story of Jim's hunting prowess.

During the winter Jim trapped as usual, shoveled snow and worked at anything he could find. Most of the family, including Jim, and many others in town came down with the grippe that winter. Crowe-Wesener opened a new shoe store in March and Jim went to work there for fifty cents each Saturday.

J. Oliver had seemed to bring him luck, and Jim decided something fancier might be even better. He had some letterhead printed, calling himself "J. Olivier Curwood."

Fred Frieseke was another hometown boy making a name for himself. A painter, Frieseke had attended art school in Chicago, then worked for a time as an illustrator in New York. Now he was in Paris and winning honors at an artist's school.

Company G went off to the Spanish-American War in April with great fanfare and tearful farewells.

The rest of Jim's class graduated in June and Nellie Carpenter got a whole bunch of bananas delivered to her, fulfillment of an often-expressed wish.

Four O'Clock Magazine published that old story of The Girl With the Rarerip Lips, etc., under a new title, "The Poison of Heredity," and said that someday they'd be able to pay their loyal writers.

And *Gray Goose Magazine* wrote they were accepting his story "Glenville of the Lonely Peak" (it had been the "Lone" Peak in the *Detroit Journal* the year before) and would pay him for it. Pay him? Finally, he was going to be paid for a story! He rushed over to Janette's to tell them the news, then raced home to write all the editors who'd been turning down his work to tell them how they'd missed out.

Then in August the mail brought a check from *Gray Goose* for ten dollars, the reward for ten years work and hundreds of thousands of words. He was a success at last!

James had bought a house on John Street near the bend in the river and had been making improvements for some weeks. In September, as Jim prepared to leave for college, they moved into their new home.

On September 5, the biggest fire in Owosso's history broke out. Woodard's furniture factory on Main Street, the brewery and cold storage house, Crowe & Payne's farm implement business and barn, Dr. Jopling's livery barn and Barie's meat market were all either burned to the ground or severely damaged. Even the Main Street bridge caught on fire. Other smaller places were lost, or nearly so. Every hand was needed. Volunteers were paid and Jim added his pay to his savings. He had $120 and he hoped it would be enough.

In mid-September Jim quit his job with Crowe-Wesener, packed his telescoping suitcase, and put his typewriter, paper and manuscripts in a box. On the last day of the month he told his family good-bye, and went down to the junction to take the train for Ann Arbor to enter the University. All he had to do was pass that entrance examination.

If I fail, Jim said to himself, I'll never come back.

He checked his baggage at the station in Ann Arbor, just in case, and set out for the university to take the exam. Seated in the room with a number of other students, he looked over the questions and realized that he didn't know the answer to any of them. What was he to do? He couldn't go slinking home again if he failed.

Reading over the first question again, his curiosity was aroused. And he was a writer, wasn't he? He could write something, couldn't he? He considered each question again and began to write—what he knew about it, or if he knew nothing, then how he felt about it, or why it was a mystery to him. And he passed the exam.

He set out in search of a room he could afford. Every penny had to count. He found one for a dollar a week, a small room with one chair, a small table and lamp, and a single bed, but no heat. Two dollars for a rug and four dollars for a stove and a piece of stovepipe, found at a second-hand shop, and his few possessions in place, made the place comfortable.

He made arrangements to take his meals for two dollars a week, simple but filling meals, at Mrs. Gray's boarding house on State Street near the campus, a place he'd heard about from other students who were in the same financial circumstances.

Books and fees left such a dent in his hoard of money that he went looking for a job, and found two, tending furnaces. They were a mile apart but each paid a dollar and a half a week, enough to cover his lodging and his food at Mrs. Gray's.

He settled into his new routine easily.

Professor Scott, who had conducted the examination and had seen that Jim was a writer, had suggested he might earn some money as a correspondent for newspapers. Of course he'd planned to send stories of campus life to the *Detroit Journal*, but now he turned his sights on other newspapers, too, as far away as New York and Chicago, and set about looking for stories.

Ann Arbor was, and is, a college town, with everything in the town geared to the life of the campus. Jim embraced his new life eagerly. He accepted his hazing as a freshman with surprising good grace, peeled a lot of onions, learned to climb the nearest tree to avoid upperclassmen approaching with paddles, and once got thrown into a pond among the frogs and lily pads.

His dress became more stylish. He thought his legs too skinny and took up the current fad of calf pads and leggings. He probably began smoking a pipe this year. He was a college man.

He was also a writer, something that gave him a feeling of superiority over students who might feel above him because of money or social status. Writing is really a drudgery job most of the time, hours spent alone dragging words out of your skull and transferring them onto paper, seldom satisfactorily at that, but there is a certain romance to the sound of it, and to say he was a writer gave him a sort of status that set him apart, but not isolated from, his peers.

Gray Goose Magazine accepted two more stories, "Yasodhara of the Luni" and "Across the Range to the Desert," and sent him another small check in October. In January, 1899, they published "Why the Police Subaltern Fled Jagadhri." He was still writing stories of places he'd never seen. And *Gray Goose* was only a small magazine.

Jim went home briefly at Thanksgiving. At Christmas James was in bed with the grippe and the usual family gatherings were somewhat subdued, due to that and another Christmas baby, Jack and Amy's second daughter, Marguerite, born the day after the holiday.

In January the *Argus* gave him a writeup that heightened his prestige. "We have made much before of the excellent literary work done by James O. Curwood of this city," the article stated, calling its readers' attention to Jim's story in the current issue of *Gray Goose* and to one coming up. His mother proudly sent him the clipping.

Now it was the *Detroit News-Tribune*, not the *Journal*, that was publishing his work, and paying for it. Confident from his literary successes, Jim gave up his furnace tending jobs to spend more time writing. There were stories everywhere. He learned that a mysterious professor now missing in Arizona had been supplying the university with artifacts from the Southwest, and he wrote it up for the *Journal*. He met an old man who was descended from a Prussian baron and had been a captive on a desert island, and two students from South Africa who were members of one of the families deeply involved in the growing conflict between England and the Boers. He let these people tell their stories themselves so that the reader felt as though he were there himself.

All winter and spring he took long walks through the woods and fields that surrounded Ann Arbor, as far as the neighboring villages and towns. He climbed the hills and bluffs along the river that wound through Ann Arbor, and found unfrequented spots where he could think and plot his stories. In the spring he rented a canoe and paddled his way up and down the river.

One of his favorite places was a secluded spot above a ravine called Schoolgirl Glen, a spot that overlooked the river and from where he could see the university buildings and the city. It was his private place, no one else seemed ever to go there.

The *Argus* took note of Jim again in April while he was home for spring vacation. "James O. Curwood, of this city, who is a student at the University of Michigan, is a regular correspondent to the *Detroit News-Tribune*, and has done excellent work during the year." He rode the train back to school further encouraged.

His visit home that summer was brief. Professor Adams, one of his instructors, was doing some railway statistical work for the government during summer vacation and hired several students—Jim was one—at $75 per month. He was able to be out-of-doors and be paid for it.

Sometime during that summer of 1899, Ethel Greenwood left the Doctor Crums, probably when Mrs. Crum and the children went to their summer cottage—they certainly didn't take her with them—and went to live with Bert and Louise Sullivan, whose daughter, Ruth, was born in July.

In August Jim was home for a brief visit before his return to classes.

Cement sidewalks were being laid downtown, some of the streets were now paved—a vast improvement—and more sewers were being installed. The county offices moved into the new courthouse in Corunna, built at a cost of $4,500, with $125 left over after all the furniture was bought.

There were the usual family suppers and fishing trips on the river, and a short hunting trip for James, Jim and Ralph to the marshes. Queen, stopping to watch the candy makers working in the window of the Sugar Bowl Restaurant downtown, fell through the sidewalk grating into the basement, suffering bruises, a bloody nose and a trip to Dr. Ward.

Before he went back to school, Jim investigated an old story about an Indian battle at Hopkins Lake, on Owosso's south side, and sold this story to the *Journal*.

In September and back at the university, Jim threw himself into writing articles. Classes were secondary now. In three months time, the *News-Tribune* printed nine of his articles. One article in October, his interview with three university professors who analyzed and discussed the theories of Christian Science, did not carry his byline, something he would seldom fail to get in his writing career.

His byline changed to J. Olivier for two stories published in the *Journal*, one about a man shanghaied onto a ship and then left on an island of savages, and one about the experiences of the well diggers who were drilling an artesian well on campus. It changed to J. Oliver for "Into a Hades of Bullets," about soldiers fighting in Cuba, and back to J. Olivier for "The Song of the Dying Lepers," about the leper colony in the Hawaiian Islands. It was as though he couldn't make up his mind.

"Hallucinations of P. Hontus VanGaff"—he'd used that name in his story of a voyage through the center of the earth; he would often use the same names and events over and over again—was published in the *News-Tribune* in December. This time it was a fiction story about a man without a country. "Scraggs (the main character) had trotted the globe until he was foot-sore. He was an ordinary man with the capabilities of an extraordinary genius that hadn't yet been put to a test." There was, of course, a girl with, of course, long hair, in this instance "raven curls tumbling low over her pink cheeks in such soft lustrous clusters...." Later, in 1901, he sold this story again, to *Redfield's Magazine* for eight dollars.

Sales to magazines, bigger and better-known than *Gray Goose* and *Four-O-Clock*, were sure to follow soon. He was on his way to success. He wasn't even sure he needed to attend classes anymore.

That was his attitude when two events happened in quick succession to bring about a radical change in his life—he got a job as a newspaper reporter and he got married. The two were tied together, and neither James nor Abby could dissuade him from either.

Chapter 8

Jim came up the path into the clearing overlooking the river and there she was, his dream girl come to life from the pages of one of his stories. The girl with the rarerip lips and raven hair, perhaps, with "ravishingly crimson lips, such a face of warmth and glow." Or a "marvelously pretty face, framed in a wealth of waving brown hair that curled low over her beautiful brow," straight from the pages of "The Angel of Heaven," written for the *Detroit Journal* two years before.

But no, this girl was alive and real, and right now she was blushing prettily at having been discovered dreaming in this secluded place above Schoolgirl Glen.

Cora Leon Johnson was 16, a lovely maiden with curling brown hair and laughing eyes. Daughter of a well-to-do family from Albany, New York, she was in Ann Arbor to study art. A skilled horsewoman, she loved the out-of-doors.

"Hello, I thought this was my retreat and I cannot recall having invited anyone to share it with me," the girl said to Jim who was momentarily speechless.

Then smiling up at him, she invited him to sit down. With a sweep of her arm, she indicated the autumn scene of red and gold before them. "Don't you think it's beautiful and inspiring?" she asked. "I love it." He found not only the scene but the girl inspiring, too. It was a whirlwind romance.

About this time Jim received a telegram from Pat Baker, news editor at the *Detroit News*. "Do you want a job as a reporter?" he asked. Baker was a big, gruff Irishman, respected among journalists, loved by his friends and feared by his enemies. Jim had met him before in the *News* office. He thought Baker an "ogre," and was afraid of him. Nevertheless, Jim quickly accepted the job.

"I saw fortune and glory ahead of me," he wrote in his autobiography. "Even nature and my story-writing were forgotten in the wild thrill of the moment."

Abby and James came down at Thanksgiving but they were unable to persuade Jim to stay in school. Jim dropped everything and went, bag and baggage, to become "the dumbest reporter that ever lived." It was December, 1899.

The move was highly disappointing. The first thing Baker told him was to get a haircut. Then he put him to work writing up funerals. Jim found that chasing fires, reading police reports and attending funerals weren't much fun, and writing what someone told him to write about was not only harder than finding his own stories, but definitely unsatisfying.

His first payday was a shock. When he opened his pay envelope the end of the first week, he took out only eight dollars. Eight dollars? He'd been making three and four times that a week selling stories and articles on his own.

Fred Janette was writing for the *News* now, too, but he was an editor and Jim was on the lowest reportorial level and feeling very small and trivial.

If Baker was an ogre, City Editor Ed Beck was an angel in Jim's eyes. Beck taught him not to make romantic features out of the funeral notices. In early January, when Jim and another reporter were sent to cover a big fire at the Parisian Laundry, Jim came back excited and enthusiastically wrote pages of description. Baker cut it down to three paragraphs and said it was fine. When Jim and Kiltie Stewart went over to the Canadian side of the river in early February to cover a hanging, Jim nearly fainted but he wrote his share of the story. Nearly all of this, too, was cut out.

Jim's imagination had run free for so long he found it difficult to confine himself to mere details and facts. He missed the free and easy life at the university.

He wasn't sure he was worth even eight dollars.

Jim had told Baker he was married, believing he'd be considered more mature and the pay might be a little better. So he needed a bride. Jim and Cora Leon Johnson, known as Leon, were married January 21, 1900 by a justice of the peace in Windsor, Ontario, across the river from Detroit so that the marriage wouldn't be discovered by a reporter at city hall in Detroit. He brought his new bride to his rooms at 45 Elm Street, close to the *Detroit News* offices.

Love in the autumn sunshine is not the same as dirty dishes and an unmade bed in a cold, grimy flat in the heart of the city.

Leon couldn't cook. She didn't know how to keep house. Her world had been fun and laughter up to now. How could she recognize in this brooding, intense young man the romantic lover who had swept her off her feet? And Jim, impatient, disappointed, dismayed at being responsible now not only for himself but for this dependent creature too, was anything but an ideal husband.

To make matters worse, Jim was fired from the *News* almost before the ink on the wedding license was dry. He had committed the unforgivable sin in newspaper reporting—he'd gotten someone's name wrong.

Hanging around city hall one day in February, he picked up a "scoop" about a window peeper, not particularly exciting in itself. This man, however, had tried to peep through a board fence at two women who had promptly and soundly horsewhipped him. That had possibilities for a big story and Jim raced back to the office to write it up. Surely this would get him recognition and, he hoped, a raise.

The story made the front page, but Jim's recognition was not what he had in mind.

When he reported for work the next morning, he was called into the editor's office. He'd had the last name of the window peeper right, but the first name was wrong and the one he'd used was that of a respectable citizen who failed to appreciate his sudden notoriety. He was, the irate citizen declared, "not in the habit of peeping through knotholes." He demanded an apology and retraction.

Jim was fired.

For weeks Jim tramped the streets looking for work, any kind of work. He spent a week shoveling coal. Neat, fastidious Jim Curwood shoveling coal. It was almost more than he could bear.

He struck out at the nearest object, his new bride. Leon testified at their divorce trial eight years later than he struck her for the first time only two weeks after they were married.

Everything had gone wrong from the very beginning in both the job and the marriage.

The only bright spot that February seemed to be that *Gray Goose* carried his story, "A Whisper from the Klondike," for which he'd gotten another small check. Again, he was writing about some place he'd never been.

There was a silver lining to all this trouble, as there usually is to any black cloud we encounter in life. The *News* office and Elm Street are downtown Detroit, which is along the riverfront. The train depot was here, and the docks and factories and warehouses and shipyards. The life of the river was here, ships and sailors and goods from all the ports of the world. He had seen the ships passing far out on Lake Erie when he was a boy in Ohio. Here, he saw them up close, got a glimpse of the world, talked to people who had actually been to India and Athabasca and the Klondike, all the places he'd been writing about, people from everywhere. He spent hours at the Seamen's Mission on Cadillac Square listening to old sailors tell tales of their adventures, his eager young mind soaking them all up, then he went home and put them down on paper.

It was cold that winter. A blizzard the end of February left 14 inches of snow piled up in impassable drifts. But even in winter the river was a busy place. Ice boating was the latest craze, and there was skating across to Canada, sleighing and tobogganing.

Whenever Jim wasn't job-hunting, he wrote. *Four O'Clock Magazine*, in its March issue, published his story "Veronica Haskelle," an old story originally titled "The Towers of Silence" which he'd tried to sell to *McClure's* in 1897. Was he thinking of Vera Haskell when he wrote it, or did he just use her name, as he so often would use names of his friends? The story takes place in Bombay.

Back home, the *Evening Argus* was wondering, too. "Veronica Haskell is the name of an Owosso young lady well known in local circles as a violinist of considerable ability," it reported (her name was actually Vera, of course). That, too, it noted, was the name of the heroine in Jim's story. "We see nothing in the story to suggest Miss Haskell unless the writer,...lets the thought be father of the wish—but no, Jim is already a married man. It was done out of compliment." Leon may have wondered, too.

Even though Jim had been fired as a reporter, the *News-Tribune* continued to publish his stories, buying them on his old free-lance basis. There was "The Pathetic Story of a Social Outcast" in March, "'Sailor Jim' and His Precious Bible" in April, "Mulvaney Lies in a Sandwich Grave" in September (Sandwich was Windsor, Ontario, across the river from Detroit). He sought out bums and bankers, lumbermen and lawyers for his stories. He was open to them all, went everywhere, to the missions on the waterfronts and to fancy office buildings, was observant and attentive, willing to listen to anyone no matter how odd a character he or she might be.

Abby and Amy came down in May for a few days. They brought Jim up to date on hometown news. Someone had run into his boyhood friend of the old West Town days, Charlie Miller, up at the Soo (Saulte Ste. Marie in Michigan's Upper Pensinsula), and Charlie had conned him out of some money. Fred Frieseke, now in Paris, had sold a painting for $50. His Infallible Blood Purifier friend, Leslie Hanes, was now in London representing a zither company and had just married an English girl.

The *Argus* was saying that he'd left his job with the *News* to write stories for the *McClure* syndicate. In fact, he'd sent stories to *McClure's* and once told the *Argus* one had been accepted, but *McClure's* had yet to publish any of them.

James and Abby came for a ten-day visit in August. Shortly after they went home, Abby was struck by a bicycle and injured. "This is another evidence of reckless riding which can not be too severely condemned," the *Argus* stated.

Teddy Roosevelt stopped by in Owosso for 25 minutes. Leslie Hanes came home from England. Ethel Greenwood was treasurer of the junior class at Owosso High School. Martha Pier of Flint married Frederick Woodard of Owosso and they planned to build a house on John Street, just a few doors down from where the Curwoods lived along the river.

It was not, however, a good time for Jim. He prowled downtown.

Going through one of the big office buildings one day, looking for work and for stories, he stopped at random in the office of an old gentleman. They sat and talked for an hour. This was Alfred Russell, a lawyer of some prominence in Detroit. When he left, Jim carried with him a letter from Russell to Harry Stillman of Parke-Davis and Company, makers of pharmaceuticals in a plant along the river off Jefferson Avenue.

It wasn't exactly a writing job. In fact, he wasn't a writer at all, not at first. Put simply, he was a pillroller. How could he let the folks back home know what he was doing in Detroit when he'd kept them so supplied with news of his progress? How could he tell them he was now making hair tonic, or was working in the cod liver oil department? Assaulted by the sounds of machinery and the smells of the oils and other ingredients from which they were made, he made pills of all shapes, sizes and colors. Americans, he learned, were tremendous pill eaters.

But, as always, he kept his eyes and his ears open, taking note of everything. His apprenticeship eventually brought its rewards. In January, 1904, *Leslie's Weekly* published "Pills, An American Staple," and in September, 1910, *World To-Day* published "Americans a Nation of Pill Eaters."

Having experienced all the various workings of a pill company, Jim went to work in its correspondence department; in other words, he went into advertising. But he made more money than at the *News*.

Of course he continued to write, and the *News* occasionally bought his stories. Nevertheless, it was a year after his story of a young man who'd bummed his way to England was published in November that he made another sale. "The Fourteenth Floater o' Jacob Strauss" appeared in *Wayside Tales* in December 1901. It was a short fiction story of a freighter on Lake St. Clair, written in dialect and including a poem by Charles B. Parsons, a Detroit poet.

That was the first of his lake stories.

In the meantime, though, January 1, 1901, was the beginning of a new century, and things were looking up for Jim. He and Leon moved to a better apartment, on Lysander Street. Jim was working and writing, and spending his spare time searching the city for stories. Leon very likely found little changed except the move to Lysander Street.

Jack and Amy caused a sensation in Chesaning in August 1901 by arriving in an automobile. It had no windshield, no top and no radiator, was steered by means of a tiller, and had tires not much larger than those of a bicycle. Jack gave the local ladies rides around town. The auto, a Mobile Steamer, didn't belong to Jack, of course, but to J.C. Shattuck, owner of the Michigan Sewing Machine and Organ Company in Owosso, for whom Jack often worked, and it was the only automobile in three counties. A few days later, Jack led a circus parade in Owosso, something only a very few auto drivers had ever done in the entire country.

President McKinley, shot at the Pan American Exposition in Buffalo, died of his wounds and the *Detroit Journal* sent Fred Janette to cover the funeral.

Jim and Leon went to Owosso in October for a vacation, and with James, Abby and Ralph went camping at the Saginaw Marshes, part of the St. Charles Flats where he'd spent those spring weeks so long ago. They hunted and fished, though the hunting was poor. Jack, Amy and Merrick Blair also came up for a few days' fishing.

In early December Abby was very ill. Jim and Leon came home and Ed and Stella came from Ohio. By the holidays the crisis had passed and Abby was much improved.

Jack dressed up as Santa and drove around town in the automobile, delighting his young daughters and the other children in town. The world was getting a bit beyond him, Santa told the children, what with telephones and electric lights. There was no telling what they'd be expecting in their stockings these days, probably things like roller skates and bicycles instead of dolls and sleds. Not even Queen and Marguerite recognized their father.

Magazines besides *Gray Goose* were now looking favorably at his work. He copied his old story, "Why the Police Subaltern Fled Jagadhri," retitled it "The Red-Headed Tigress," and sent it to *Wayside Tales* where it was published in February, 1902. He was paid $25 for that and his "Fourteenth Floater" story.

The *News-Tribune* was buying again, and *Redfield's Magazine* took a couple of his old stories which had been published before. He was learning about reprints, the publishing of something that has appeared elsewhere before.

Jim was like a sponge, soaking up everything around him and pouring it out again in his stories. At some time or other, almost everything he saw or heard or felt found its way into his writing.

The ice-boating craze on the Detroit River led to a story, "The Wreck of the Winsome Winny," an exciting story about a boy and his uncle on their way from Detroit to Sandusky by ice-boat who come across some "sheep smugglers" on their way from the Canadian side to the Michigan shore. It was published in March, 1903, in *The American Boy*. He would sell a lot of stories and articles to *American Boy*, articles on how to grow peanuts at home, how to hunt muskrats and to trap moles, on federal fisheries and sunken ships in the Detroit River, and fiction like the Winsome Winny story and one about a boy hunting in Arizona.

In the spring of 1902 Mason Wood, James' old friend, died. And up at St. Charles, plans were underway to drain 5,000 acres of the swamp Jim had explored years before.

In May, the *News* hired Jim again, this time as a special writer for the Sunday section. His boss this time was Annesley Burrowes, an Englishman much older than Jim and a longtime newspaperman. The two became good friends. The Sunday section offices were on the second floor of the *News* building on Shelby Street. Jim stayed five years.

Working for Parke-Davis and then the News brought security. Detroit put him in touch with story sources that would bring him stature in the field of writing. His first successes were in Detroit. Later, he kept rooms there, talked of moving back there, escaped to the city as a haven from troubles at home after he'd moved back to Owosso, and went there often on business. But his heart was never there.

"God meant for us to taste the bitter with the sweet," Jim said later, "and those years in Detroit were the bitter."

Chapter 9

Malcom V. MacInnes, "Mac," was a Canadian colonization agent stationed in Detroit. A jovial, slightly portly, mustachioed man, some years older than Jim, Mac's mind was filled with vivid pictures of his beloved Canada.

Jim met him in 1902 and Mac began painting for Jim scenes of the vast landscapes beyond the Great Lakes. He talked of the sweep of the prairies that lay waiting for someone to touch them with plow and scythe and transform them into giant fields of grain. There were, he said, forests and mountains such as Jim could never imagine, rivers more awesome than the Shiawassee during spring flood, game so plentiful there would be enough for all the hunters who might ever come, the Barren Lands, wind-swept plains too cold even for snow. Jim was enthralled.

Mac introduced Jim to immigration officers, members of Parliament, Hudson's Bay Company people, men of the Canadian Pacific and Grand Trunk railroads, and of the Royal North West Mounted Police. Many of these men would be extremely important to Jim in the years ahead, and he did not forget their kindnesses and their help.

Mac was another turning point. He probably influenced Jim's writing more than anyone else he met, more than Fred who had given him that early encouragement, more than Ed Beck who'd ridden herd on his flamboyant prose, even more than Abby and Amy whose belief in Jim began early and never wavered.

Jim looked at Canada and found the source of material and inspiration that would carry him on to the success he dreamed of—to be read by people everywhere, and to be paid and paid well.

But not yet.

Jim spent his free time along the Detroit riverfront. He talked with the men of the lakes, from seaman to captain to ship owner.

The ships that ply the Great Lakes are long, workhorse carriers of grain and iron ore and steel, riding low in the water as they steam down from the upper lakes loaded with ore and grain for the ports of the east or northbound with steel and coal, bouyantly high when their holds are empty. They have been ploughing these inland seas since the opening of the Erie Canal, for what would be the use of the wealth of grain in Alberta, Saskatchewan, the Dakotas and eastern Montana without the ships to transport it to the hungry world? What would the mines of Minnesota and Wisconsin and Michigan's Upper Peninsula do without the lake freighters to haul copper and iron ore to the smelters in Pennsylvania and New York?

The seas they sail are as wicked as any to be found, as wild and untamed as any ocean, the only predictability being that, come spring and fall, no vessel is safe from the storms that rage, and each season, any ship that dares to sail them may not reach port. In winter, the lakes are locked in with ice; it is the last weeks of autumn that are the most treacherous. Of all the lakes, Lake Superior is the deepest, the coldest, the most treacherous. Once a ship clears the St. Mary's Rapids, where Michigan's Upper Peninsula and Canada nearly touch at the Soo, and goes west through the Locks into the waters of Lake Superior, the ship and its crew are at the mercy of the waves—and the Lord.

Jim was now taking short sails on the lakes. He wrote about the ships, about the sailors who rode them and the men who owned them. He was young and eager, brash and likeable, and the men of the lakes, from seaman to captain, talked freely of their lives. Sometimes he wrote the stories they told him as his own, sometimes as interviews. He learned about copyrighting his work.

At home, things were not going well. He didn't know how to deal with marriage. In the fall of 1902, Leon was pregnant. He was trapped, bound to a desk and a job that satisfied him only in that it gave him time to write and brought him into contact with story sources. Out of frustration, anger, fear, whatever drives a man to do this, he struck Leon a blow that left a lasting scar, one she would later show the judge to prove her divorce plea. She said he struck and cursed her often during her pregnancy.

Nowhere is there any record of Jim's side of their domestic difficulties. How much of what Leon claimed was true or whether she may have provoked him was never revealed publicly. He did not contest the divorce. He denied Leon's charges that he beat her, and took upon himself the blame for the failure of their marriage.

Whenever he could, he went home to Owosso and his family, sometimes with Leon, sometimes without.

In September, the *Evening Argus* carried an article about Jim. It said he had been "quite successful in the way of discovering publishers for his original stories, articles and poems." He had had, the paper reported, 18 stories and six poems published since January. Of course, it also said he'd graduated from the University of Michigan in the Class of 1899, and of course he hadn't graduated at all. And that he'd made the longest bicycle trip on record, six thousand miles, but that too, was incorrect, and besides, Leslie Hanes, now back in the States and living in New York, had also made the trip and he, too, was a former Owosso boy. Jim, however, who probably wrote the article, was tooting his own horn. He was working on a book about Canada, or so he said. Such a book was never published, although almost all of his novels were set in Canada.

In September, too, a story appeared in the *News-Tribune* on "How I

Caught 1,000 Sea Lions" under the byline of Capt. J R. Mullet of Detroit, but copyrighted by J. Olivier Curwood. He turned this into his own adventure, telling the story as though he had been on the boat off the California coast, when it was published in *The Era Magazine* in February 1904 as "With the Lions of Anacapa" under his own byline. He never, then or later, went to California.

"Moogwa, the Three Thieves and the Man-Squaw," was published in September 1902 in *The Era*. He was paid twenty dollars for this somewhat confusing story set in the Southwest. "Coraleone, the Story of a Beautiful Spook," which appeared in the December issue of *Redfield's Magazine*, took its theme from the popularity of seances and mediums, and its name, of course, from Leon.

Ethel Greenwood graduated from Owosso High School in June that year as vice president of her class, and took some summer classes at Ypsilanti Normal near Ann Arbor. She began teaching in Laingsburg, a village south of Owosso. She was 19. Street and sidewalk paving was continuing in Owosso. The Fred Woodards had a son named Pier.

Jack was still getting attention driving Shattuck's car. In May he'd taken a rural mailman on his rounds and they cut the time for the 27-mile route in half, down to three hours, and would have done it faster if there had not been a strong head wind. He drove it in the Labor Day parade, with a frame built around it resembling a ship, with advertising signs plastered on the sides.

Woodard Manufacturing, of which Fred Woodard was manager, was building a new furniture factory, and the Estey company was in bankruptcy. Vera Haskell, studying at the American Conservatory in Detroit, was now an assistant teacher there.

President Theodore Roosevelt's carriage was struck by a trolley car in Pittsfield, Massachusetts. The *Flint Journal* raised the question of electric cars speeding down Saginaw Street: How did we ever get along without them? Michigan was now the number one bean growing state.

Amy came down to visit in December. Ed and Stella and their infant son, Guy, were in Owosso for New Year's, but Jim and Leon, six-and-a-half months pregnant, stayed in Detroit for the holidays.

In his capacity as special writer, Jim did feature stories for the *News-Tribune*, the Sunday edition of the combined *News* and *Tribune* which were separate during the week.

Carlotta was born in March, 1903. Jim had just received a check for one of his stories. Elated, he cashed it and took his money in one dollar bills, went home and tossed it into the air over Leon in bed. She didn't find it funny. Leon, who was the gay half of this marriage, had apparently lost her sense of humor.

Jim and Leon had moved again, to Third Avenue, still downtown. The street was only three blocks long, the first one being paved with brick and the other two, including in front of Jim's house, with cedar.

This year, 1903, Jim got acquainted with two young men who were just starting a magazine called *Twentieth Century Review*. They eagerly accepted Jim's stories, the first one being "The Most Remarkable Town in North America," about Rosthern, Saskatchewan. Mac surely supplied the information for this. They gave him a big, front page announcement, which Jim proudly showed to everyone, and promised to pay him soon. Each time he stopped by their offices, however, the safe was empty. Nevertheless, he continued to write for the magazine. "Lost in Madagascar" was a six-part serial which began in May. "Son of a Hero" appeared in August. Eventually he received as pay, for his serial and the two short stories, a B-B gun.

Jim was doing a tremendous amount of work now. There was his job at the *News-Tribune* and his free lancing. He wrote, either at the office or at home, seven days a week.

His article in *Overland Monthly* in May on the "American Invasion of Canada" questioned the Canadian government's method of colonization, importing people from the United States. A number of families from Owosso had gone north after an agent visited there. What about when all these people had earned the right to vote? Wouldn't they Americanize the provinces, he wondered.

Otherwise the several articles he wrote on Canada were full of praise for the way the prairie was being settled, with cities growing up there almost overnight as the railroad lines were pushed westward. Most of his information certainly came from Mac, though he had begun to take a few quick train trips out from Thunder Bay, seeing for himself the expanse of the prairie land he was writing about.

There was little time for family, although he did go to see his mother shortly after Carlotta was born. They all went to Owosso in April, or it may be that he took Leon and the baby on that first visit and left them with his mother, bringing them home in April. If so, he would have had many peaceful days to write without the annoyance of wife and child, something that would have pleased him.

That summer, Amy and eight-year-old Queen came down to visit. Queen thought Aunt Leon fun and her Uncle Jim stern.

Jim was now acting managing editor of the Sunday edition while Annesley Burrowes was on a three-month vacation. He was preoccupied with his work, but at home the rest of the family spent their days in games and play. Leon taught Queen how to spell Mississippi: "M, i, crooked letter, crooked letter, i, crooked letter, crooked letter, i, p, p, i." One day, as Amy lay on the bed holding Carlotta over her head and tickling her, one of the slats broke and the bed fell down. They all laughed and laughed, while the dishes waited to be washed and dinner to be cooked.

Jim did take time out to go with them to Log Cabin Park on the trolley, but the windows of the car were open and he worried that Carlotta might take cold from the breeze blowing in since Leon had only wrapped her in a thin cashmere sweater. In July, James, Abby and Cora stopped to visit on their way home from a trip to see Ed and Stella who now lived in Oberlin, Ohio.

Ralph was working for Hunt's Grocery. A Rambler Touring car made the nearly 100 miles from Detroit to Owosso in less than a day; in fact, it made 54 miles in only three hours! Johnny Shotwell, boy wonder of the pitching mound, was playing baseball for Laingsburg that summer, but it was indoor baseball that would make "Shotty" famous throughout the state.

That fall, Ethel Greenwood went to Vernon, another nearby village, to teach the grammar class.

In September Jim, Leon and Carlotta were in Owosso on vacation. Jim spent part of the time in the St. Charles marshes.

In "A Commonsense View of Trusts" in *Overland Monthly* that September, Jim was introduced to his readers as J. Olivier Curwood, B A., B.PH. Just what the letters meant wasn't explained, but the blurb by his picture said he'd "made a special study of economics," and had given up a year to study the "race question, visiting every Southern State East of the Mississippi," none of which was true, of course. His photo shows him with his hair parted in the middle and a faint smile on his full mouth. He was taking himself very seriously now.

"Unsatisfied," Jim's poem in *Overland Monthly* in December, was a rather strange departure from his usual virile stories of the lakes, beginning

> "I think that man would die of weariness
> Were there no seas too deep for him to wade,
> No wastes of sky to make his thought afraid,
> No unclimbed peaks with pure snow passionless,
> No still receding aim above success,
> No depths of joy and grief, of light and shade,
> But all things equable and smooth and staid . . ."
> and ends,
> "Ah, let life never not be marvelous,
> For love, like him of Judah sent by God,
> Dies if he goes by the old ways again."

His byline was J. Olivier Curwood. He often wrote poetry, but this is apparently the only poem of his ever published.

"Pills, An American Staple" was published in the January 1904 issue of *Leslie's Illustrated Weekly*. "The pill and civilization walk hand in hand," he wrote. "Where the pill is, there, also, is civilized man." Detroit, then, he said, remembering his days at Parke, Davis, was the center of civilization, "for she is the world's most prolific, tireless and versatile producer of pills."

He was paid $60 for his article, the most he'd received so far. "And remember, it is our custom to pay old friends still better than new ones," Ellery Sedgewick wrote him. *Leslie's* published more than fifty of Jim's stories and articles, and they paid him very well indeed.

He began to write serious non-fiction of the lakes, stories of the Inland Seas, and added *Woman's Home Companion* to his list of magazines in which he was now published.

That August Jim took his first hunting trip into Canada. With his guide, Mose Meuse, he went from Thunder Bay north toward Lake Nipigon to hunt. He learned quickly to follow the advice of his guide. He and the Indian in his canoe chose to shoot a "fools rapids," rapids that should never be shot when "a good hundred miles lies between you and any other provision than that at your feet. Of course we lost our beans; we lost our bacon; we lost our flour," he said in an article later. But he found a hunter's paradise, a land where game abounded.

Sitting beside the evening campfire on that first clear, still night bright with stars, he listened to the silence as he watched the rim of the moon rise over the treetops, unbroken wilderness stretching endlessly beyond. This is what he had yearned for, this was life, and in the Canadian wilderness, sampled only sparsely on this first hunting trip, he would find adventure and romance to satisfy his soul—and to fill more than two dozen books.

"At last—good boy!" Frank A. Munsey wrote Jim in December of 1904, and sent a check for $75 for "Captain of the Christopher Duggan." This was the first of many of Jim's stories Munsey would publish in his various magazines, which included *Munsey's, Argosy* and *Cavalier.*

He had arrived at last! Jim decided to quit the *News* to write full-time, but Annesley talked him out of it. Before the year was out, Annesley's failing eyesight forced him to quit and Jim was named Sunday managing editor with a raise to $30 a week.

In addition to his work on the *News-Tribune* and his story and article writing, he began editing some local paint manufacturing and banking publications. No wonder he had no time or energy left for his family.

The variety of his stories continued, though he had less time to spend now among the seamen and dock workers. He met a Detroit millionaire who quietly collected art objects and as quietly donated much of his collection to the Smithsonian Institute. He met Fannie Baker, the only female deep sea diver searching for sunken ships in the Great Lakes.

In 1905, Jim had a house built on Woodland out at the end of the trolley line in Highland Park on Detroit's northwest side. It was the last move he and Leon would make together.

That fall he went hunting in Canada again, this time with Teddy Brown as his guide. He'd also taken a train trip as far as Saskatoon, and gone on horseback out upon the prairie to feel for himself the grandeur of the open plains and to meet the people who had come to tame this wild limitless land. One of these was a young rancher named Frank Cahill who would be the subject for a story a few years later, and of much help to an old friend like Jim Curwood.

Thrilling tales of adventure on the Lakes were now mixed equally with tender love stories. In "The Copper Ship," based on the sinking of a real copper ship, his hero, named Jimmy—from here on, many of his heroes would be named Jim—was blinded in a fight with a mutinous crew. There was a girl on board—it was not unusual for wives or daughters of the captain to sail on freighters, and often the cook was the wife of one of the crew—with, of course, "rich waves of hair falling about her cheeks." In "The Lake Breed," the heroine on board was named Jeanne. She, too, had long and beautiful hair.

Jim had the ability to put his readers into the midst of the action, to make them feel the spray of the waves washing over the ship, feel the heat of fire, strain to see through the fog, and to keep them coming back for more.

Ralph, now 22, married Vera B. "Vee" Morris in April. He'd wanted to come to Detroit and had written his Uncle Jim about finding work. Jim wrote back that he had "high hope of getting you something to do before long." Would he like something on a lake passenger boat? Jim had "somewhat of a pull" with one of them. Instead, Ralph took a job with the railroad in Ann Arbor.

Jack quit Michigan Central Railroad at last and went to work for the Ideal Engine Company.

Another daughter, Viola, was born to Jim and Leon on June 30, 1906. Leon was ill for a time afterward, and Amy came down to take care of her. When Amy went home, James brought Queen down on the train to stay a week. Queen had been to Detroit before, of course, but this time she was staying on by herself. As soon as James left, Queen began to cry. And she continued to cry. Jim, standing at the top of the stairs, running his hands through his hair, lost his patience.

"For heaven's sake, shut up," he yelled at Queen. "I'll send you home if it's the last thing I do." On Tuesday, he did just that, putting her on the train alone with admonitions from both him and Leon not to talk to strangers. She spent most of the trip on her knees, leaning over the back of her seat talking to the man behind her.

Almost everyone in the family went down to visit Jim and Leon now and then. Closer at hand was his cousin Golda Clarke, now 21 and working in Detroit. She and her fiance, Elwood Stretch, came often. They liked Leon, and found her fun to be with.

Ethel Greenwood, after a year at Fennville on the Lake Michigan shore, was back with the Vernon schools. Fred Janette, now state editor on the News, had just had a book for boys published, *Captain Tip-Top*.

Jim's reputation as a writer of stories of the Great Lakes, both fiction and nonfiction, brought him to the attention of Hewitt Hanson Howland, editor of *The Reader Magazine*. He wrote Jim in July and suggested a series on the Lakes and the ships. Jim began at once.

Jim also began a book, a novel he titled "The Courage of Captain Plum," about the Mormon colony on Lake Michigan's Beaver Island ruled by the notorious "King" Strang. He had met a descendant of Strang aboard a lake freighter and, using the seaman's story of his relative as background, Jim fictionalized the story and turned it into a rousing adventure story.

In September, Jim, Leon and the girls went up to Owosso. Jim went on to Canada to hunt again, again with Mose Meuse. From Mose and from Teddy Brown he was learning there was more to hunting than just shooting. It was far more interesting to learn the creature's habits and its character, and he began a life-long love affair with bears, the "most lovable creatures of the wild."

It was people, though, that interested him most. As he had done with the seamen, he now spent hours listening to tales of the stalwart men and virtuous women of the northland, to Indian legends and stories of heroism, to tales of the Royal North West Mounted Police. He also began to learn the Cree language. He thought it the most beautiful of languages.

It may have been on this trip that he met an Indian girl, "the sweet-voiced, dark-eyed little half-Cree maiden" to whom he later dedicated a book, and had an "affair," as Leon hinted when she was suing for divorce. Or he may have been merely impressed by the beauty and innocence of the many half-Indian, half-French women he met in the north.

Moving pictures had come to Owosso and were shown at the Opera House, in color, the first real moving picture shows in Owosso. Going out to eat somewhere fancy meant the New National Hotel where the menu included an entree of frog's legs, with soup, meats, pasta, bread, relishes, vegetables, white and sweet potatoes, Waldorf salad, pies, watermelon, ice cream and other desserts, nuts, cheese and beverages, all for 35 cents.

Ed and Stella now lived in Conneaut, Ohio, and ran a general store. The family—James and Abby, Amy and Jack, and some of the others—went there often, stopping off in Detroit on their way to and from Ohio.

As always, there were frequent visits home to Owosso, the train making the trip quick and easy. In the fall, Ed and Stella were there, too, and of course, there was a short camping trip up to the marshes.

Perriton Maxwell, editor of *Cosmopolitan*, in accepting Jim's story, "Captain Kidd of the Underground," said he would pay the standard rate of $20 per thousand words, and have the story "splendidly illustrated. Send us more of your Great Lakes stories if you care to and I will give you special editorial answer," he wrote, and asked Jim to send a photo of himself if he had one.

Howland suggested the Lakes series be published as a book after its run in the magazine. This was something Jim would later use over and over again—magazine serialization followed by book publication. The system would make him rich.

By the end of 1906, Jim was working on his novel, his series on the Lakes for *The Reader*, his job at the *News*, and his lake stories of fish pirates and salvage, beautiful women and brave men in love. He was doing articles about Canada and editing the banking publication, working on them at the office, working on the books and stories at home.

If he was lucky, he got five hours of sleep a night. He had no time for an unhappy wife and two small girls. He was affable and charming when seeking stories, but his arrival home was more to be dreaded than welcomed.

His stories and articles nearly always sold the first time out. Money was no longer a worry. His salary at the *News* was minor compared to what he earned with his other writing. He was married, the father of two daughters. They lived in a fine new home in a fashionable suburb, and he had a wide circle of friends and acquaintances. He could consider himself an up-and-coming young man. He was 28 years old.

Chapter 10

The news in 1908 of Jim's death in the Canadian wilds may have caused great distress to his family, but it amused Leon. When a *Detroit News* reporter called to ask her about it, she scoffed at the story and called it a publicity stunt.

Jim's "death" did come at a convenient time. His first two books were about to be released by Bobbs-Merrill Company, he had a contract to produce four more for them, and G. P. Putnam's Sons was putting his series on the Great Lakes into book form.

The dispatch from Winnipeg said Jim had been shot by Indians in the Lac La Ronge country. The white man who brought in the first report said Jim had instigated the trouble by shooting one of the Indians, the rest then retaliating. The Mounted Police were investigating. Jim contradicted this version when he got back out to "civilization." He said the trouble was among his guides and that he was not involved at all.

The day after the Winnipeg report was issued, a *News* reporter called on Leon. What did she know about it? "Jack London was reported lost at sea at the psychological moment, and then came to life again. You know Curwood. I take no stock in the report," Leon said.

"I don't want to be represented as laughing at the report of his death from Winnipeg, but its an improbable tale," she added. She had just sued Jim for divorce.

The hunting and exploring trip into the Canadian wilds was the first of Jim's ventures as a full-time free-lance writer and as a free man again.

The year before, 1907, had been an extremely busy one, with at least fifteen major stories published. He was now hitting the better magazines: *McCall's*, *Red Book* and *Cosmopolitan*, *People's Magazine* for the first time, *Munsey's* again, and others. Not only was he producing a lot of material, it was of great variety.

He had branched out into humor, as with "Miss Evangeline" in *Red Book's* August issue. Humorless as he was about himself, he had a fine hand with satire and wit which appeared in those years before he became primarily a book writer, showed up again when he began writing for the young movie industry, and then virtually disappeared in his later years.

There were serious works, such as "Commerce on the Great Lakes" for *World's Work*, and his articles for *The Reader* which included the Great Lakes series. There was drama in "The Bannockburn Widow," published in *Cosmoplitan* in May, and "Salvage" in *Munsey's* May issue. He ended the year with "In the Wilderness," one of his many hunting articles, published by *The Reader* in December. Six of the stories that would be included in the posthumous *Falkner of the Inland Seas* were published this year, altered later to make the stories coherent as a series.

All this was in addition, of course, to his work at the News, his various other publicity writing, his articles on Canada, and work on three books.

He spent long hours away from home and long hours at his typewriter when he was home. It left little time or thought for his family, which was just as well for Leon and the girls. When he did take notice, it was usually with anger. He was to regret his extreme behavior later and feel shamed by it. Surprisingly, it did not estrange either Leon or his daughters as it might very well have done.

Since he tended to inform everyone of his successes, and surely made no secret of his distaste for his job, he did not endear himself to many people at the *News*, which led to the caustic report of his death.

When it came to men in the publishing industry, however, Jim was a different person. He wrote friendly letters, confided his hopes and plans, asked—and took—their advice, and chided them when someone else published something they had turned down. He kept relations cordial even when he went over to competitors, and seldom did anyone seem to mind when he did so, except to regret that they were no longer publishing his work.

In 1907 he tried an agent and sent him a story called "Misery of the Millions." It apparently dealt with divorce and how to avoid it. "If more men and women followed your hero's example there might be fewer divorces," the agent wrote. The story was never published, and in spite of his hero's "example," it failed to prevent his own divorce the next year. He went back to marketing his work himself.

The Great Lakes was a fruitful field for both fiction and nonfiction. Jim's long association with the men of the Lakes brought him entré to much information. He knew not only the men who sailed the ships and the men who owned them, but he was well acquainted with those in power—William Livingstone, president of the Lake Carriers Association, and James A. Calbich, president of the Lumber Carriers Association, and others. It was Livingstone who gave him the idea of telling what the ships carry in their journeys up and down the Lakes by "building" an imaginary city with their cargoes.

Jim sought out these men for information for his series and other articles, got permission to investigate at will the building of the ships and their loads of steel and ore, free rein to explore the ships from stem to stern and invitations to sail aboard them. Lake freighters, in spite of their rough exterior, often had passenger accommodations as luxurious as ocean liners.

In his articles he began to stress the importance of Lake shipping, trying to make his readers see the romance and tragedy it held, as thrilling as any stories of ocean travel. He couldn't understand how people couldn't see what lay there before their eyes, or why they thought it was only on an ocean voyage that they could find adventure.

Jim's trips on the lakes took him to nearly every port the ships visited, but mainly he traveled from Detroit to the Thunder Bay region at the western end of Lake Superior. Soon he knew the men at the northern end of the run almost as well as those in Detroit. It was a natural progression, then, that his hunting trips began at Thunder Bay, trips that began as pleasurable hunting excursions but soon grew into sources for stories.

His many articles on Canada, fed him by Mac or from brief trips west and north of Thunder Bay, soon convinced the Canadian government to do what it had never done before, hire an American as a public relations writer to encourage settlement of its western provinces. At Mac's urging, the Canadian Immigration Department offered him a salary of $1,800 a year, plus expenses, to explore the west and write articles that would bring in more settlers, in spite of the fact that some of his early articles had questioned the government's methods of colonization with people from the United States.

With passes to ride the railroads for free, and the camera and other photographic materials Mac had also secured for him—the finest of equipment; Jim never skimped on things important to himself—Jim began to delve deeper into the Canadian wilderness than his short hunting trips had taken him to date.

In April Jim went up to see his father who was having trouble with muscular rheumatism. Owosso now had two movie theaters, with another one coming soon. Alex Johnson, Owosso's colored barber and a Civil War veteran, died. Johnson was a well-liked member of the Grand Army of the Republic, flag bearer when the Owosso contingent went to Washington, D.C. for a parade some years earlier. The town turned out for his funeral.

Perhaps because the town respected a black man, or perhaps because he had an inborn sense of justice, Jim was not only blind to differences in race—Owosso also had a Chinese laundry—but to religion, wealth, power, or any other divisive differences in his fellow human beings.

In May Jim met Howland in Chicago to discuss the Great Lakes series. Thereafter he often went to Chicago, Indianapolis, and then New York to talk to editors and film makers.

Alton Rundell was elected vice president of the Michigan Sportsmen's Association. The sportsmen in Owosso and all of Shiawassee County were becoming a voice in the state.

In May, too, he went on a spring bear hunting trip with Teddy Brown. If there was a nadir in Jim's life as a killer of wild life, this was it. He wanted a bear cub as a pet. When he came face to face with a female with two cubs, and the bear turned off the path to avoid him, he foolishly shot her with buckshot, and wounded one of the cubs in the process, blinding it in one eye. The bear, of course, was now ready for fight. Jim dropped his useless gun and ran. His young and inexperienced dog also took flight. Later, when Teddy had arrived and the dogs had treed the bear and her cubs, Jim shot the mother. He and Teddy captured the cubs, but they could never tame them.

He exposed his own cruelty and cowardice to his readers three years later in an article for *Outing Magazine*, "The Poetic Justice of Uko San," for that is what he'd named the cub, and revealed the ending of the story in which, on a subsequent hunting trip with Teddy, he had come face to face with Uko San again, the young hunting dog dead between its forepaws. This time, he lowered his gun and let the bear go.

Leon was sick that spring, and in the hospital when Carlotta was bitten by a neighbor's dog in late May. When the dog died, Jim and Leon, out of the hospital but still sick, took her to the Pasteur Institute at the University of Michigan in Ann Arbor for a series of painful rabies shots.

The advertising side of magazines had never been part of Jim's concern, but now Howland explained how *The Reader* wanted to combine advertising and circulation with the Lakes series so as to get the most from it. Jim began to see the practical side to magazine publication. Thereafter he better understood his editors when they juggled, rejected or hurried his work, or asked him to write certain stories.

The *Reader Magazine* was published by Bobbs-Merrill Company, and Howland talked with both Mr. Bobbs and Mr. Merrill about publishing the series as a book. In the end, however, Bobbs-Merrill published only Jim's fiction and G. P. Putnam's & Sons published *The Great Lakes*.

Jim proposed an article on big game hunting for *The Reader*. It should be, Howland said, an article "for the hunter and as you are a Nimrod and I am not,..." Write about what kind of game, where it was, how to get it, and so on. They published it in December as "In the Wilderness." It was a practical guide to hunting big game. It was the first of his hunting or nature stories.

One night, working on the book about the Mormon colony, there was a knock at the door. Jim opened it to a man who said he was one of King Strang's sons and asked to read the manuscript. While he read, Jim nervously eyed the door. When the man had finished, he offered Jim a check for $10,000 in exchange for the manuscript and Jim's promise to forget the story. Jim accepted with relief.

It was Sunday so he couldn't cash the check until the next day. That night a package arrived by special delivery. Opening it, he found his manuscript and a note. "Stung. The suppers are on you." It was signed by a dozen of his friends.

They went to supper and lit their cigars with the worthless check.

Why not turn some of his hunting experiences into a book for boys, Jim wondered. Bobbs-Merrill was getting into juveniles but was interested in a series. A "stray juvenile published alone stands small chance of success, but if a man can work out a series...there is sale for them and money in them," they wrote him. Each one helps sell the ones before; it would take about three in a series to get any real results.

He began work immediately on *The Wolf Hunters*, about a youth who goes hunting in Ontario with a young Indian whom he had met at school in Detroit.

Bobbs-Merrill offered Jim its standard book contract, with ten percent royalty, but "it is not the size of the percentage that counts but the size of the check he (the author) receives at the end of the royalty period, which by the way is every six months," Howland wrote him. The contract called for Jim to write five books, not to include "The Courage of Captain Plum," nor the Great Lakes series which was to be published by Putnam's.

Two fiction books now, the series on the lakes and its resultant book, articles and short stories—Jim was working feverishly to do them all. He sent Viola, now one year old, to Abby and James for the winter, and though they had planned on going down to Florida, out of the cold, they stayed home.

Jim was to receive $150 each for his Great Lakes articles, other magazines were paying $50-$100 for stories and articles, the Canadian government was paying him a salary and financing his travels. Now, at last, he could quit his job at the *News*. He did so promptly, with publicity, of course.

Pleased with the articles Jim had written about Canada, the Canadian immigration officials were only too glad to pave the way for his trips, providing him with information, photographs and introductions, and sometimes even written articles that Jim had only to rework into his own style and add his name to.

Grand Trunk Railroad sent transportation for Jim and a photographer. His first choice was his brother Ed, but when Ed couldn't get away, he asked his cousin, Leon Griffin. So in spite of all his other commitments—the Lake series, the books, and other articles and stories he had promised—the two men set off in October of 1907 for the wilds of Ontario.

Indian guides were waiting for them at Wabinosh House, a Hudson's Bay Post north of Thunder Bay, Jim told the *Argus*, and in the spring they would go overland to Hudson Bay. Actually, they were gone about three weeks.

While he was gone, Howland, feeling that a change in Jim's byline was important and not being able to reach him, bylined Jim's story on the Thunder Bay region J. O. Curwood. He hoped that was alright, he wrote Jim.

"Better start right, or what seems right to us, now that you are entering the national field," Howland wrote. "There is great value in having a name people can remember and pronounce easily. J.O. Curwood is short, sharp and memorable." Jim, who had used J.O. before, approved. "It is good of you to take in such friendly spirit our suggestion," Howland replied.

The *Detroit News* might scoff at Jim, but the *Journal* was still willing to publicize his literary efforts and did so with an article in December, expounding on his knowledge of the lakes, his hunting and his membership in a Detroit troop of calvary. All his life, Jim was an enthusiastic horseman, and took pride in his skill on horseback.

"The Building of the Ships," the first of "The Romance of the Great Lakes" series, was published in *The Reader Magazine* January 1908. But right away there was bad news. *The Reader* has been "caught in a squeeze," Howland wrote, and is consolidating with *Putnam's Magazine*. It is a disappointment, he said. The magazines will carry both titles in March and be published from New York. J.B. Gilder of *Putnam's* dealt with the series now, and although they already had a series on the lakes, decided to continue Jim's but cut his pay to $125 for each story. "I regret this is the best arrangement...we could make."

Jim had another name change, this one the final one. He asked Gilder to use his full name from thereon.

At Bobbs-Merrill, where Howland was back at his old job of editor of the book department, *The Wolf Hunters* had been accepted. "It looks to me as if you had struck your gait and that it's a gait which, if maintained, will put you in the front rank of American juvenile authors." In keeping with their advice to make it part of a series, Jim had the wolf hunters find signs of gold at the end of the book. The two youths, Rod, the boy from Detroit, and Wabi, the young Indian, made a pact to look for it the next year. At the end, as Rod is leaving for home, Wabi asks, "And you'll come back as soon as you can?" If I'm alive, Rod answers.

"And then—the gold!"

"For the gold!"

All of this leading, of course, to the next book, which Jim was already writing, *The Trail of Gold*, titled eventually *The Gold Hunters*. Although he ended this book set up for a sequel, there was no third book in the series.

The Wolf Hunters went to the printer on February 1, with the first run scheduled for 3,000 copies. Jim's dedication read, "To my comrades of the great northern wilderness, those faithful companions with whom I have shared the joys and hardships of the 'long silent trail,' and especially to Mukoki, my red guide and beloved friend, does the writer gratefully dedicate this volume."

Howland cautioned him that one book a year was about all the market could stand. Nevertheless, both *The Wolf Hunters* and *The Courage of Captain Plum* were published October 24, 1908. Mac advised him to invest the big money he expected to get from them in Canadian lands.

The Great Lakes, begun before either of the other two books, was published by Putnam's May 1, 1909. It was handsomely bound, subtitled *The Vessels That Plough Them, The Owners, The Sailors, and Their Cargoes*, and had 72 photographs and a map. He added a second section that included a brief history of the lakes. It sold for three dollars and a half. But it did not sell well.

Owosso folks were kept informed of his success. Young Johnny Shotwell, better known as "Shottie," was also making a name for himself as a winning pitcher for the West Side indoor baseball team. Ethel Greenwood was now teaching in Owosso. Connors Ice Cream Company, now headed by John McDonald who had worked his way up the ladder at Connors, was branching out with its newly formed Lansing Ice Cream Company.

In February, Jim had the grippe, but he continued to work. Just the correspondence alone concerning all of his stories, articles and books was becoming a heavy task.

"The Fish Pirates," published by *People Magazine* in March, as "Salvage" the year before in *Munsey's* and "Captain Kidd of the Underground" in *Cosmopolitan*, took a look at the seamier side of life on the Great Lakes. Later, in his stories of the Canadian northwest, Jim's characters would not always follow the path of law and order.

Cosmopolitan published "The Amateur Pirates" in May. In it Jim drew from his memories adrift on his makeshift raft in Lake Erie to write a story about a gang of ragamuffin boys who turn pirates and set out to capture a ship, only to get captured themselves and fall into the midst of a love story.

By May, Jim, exhausted and distracted, went home to James and Abby's house for ten days to get some writing done. This was his retreat. The words came easier in the old room upstairs, with his parents listening to the tapping of the keys and knowing he was doing his literary work.

The respite didn't help the situation at home. Back in Detroit, he continued to lash out at Leon, and sometimes even the girls. But he was not home much.

By the first of July he had made up his mind to move back to Owosso, and announced his intentions to his old friend George Campbell at the *Evening Argus*.

On July 23, Jim and Leon had a nasty quarrel. Jim swore at her. She glared at him and he forced her back on the bed. The next day he left for a trip on the lakes, to be gone two weeks. He was back a little early, about midnight August 2. Leon wouldn't let him in the bedroom and he kicked in the door. There was such a fuss the neighbors called the police.

Jim packed his things and went home to Owosso. He planned another trip to Canada, announcing his plans in the *Evening Argus*, of course, with the usual embellishments. Remembering Mac's advice to invest in Canadian land, he made a deal with a group of Port Arthur businessmen to swap some articles advertising the Thunder Bay region for title to some city lots.

He went north of Saskatoon to Prince Albert and on up into the Lac La Ronge area by dog team. It was from here the report of his death had come. Like Mark Twain, he said when he arrived back in Winnipeg, his death had been greatly exaggerated. The quarrel, he said, was between two of his guides and some other Indians. It was just a petty fight which he didn't understand because he didn't understand the language. The *Detroit News* articles "deeply grieved" him, he told the *Evening Argus* once he was home, and were prompted by "private animosity" felt against him by some of the staff of that paper.

Nevertheless, like Mark Twain and Jack London, the erroneous report of his death gained him literary notice. His portrait appeared in November in *Bookman*, a literary trade magazine.

He was back in Detroit in time for the divorce.

To get a divorce in 1908 it was necessary to show cruelty. Leon testified that Jim had begun striking her shortly after they were married, that he hit her when she was pregnant, that he once struck her so hard that she had to be hospitalized, and that she had a scar on her upper lip as a result of one of his blows. She said he was guilty of "insane jealousy." Lorene Moore, their maid, confirmed Leon's testimony. Other than to deny the beatings, Jim didn't contest the divorce.

It was surely a relief to them both.

An amicable agreement had already been reached in the matter of alimony and the house. Jim would pay $250 temporary and permanent alimony, the solicitor's fees and support for the children. Leon didn't ask for more than this. She was also to have the house and furniture. Jim would pay the remaining paving assessments as they came due and taxes for the present year.

Leon was granted custody of the girls until they reached the age of 14. Jim could have them for a month at a time as long as it didn't interfere with their schooling. If Leon married again, she was to set aside $1,000 for each of the girls. If she moved out of the state, Jim would get custody of Carlotta and pay expenses for her to visit her mother.

Judge Murfin approved the settlement. The divorce was suppressed but the *Detroit News* got wind of it and sent a reporter to the trial. The story made page one.

Jim's cousin Golda and her husband Elwood Stretch—they had recently married—had long been friends of Jim and Leon, and visited often at the house on Woodland Street. "I believe there was affection remaining between Jim and Leon all the days of their lives," Elwood said many years later. "Leon at long intervals used to come to Detroit to see Jim. I believe he continued to help her at times.

"These visits," he said, "were not of public notice."

Leon got custody of the girls, but Jim, back in Detroit in early December to give a talk on the Hudson Bay country, took Carlotta back to Owosso with him. Hand in hand, they walked away from the house on Woodland Street and didn't look back.

Chapter 11

James and Abby were at Ed's in Ohio that winter. Carlotta stayed at Amy's. Jim had the house on John Street all to himself. He fixed up his old room with a stove, put his typewriter on the yellow oilcloth-covered sewing machine stand, and felt at home. He could always write better there.

He finished his newest book, *The Trail of Gold*, sequel to *The Wolf Hunters*. When it went to press in April of 1909, however, it was titled *A Fight for the Treasure*, and was finally published in October of that year as *The Gold Hunters*.

Jim began his fourth novel for Bobbs-Merrill, eager to fill out his contract in spite of their warning that one book a year was enough.

He worked on the Great Lakes series for Reader-Putnam's, getting them ready for publishing in book form, and wrote his articles for Canadian papers and magazines. And, of course, he was writing short stories.

Carlotta had been late in entering school—it was mid-November 1908 when the divorce was final—and Jim spent hours helping her catch up that winter, teaching her the ABC's on the blackboard Amy's children had used. He was usually patient but there were also stormy sessions. Both of them had been through a great deal and it had been especially hard on Carlotta, who was only five. And they both had tempers.

Ralph and Vee lived just a few doors down the street from Amy, and Jim spent nearly every evening there playing cards. These were sometimes stormy sessions, too, with both Jim and Ralph losing their tempers and shouting at each other. The family liked fan tan and hearts, and they played them with vigor; Jim loved to give the Queen of Spades to others, but he didn't like getting it himself.

Good-natured Vee finally had enough of sitting by herself while the two wrangled. One evening she walked over to the table where they were playing, gathered up the cards and threw them in the stove.

Jim and Ralph moved their card games over to Amy's, but this soon ran into a snag, too. They were playing their usual heated game one night when the minister came to call. Amy was embarrassed and ashamed, and after that, the card games were kept toned down or abandoned when tempers flared.

Jim spent a lot of time at Ralph's. They had always been more like cousins than uncle and nephew. Jim naturally helped out with some of the chores. He went out to empty the ashes one day, and when he came in Ralph asked him, "Where is the ash pan?" Jim looked bewildered. He'd absent-mindedly thrown it out with the ashes. Absent-mindedness was a family trait, one that got them all a lot of good-natured kidding. In Jim was added the complication that his mind was so often on his writing.

If Jim had been passed by when invitations were sent out when he was a boy, he was not now. He entered into the social life of Owosso with a vigor. He had no intention of staying single and he was looking for a wife.

He met Ethel Greenwood at a chicken pie supper at the Congregational Church shortly after he moved back to Owosso, and sent her a Christmas note. Ethel lived in the Dudley Apartments down the street from Abby's, at the corner of West Main street.

There were a lot of single women in town though, and he was still looking around. He dated Edna Geeck, whom he'd known all his life, but nothing came of that.

There was a favorable review of *The Courage of Captain Plum* in *Bookman* in December, and in January there was one of *The Wolf Hunters*. In Detroit, *The Great Lakes* ranked number three in popularity among nonfiction books. Nevertheless, this book never did well, selling less than 1,500 copies in all.

Putnam's carried an article about him in January.

Hudson's Bay Company offered Jim a job as factor of a trading post in northern Ontario, where the factor had died under suspicious circumstances. It would be a wonderful opportunity to live close to the people and the land he had come to admire, but it was too restrictive, and Jim turned it down.

In late January, Jim gave a talk to the boys at the YMCA on Hudson Bay and his travels there and got a fine reception. Among the things he emphasized to them about the Indians he'd met was their honesty and their respect for old age, something he said the boys of Owosso "might well emulate."

Owosso was a growing, prosperous town and Jim was glad to be back. The new moving picture shows were becoming the rage in Owosso and even West Town had its own theatre. A Canadian visiting Owosso said all records for immigration of farmers from the United States to Canada would soon be broken and several Owosso families went back with him.

The Rev. W.S. Ament of Owosso, greatly respected for his many years of missionary work in the Orient, died in San Francisco on his way home and was brought home for burial.

The townspeople were trying to find a slogan for their city. Woodard's, Connors Ice Cream Company and other old businesses were flourishing and there were a number of new factories: Reliance Motor Truck Company—Owosso was really getting into the automobile business now—and Independent Stove Company, which had moved up from Detroit.

The West Town indoor baseball team became world champions in February, winning three out of five exciting games from the Chicago Spaldings, and there was a big celebration down at Symes Tavern in West Town.

Vera Haskell was back in Owosso and had formed her own orchestra which played for the vaudeville shows at the Ideal Theatre.

The weather was very bad that winter, with a lot of snow but not enough ice to suit the local icemen who predicted a shortage come summer.

Jim got a check for $250 from the Canadian Immigration Department to cover his expenses and salary for December and January. The department supplied him with photos to illustrate his stories and, most likely, his talks.

In February, *The Gold Hunters* was on its way to the printers.

Gifford Pinchot was named the country's first chief forester, heralding the beginning of the conservation movement. Jim was a nature lover, but he hadn't yet seen the need for conserving what appeared to be a wealth of wild life.

A long letter came from *Outing Magazine* in April. They wanted to use "Honor of the Big Snows" if he'd take one and one-half cents a word for it, "assuming your article contains 5,600 words as noted in your manuscript." His pay came to $84. They'd use the bear hunting story, too, if he could send some photos, but returned a short story.

"We are anxious to secure a class of material which you are competent to write," they said, "and it may be that we should be able to arrange a continuous assignment of some kind if we are able to get together and have a personal talk."

This tone of letters had now become common, and Jim would continue to receive such encouragement from editors of the various magazines that printed his stories and articles. His letters, too, were often chatty, full of little personal comments and offers to come for a talk or invitations to go hunting or fishing with him.

He was getting good reviews of his books, especially *The Wolf Hunters*, and Bobbs-Merrill was eager to get *The Gold Hunters* out to its youthful readers.

In the spring of 1909, Jim bought a lot and hired Bonson and Peters to build him a house, giving them $125 as a down payment for materials and labor. Fred Woodard, who lived down the street from James and Abby and with whom Jim had become friends, advised him to build up on Oliver Street, where the moneyed people in town lived. Instead, he chose a lot three blocks from his parents' house, on Williams Street, within sight of the river but on the other side.

He was now on the right side of the river, but with his back to Oliver Street and Owosso's upper "society." It was probably not done that way deliberately. The lot was a pleasant site, he could see the river, it was close to James and Abby's house where he liked to spend as much time as possible, and he was not class conscious.

The house was a two-family affair of brick veneer, built at a total cost of $3,500. He would rent one side, which would recover the cost of construction and help maintain it, and would live in the other half.

His social life consisted of church suppers, family gatherings, picnics and boating on the river. Fancy parties were not his style. He valued, instead, gatherings of family and/or friends above all other forms of relaxation and good times.

James, Abby and Cora came home from Ohio in time for Easter and for a big blurb in the *Evening Argus* about Jim's book, *The Great Lakes and the Vessels That Plough Them*, handsomely bound and selling for $3.50.

Jim continued to go to Detroit now and then. Leon and Viola were still there, and Golda and Elwood, with whom he often stayed, and many friends.

With no home or office commitments to hinder him, he soon became familiar with Chicago and Indianapolis, and with New York, the center of the publishing and movie-making industries.

The end of April there was a heavy, wet snow, followed by thunderstorms and wind. Everything flooded and some people along the river had to go about by boats.

Connors Ice Cream Company opened a restaurant serving meals as well as ice cream. Jim was inordinately fond of ice cream, and he and John McDonald, Connor's president, became close friends.

Chambers wrote from Bobbs-Merrill in May that *Cosmopolitan* was looking for a good serial and if it was alright with Jim, he would send them Jim's new manuscript. Jim wired that it was. *Cosmopolitan* had already published some of his short stories, but didn't buy this story.

Several saloon keepers were arrested that summer for violations of the liquor laws. Autos were getting to be a nuisance, but the mailman out in Vernon was now using one of the gas wagons for delivering mail and had cut several hours off his route. General Motors bought out Reliance Truck Company and many people who'd panicked and sold their stock were now regretting it; General Motors was buying up all the stock and the price had risen from $60 a share to $115.

Three of the men working on Jim's house fell from a scaffolding while working on the roof and came down in a shower of bricks and boards. Arthur Brown got hit on the head with a brick and walked to the doctor's office for stitches. He was back to work the next morning. One side of the house had already been rented before the house was finished.

A new house needed a wife, and Jim now set out in earnest to find one.

Ethel Greenwood was not only a beautiful woman, with a wealth of long, dark hair and pretty eyes, she was charming and intelligent as well. She had taught in three small schools, two nearby and one on the Lake Michigan shore, before being hired by the Owosso schools, and she lived by herself in an apartment. She was twenty-six the winter she started dating Jim.

Jim was intrigued by her "bright eyes and sweet appearance and demeanor." She'd been reading the accounts of his trips and his writing, she told him. She was "so nice and interesting that I decided to get better acquainted with her," Jim said later. She was probably looking for marriage, too.

Before long Jim decided she would make a "wonderful companion on the hundred wild trails" he was going to travel.

In August 1909, *Outing* published the story they'd purchased but under a new title, "A Test of a Code." They used an illustration from the story for the frontispiece of the magazine, the first time one of his stories had been so honored.

Almost at once Jim began expanding the story; it was published again later under its original title, "Honor of the Big Snows," by *Munsey's Magazine* from August 1910 to January 1911, ending just before it came out as the fifth book for Bobbs-Merrill, fourth in the contract.

Serialization followed by book publication was a strategy Jim used many times. Almost all of his books after this were published as serials as a matter of course, serving well for everyone concerned—magazine and book publishers and Jim, for the publicity, exposure and the added money. He made his words go twice as far this way, and earn him twice as much, or even more.

Jim made plans for another Canadian trip that fall. Both Canadian Northern and Grand Trunk Pacific railroads offered him free transportation over their lines, and the Canadian Immigration Department was extending its help, but said that "requests for ladies are repeatedly refused" for travel to the far West. A photographer had been sent West and Jim could use any of those photos when they were ready.

He was feverishly finishing "A Fight for Life," to begin in Munsey's in November, and putting the serial in shape for a book so that he could read the galley proofs while at Teddy Brown's. There were a few problems with it. Howland pointed out that he was using the names Meleese and Jean again, and people might be confused with the characters in his story "Honor of the Big Snows." In the end, the names were left as he had them.

The intense writing, overseeing the house building, plans for his coming trip to Canada, and his courtship of Ethel "clogged" his "machinery," as he wrote Howland at Bobbs-Merrill, but he managed to get out a short story for *Red Book* about a young man named Philip Steele, the son of a wealthy Chicago banker who had joined the Royal Northwest Mounted Police. He sent it off under the title "The Man Hunter."

Red Book's editor, Karl Edwin Harriman, liked it so well he agreed to Jim's suggestion that it become a series of stories at $100 each, and Jim began immediately on another story about the handsome Mountie.

Ethel had signed a contract to teach first grade in the fall, but Jim's trip to Canada soon became plans for a honeymoon trip, as he wrote to his old friend R.W. Titherington of *Munsey's*. Would *Munsey's* be interested in a narrative of their trip, Jim asked. Congratulations, Titherington replied, but such a narrative wouldn't be what they wanted for *Munsey's*. "We would rather have good fiction."

The honeymoon might have read like fiction, though. Jim and Ethel were married at six o'clock in the morning on September 27, 1909, at James and Abby's house. Immediately after the ceremony, the newlyweds carried their luggage to the train station and left on the early train, headed for the wilds of Canada.

Chapter 12

There were moonlit nights along the trap line, Jim eager to teach Ethel the ways of wildlife. She learned to snowshoe through the deep drifts, snowflakes sparkling on her dark, lustrous hair. Jim taught her to shoot. She was such an apt student that she twice went out by herself.

The stiff formal dinners each evening at the Hudson's Bay Post where they were staying were the only unpleasant thing that winter, but soon forgotten in the privacy of their own cabin.

And every day, Jim wrote. There were problems with plot and dialogue. Ethel learned what it was like to live with a man who "lived" the stories he wrote. Because, of course, his work went on, as it always would no matter what else was happening: illness, family, marriage, death of loved ones. It was his livelihood; more, it was his life.

The honeymoon trip was publicized in the *Evening Argus* as part of the wedding annoucement. Mr. and Mrs. Curwood, the report said, would be spending their first few weeks in the wilderness regions of the Thunder Bay country near Port Arthur, hunting big game. Later, when there was enough snow, they would go north by dog sled into Eskimo country and the Arctic Circle.

There was also, naturally, a plug for his books.

Jim and Ethel spent several weeks at the Post near Lake Nipigon, north of Thunder Bay, hunting and trapping and, for Jim, writing. But their trip by dog sled into the north was cancelled.

Ethel loved it all, except for that evening meal which they took with the English factor and his wife.

The first evening, as Jim and Ethel left to set traps before dinner, the factor's wife cautioned them to be back by eight o'clock for dinner. "Dressed," she added, meaning dinner clothes.

Ethel explained that she'd brought nothing formal, only outdoor clothes.

"Of course not," the factor's wife said with disapproval, "you are Americans."

Chicken was served one evening. Ethel chose white meat but Jim wanted dark. "We serve dark meat only to Indians," the woman sniffed.

But the evening meal was only a part of the day. There were hours to spend in the sparkling, invigorating snowy forests. Running their trapline after dinner, Jim taught Ethel how to tell what animals had passed along the path by the tracks they left in the snow. Together they watched the battle for survival of the wild things, and marveled at nature. At the end of their ten-mile trapline was a herd of caribou. About three miles from their cabin was a yard of moose.

They were, as Jim had hoped, true companions of the trail. Ethel was not a pampered city girl nor young, as Leon had been, but a farm girl who'd had to work hard to get ahead, just as Jim had had to do.

During the day, though, when Jim was writing, Ethel nearly ceased to exist for him. Sometimes he was hardly aware of her.

Late for lunch one day, a distraught Jim rushed into their cabin.

"Jim, what is the matter?" Ethel asked in concern.

Running his hand through his hair, he cried, "I can't make Philip die. He won't do what I want him to," and rushed out again.

It was Ethel's introduction to Jim's total concentration on his writing.

Philip Steele did not "die," but lived through several more episodes, eventually to become, of course, a book.

"Why not let all the stories revolve around a pivot of the same man," Harriman had suggested after "The Man Hunter," keeping a love interest secondary to the Mountie's adventures. Later Jim could weave them together for the book.

But find another name for the hero, he advised, because another author had already used it. Obligingly, Jim titled his series "Philip Strong, Gentleman Adventurer," but in the end he went back to Philip Steele. The series, published first in *Red Book*, became his sixth book for Bobbs-Merrill and last in the contract. It was titled *Philip Steele of the Royal Northwest Mounted Police*.

By the end of January, Jim and Ethel were home and moving into their half of the house on Williams Street. They had been gone four months.

The railroad refused to ship the four wild sled dogs Jim had bought in Canada. Dogs were one of his passions. He admired the dogs of the North—two of his books were about northern sled dogs—but he didn't get these. He did, however, get the moose head he had shipped home, but not without trouble; customs revalued it higher than he had declared.

Jim got the first set of galleys of "Fort O'God," his newest story. There was a possibility of making a play of *Honor of the Big Snows. Outing Magazine's* new department, "Campfire Stories," needed anecdotes or short yarns. "If you want to amuse yourself trying your hand at it, we'd like to see some," the editor wrote him.

Jim's royalty check from Bobbs-Merrill for the last six months of 1909 was for $17.55 and that from Putnam's for *The Great Lakes* was $98. Only two copies of *The Courage of Captain Plum* had been sold, 102 of *The Wolf Hunters* and 13 of *The Gold Hunters*. He was discouraged again. Magazine articles and short stories brought him much more than that, but his books failed to sell well, in spite of the publicity.

Nevertheless, Jim bought a Regal touring car.

"That new automobile doesn't match your royalty report," Harriman wrote, surprised at the extravagance. However, he added, "I am glad someone in the literary trade is able to have an automobile. When you bring the car over to Chicago, I shall be very glad to act as your guide."

Driving out Mulberry Street north of town one day in April, Jim ran over some broken glass in the road. He went back over the route and counted fourteen places where there were jagged pieces of broken bottles in the wagon tracks. Angered, he called the *Evening Argus* and offered a $50 reward for evidence that would convict the offender. No one ever collected.

Advice flowed to him from his editors, about how to revise stories that were not quite acceptable, what he should write next, how he should proceed. It was this assistance from the men at the other end, his publishers, that helped steer him towards ever greater success. There were still many rejections and critical comments, but since Jim treated every editor as a friendly acquaintance, whether they had met or not—and he eventually met most of them—they responded in kind.

The Danger Trail was published in April. It was illustrated in color by the popular artist, Charles Livingston Bull. The advance sales were coming along nicely, Howland reported, and sent ten complimentary copies. They were getting orders for more copies than the average novel did in a lifetime, he wrote.

By the end of April "The Honor of the Big Snows" was out to *Munsey's*, ready to begin in August. Bull was also to illustrate the book when it came time for its publication.

Jim was writing furiously now. Stories and new chapters of his series and letters went out almost daily. He was working on yet another long story, "The House of the Red Death," which he sold to *Gunter's Magazine* in May.

Not all was sweetness and help from editors. *Collier's* sent a check for $56 for an article on trapping and Jim complained to Howland about the low pay. "*Collier's* has a reputation for paying top prices," Howland replied. Hadn't he asked for an offer when he submitted it? Ask for $150, and let him know if he could be of any further help.

"You are doing pretty well for a literary youngster," he added.

Collier's eventually sent Jim another check for $44, making a total of $100 for the story, then used it only in their Canadian edition.

In spite of a check from *Munsey's* for $1,250 for the serialization of "The Honor of the Big Snows," Jim was depressed, as he would often be when he drove himself too hard. He wrote to Howland and wondered at his worth.

"I can't agree with you that you are never likely to do anything better," Howland replied. "You are too young and too earnestly ambitious to have struck twelve."

In June the stock market was booming and Jim earned $100 in one day with a "trifling purchase" in copper stock. He figured he could really increase his money and be able to pay for some expensive trips into Canada, so by the end of the second day he had bought 400 shares of stock.

He called Ethel in excitement. "We're going to be rich," he exclaimed, and ordered her a $400 piano from Shattuck's.

When he came home that afternoon, Ethel demanded to see the money, and he had to explain that it was all on paper, not in his pocket. Whenever the stock went up in price, their money increased, he said confidently.

Within a few days, however, the bubble had burst and he was poorer than ever. Jim turned to his old friend Howland at Bobbs-Merrill who immediately wired him that he could get a $1,000 advance against his book royalties anytime he wanted. "I am afraid the slump yesterday maybe wiped you out."

Jim's writing, too, was in a slump.

"There are times when we have inspiration and times when we are barren," Howland wrote him. It is often good to talk it over with a sympathetic listener, he said, one who contributes nothing but the act of listening. He'd be glad to listen. "Come some time the middle of the week."

It was one of many such sessions Jim would have with Howland and others, and especially later with Ray Long, when he would bounce ideas off them, talking out ideas and story lines, sometimes taking their advice or following their suggestions and other times following his own instincts if it varied from theirs.

Titherington of *Munsey's* now advised him that he had a "good field in the Northern wilderness of Canada. That novel atmosphere helps sell your stories— stay with what works for you...." He cautioned Jim, however, to avoid the "melodramatic."

"You have an excessive tendency towards the sensational and emotional," he said. But, he added, the public likes stories pitched high key.

Writing about the North, of course, had now supplanted the Lakes in Jim's writing, but he continued to have trouble with straying toward the "melodramatic."

There was a big write-up in the *Evening Argus* about the big writeup about Jim in *Publisher's Weekly*. Both also carried a photo of him in his "explorer's costume worn in the north woods": woolen shirt, breeches tucked into heavy socks and calf-high laced boots. He was wearing a beard, as he usually did, on his northern trips.

The Evening Argus printed "The Courage of Captain Plum" that summer.

In his article, "The Growing Power of the Business Man in Politics," published in July 1910 *Book-Keeper*, he said that a Democratic saloonkeeper in his home town of 15,000 population came within 57 votes of being nominated in the Republican primaries, in spite of the women voters, those keepers of the hearth he had depended upon to keep liquor out of town.

Leslie's Weekly was a pillar in the magazine world, and its editor, John

Sleicher, wrote him, "I like your little stories very much." He, too, guided and encouraged Jim toward writing what Leslie's liked to publish. "I wish we could pay you all you're entitled to but a great many good stories are offered to us at 1¢." He was offering Jim two cents a word, and also wanted "something for Christmas." The office rule at *Leslie's* was to pay on publication, but Sleicher gave orders that Jim was to be paid on acceptance.

In August, Ethel, five months pregnant, visited her family in Indiana, taking eight-year-old Carlotta with her. They were gone two weeks.

Ed had disposed of his business in Conneaut and decided to go overland to Oregon for his health, he told the family when he, Stella and their son, Guy, visited that summer. They stayed a month. Aunt Frankie, divorced from Van Ostran and married to Theodore Bain, lived in Owosso just down the street from Amy and Jack. She gave a party to celebrate Ed and Stella's wedding anniversary and Ed's birthday. All the family was there.

The new moving picture shows in town intrigued Jim. Why couldn't he write movie scripts? Again, he turned to Howland at Bobbs-Merrill for advice. "I can't see that it would do any harm and if the pay is worth it, take a shot," Howland said.

Jim sent a proposal off to George K. Spoor at Essanay Film Company in Chicago. Spoor replied that "we would be glad to discuss the matter into (sic) more detail." However, they weren't interested in making pictures in the far north but were looking for good comedy plots. Most movies were made in New York or New Jersey or, as with Essanay, in Chicago, although Essanay did have a western movie company which traveled around, shooting pictures when they found suitable locations.

"I don't see why you can't furnish us some good material for western pictures," Spoor wrote Jim. "The plots of many of your northern stories, it seems to me, could be twisted to fit a western locale." He enclosed a writer's guide which would show Jim that the plot ideas were simple but dramatic, the situations strong and effective. Essanay would "certainly pay more than $10 for your western stories. We will name a figure, let us say, on the first available story you send; if you don't think it worthwhile, you may discontinue."

That fall Jim sold his first movie scenario. Thanhauser filmed it as a little one reeler called *Looking Forward*.

Jim was invited to join the Famous Authors Club of Whitehall Court, London, though Mr. Bobbs of Bobbs-Merrill, who also got an application, didn't seem very impressed—"they are trying to obtain more funds by inviting everyone who owns a typewriter to become a member." Nevertheless, Jim joined.

Stories, articles, revisions and resubmissions, a new novel, coordination of the Philip Steele series for a book, and now movies: Jim was working harder and faster than ever. Keeping track of royalties, and his other financial dealings, such as his Canadian property—by now he had bought or bartered publicity for lots in Saskatoon, North Battleford and Port Arthur—took up a lot of his time, too.

The first 48,000 words of his new novel, retitled *Fort O'God*, published finally under the title *Flower of the North*, went out to Bobbs-Merrill in November. Jim corrected Howland, who had thought he was correcting Jim, that Hudson's Bay Company was correct, not Hudson Bay Company.

Jim had used the name Meleese in *The Danger Trail*, and again in *The Honor of the Big Snows*. He revised the latter to avoid confusion, but he used Meleese, and Isobel and Jeanne and Billy and Bucky and many other names over and over. Kazan was the name of a dog in several of his short stories, in books and, of course, in the book about a dog of that name.

Not only did he use names over and over again, he often patterned his people after those he knew. He put himself into nearly all of his stories, often as the hero and often with the name of James or Jim. His heroes had a tendency, too, to age along with himself, each year's book having its main male character just a little older than in the one the year before.

The French publishing industry was looking at issuing Jim's books in that language. Eventually, nearly all of Jim's books were printed not only in French but in most of the other European languages, including Russian.

James Oliver Curwood Jr. was born January 21, 1911, a Saturday. Jim was 32, Ethel just turned 28. Carlotta was eight and Viola, with her mother in Erie, Pennsylvania, was five.

Ethel disliked the entire messy process of giving birth. She decided she didn't care to go through it again. There was only one way to be sure, of course. She closed her bedroom door to Jim.

They had been married 16 months.

Chapter 13

Spring flowers perfumed the air and the outdoors beckoned the end of April, 1911, but Jim was not out to enjoy the spring. Exhausted mentally and physically, he collapsed and was in bed for weeks. It was the first time, but far from the last, when overwork would make him too ill to function.

Jim's mind always churned with stories, with business to be taken care of, with new ideas. He didn't know how to quiet it, how to stop. He couldn't simply write less, work fewer hours, cut down on the constant drain on his energies and emotions. The struggle to be recognized, to succeed, the drive to write were more powerful even than his love of the wilds or the needs of his family for his attention, or even his own health, and he poured all of himself into his work until his body rebelled.

The new year had started out so well. *The Honor of the Big Snows* was to be one of the "big two" books on Bobbs-Merrill's spring list. Jim was working on his "Philip and Hepzibah" series, "which, to my mind," he wrote Howland at Bobbs-Merrill, "are about the nobbiest things I've done. Have you ever noticed how inflated I get with every new thing I take up—just like a balloon that's never out of gas; but you probably understand the animal a little bit by this time, and will excuse him."

Then so many distractions crept in. Bobbs-Merrill wanted a new picture of him, but "I haven't changed since the old ones were made so couldn't they do?" Jim protested.

Leon came to see Jim while Ethel was still in bed after Jimmy was born. "Get her out of here," Ethel demanded.

The new baby disrupted the whole household. "The little cuss that arrived at our house three or four weeks ago has been making so much noise lately that I've rather had to take a week or so off," he wrote one of his editors.

Ray Long, editor of *Hampton's Magazine*, lost a manuscript of Jim's and he wanted to know if Jim had a carbon of it. "I'm tremendously sorry about this," he wrote.

Jim and Howland wrestled with the problem of a book title for the Philip Steele series all spring. "Do you like 'Philip Steele, Gentleman Adventurer' or is there something better?" Jim asked Howland. "Would 'The Man Hunter' look well?" Howland liked Jim's idea of "A Knight of the Royal Mounted," but at the end they settled on *Philip Steele of the Royal Northwest Mounted Police.*

Bobbs-Merrill wanted the manuscript by the first of April and at first Jim had trouble stringing the stories together but, he wrote Howland, "I've been

79

working like a horse and the shrewdest critic in the country won't be able to tell that the first 20,000 words has anything to do with short stories." He added a new chapter to follow the first story that had appeared in *Red Book* Magazine, "making the love interest ten times as strong." The girl had only figured in the first and last of the magazine stories, now he had to keep her at least in Philip's mind all through the book.

By mid-March he had it done and sent his only copy of the manuscript, now 53,000 words, to Howland to be copied. Jim was a terrible typist. His grammer and sentence structure, too, were often faulty. He relied on the publishers of his material to clean up his copy, which most of them were only too willing to do in order to get his stories. Later, a succession of secretaries and literary assistants would take care of these details for him.

Not all of Jim's Mounties were heroes. In the Philip Steele series he introduced Bucky Nome, a Mounted Policeman gone bad. The RNWMP didn't like it, and later they banned this book in Canada, and the movie later made from it.

Jim got his stories from the blue books and musty files of the RNWMP itself, when he was still welcome in its offices, and he wrote many stories of their heroism. He admired the Mounted Police and their motto of "Don't come back without your man," their intrepid tracking of wanted men across unpeopled wastes, their bravery and willingness to undergo terrible hardship to carry out their duty. One of the characters he used several times was a policeman named Pelletier, a real Mountie who, with three others, traveled nearly 3,500 miles across the unexplored wasteland from Fort Saskatchewan to Hudson Bay, and—unlike some well-provisioned heralded explorers of the Arctic—without making any fuss over it.

In March, Jim wrote Howland a long letter. "If I didn't know that you would take what I'm going to say as a gentleman, and feel, perhaps, that it comes from one," he began, trying to soften what he wanted to say.

"A little bug is working in me—and I don't want to call it Dissatisfaction, and won't," he said. "But it stirs me up to write you, anyway. The Bobbs-Merrill Company has published five of my books, they have got them out in splendid style, and yet four of those books have fallen flat—have not been worth the writing."

New writers were getting big publicity, he said, but there was nothing for his books. His *Honor of the Big Snows* was to be advertised hardly at all, while books by other authors are "pushed to the queen's taste."

"Is it because the people do not want out-of-door stuff?" he asked. It is the "sales and booming that counts; and when you flood the country with the advertisments of one or two books, doesn't the one NOT included have to suffer?

"I feel that if I am wrong you will set me straight on this; and that whatever you say, it will be in a most friendly fashion."

The next day he wrote a contrite letter. "I've felt better—and worse—since I wrote you that long letter of yesterday. Got the bile out of my system at least, and I hope you have taken it all in good spirit."

Howland, by now familiar with Jim's volatile nature, accepted Jim's apology. "You have always been most generous and loyal in your attitude towards us and the warm personal feelings that I have always felt for you would be weak indeed if it would not stand the strain of such a letter."

Howland was now even handling some marketing of Jim's short stories, sending them out to magazines he thought might use them.

Jim turned to him constantly for advice about the publishing field. He wanted to know how book sales worked. If he was breaking the rules to ask, "please forgive my ignorance. All I've learned in the book business I've learned from Bobbs-Merrill."

There are no rules, Howland replied, and if there were, "you could not violate them if you tried."

To relieve some of the strain on Jim, Howland urged him to give up the proof reading and leave it to them.

With *Philip Steele* gone to the printers, Jim looked about for another book idea. He sent Howland a copy of a short story, "The First People," which had appeared in *Success Magazine*. Was it a possible book if he added to it? Bobbs-Merrill was not enthusiastic and he chose, instead, another of his stories published in *Success Magazine*, "Little Mystery." This story, too, would go through many changes, from this short story eventually to a book, and many titles: *The Blue Flower, Ice-Bound Hearts,* and its final book title, *Isobel.*

Those first months of 1911, Jim wrote more than two dozen stories and articles. His income now averaged about $15,000 a year, almost as much as Jack London's.

Then he fell ill. For nearly a week his body burned with fever. It was two weeks before he was allowed out of bed even briefly. He ordered his typewriter brought to his bedroom and wrote a few lines to his old friend Howland.

During the weeks that followed, Jim lay in bed thinking up plots for new stories. As soon as he was able to be up again, he was back at his typewriter. In two days of furious writing he wrote "Jim Falkner, Pirate," then collapsed again and was ill another two weeks. He sold the story to the *Saturday Evening Post* for three hundred dollars.

In May Jim ventured out for a ride in his automobile, but his fever rose again and he was ordered back to bed. His recovery dragged on as he suffered relapse after relapse. He was writing regularly for *Leslie's* now, as well as *Munsey's* and several other magazines, and his commitments to them drove him to keep working.

Lying in bed, Jim couldn't help but think about his association with

Bobbs-Merrill. He had now written six books for them, but none of them had sold well. Other books were being heavily advertised, but not his and they weren't selling. He had his typewriter brought to his bedroom again and wrote another long letter to Howland.

"Am still in bed, with half hour 'ups,' and I'm taking advantage of one of these to answer your letter," he wrote. He had been thinking about why his books weren't doing well. Can't we do something to make this book (*Philip Steele*) sell a little? He had some ideas for a cover illustration that would "arouse the prospective buyer's interest," if he could only talk to the illustrator.

"One more thing, and then I'll go back to bed to sweat and swear," he wrote. When he was editor at the *Detroit News* he signed checks for every serial they ever published. *The Danger Trail* was now in syndication; shouldn't the author "get a look-in?"

Still thinking of the lack of advertising, he wondered if the financial and advertising returns they received from one of his stories went to advertise someone else's.

"I don't suppose I'd think anything about this if I saw any hope of you doing something with one of my books. But, honestly, if you'd written six of 'em, and saw them all go down in the well, one after another, wouldn't you have glum thoughts? And, if you were 'it,' wouldn't you, like I am doing, ask that with the seventh book some special effort be made to get it 'on'?"

He began to consider finding another publisher.

Carlotta, helping Ethel in the kitchen, spilled a pan of boiling water on herself and was badly burned, though the doctor assured them it wouldn't leave a scar.

In late June, Ethel left to visit friends for a few days.

A rumor had begun circulating in March that Jim was selling his flat in Owosso and moving back to Detroit, after a business and pleasure trip to Chicago, New York and Indianapolis, "publishing centers where he is not a stranger," as the *Argus* put it. He quickly denied it. But truthfully, he was considering it. As before, his work was everything and wife and family were interruptions he could not tolerate.

Besides, he missed the contacts Detroit offered. He had written Howland in April that he depended on him for all the news, "But I get back to the city this summer, and then, when I've got people who know something about me, things are going to happen. If you don't believe that a small town can kill you, try one for two years, as I have. No wonder I'm getting gray-headed. But 'It's an ill wind that blows no good.' I at least have got rid of my corns."

He felt buried away in Owosso, but he was, in fact, spending a lot of time in Detroit. He liked dining out and going to the theatre and taking in the city sights. He ate steak and recounted a time in Canada when he'd eaten mastodon, dug up out of the frozen tundra, and of course wrote it all up for the Detroit papers.

In July, still recuperating from his long illness, Jim took a cottage on a small lake at Clarkston, northwest of Detroit, where he could write without the distractions of home.

Among the matters Jim took care of that summer was the dedication of *Philip Steele*—"To My Wife."

Bobbs-Merrill decided they wanted new pictures after all, but Jim wrote, "I'm a mighty poor looking specimen now.... They'd rather belie my reputation as a big game hunter and northwoods man." Nevertheless, he had new photos made in August.

His stories were bringing $150 to $325 now. His short stuff was "walking off like hot cakes," he said. In spite of his concentration on Northwest adventure stories and his battle with fatigue, he was able now and then to turn to more light-hearted stuff like "Mrs. Tommy's Indiscretion" and "Thomas Jefferson Brown." His touch was light with this kind of story, his prose loose and witty, and there was nearly always a bit of adventure thrown in to make the stories lively.

"His First Penitent," though, was a short story about a train stalled in the snow in the Canadian forest and a priest talking about the first confession he'd heard. Published in August in *Munsey's*, the story is vivid with the penetrating cold seeping into the train, the storm raging outside, the little group enthralled with the priest's story, the surprise ending. He told it with clarity and feeling, illustrating that so much in life is guided by little things, small happenings that turn us this way or that. He knew the role of circumstance in one's life, and it was a philosophy he would enlarge and repeat often.

Jim was pleased with himself with this story, and it became one of his favorites.

Pearson's accepted his new novel, "Fort O'God," to run as a serial. He was now getting prices on a level with London, Stewart Edward White and other popular writers. He announced that he'd be dividing the winter between New York and Detroit.

Nevertheless, he moved home again in September.

Jim's magazine sales were pulling in a lot of money now—he counted up his sales of short stories and found he had earned $4,280 from these sales alone so far in 1911. In his last letter to Howland before leaving the lake, he recounted some of his most recent successful sales, and asked if Howland thought there might be a short book in "The Valley of Silent Men," should he enlarge the story.

By now both Jim and Bobbs-Merrill were dissatisifed with the sales of his books. By mutual agreement, he sought a new publisher and chose Harper & Bros. who agreed to split 50-50 with him on sales to the papers.

On November 11—11/11/11—a tornado struck Owosso causing great damage. Two people were killed and many streets, including Williams Street where Jim and Ethel lived, were blocked by fallen trees and debris. Jim and Ethel, however, were on a long trip in the East, visiting publishers of his work. Their home life might be stormy—and local gossip about loud arguments and violent threats gave credence to this—but they took many such business trips together, as well as hunting and later research trips into Canada, and presented a picture of domestic harmony to all who did not know them well.

The *Saturday Evening Post* paid Jim $400, his largest pay to date for a short story, for "The Lawless Godliness of Billy Smoke," and published it in its December 23, 1911 issue.

Pearson's editor wrote Jim that he liked "Fort O'God" but they couldn't pay much and couldn't publish it until November of the next year. "Why do you never come to New York? We could come to a better understanding if we talked." But Jim, of course, had just returned from an extended trip through the East, seeing other publishers.

During the fall and winter, Jim enlarged "Little Mystery" and retitled it "The Blue Flower." The heroine's name was Isobel.

Most of December of 1911, Jim spent at Ed's in Conneaut, Ohio. His mail followed him around whether he was in Owosso, Clarkston, Detroit, Conneaut, or in the Canadian wilds.

His troubles followed, too. In an effort to make some money from the newspaper serialization of his stories, he sought to straighten out the contracts he'd signed with *Munsey's* for his stories, especially concerning "Honor of the Big Snows," which he was beginning to wish now he'd never written. Jim regretted any problems with *Munsey's* as they had paid him better than any other magazine.

Parting from Bobbs-Merrill, he asked Howland "to 'fire' me in a perfectly good spirit, leaving me an opening to come back some time...."

Then he signed the contract with Harper's to publish "Fort O'God" in the spring and "Little Mystery" in the fall, the former eventually titled *Flower of the North* and the latter *Isobel*.

Ralph and Jack were both now working and traveling for Reliance Motor Truck Company. The company asked them to move to New York. Only Ralph went, with Vee and five-year-old Virginia. James, Abby and Cora at last went to Florida for the winter. Jack and Amy, with Queen and Marquerite, joined them in January. Ed, Stella and Guy went down, too. Jim spent most of the winter in Detroit, taking up more or less permanent lodgings at 14 Madison Avenue. Ethel, Jimmy and Carlotta stayed in Owosso.

It was a mean winter that year in Michigan, with a terrible blizzard raging in February, immobilizing most of the Midwest and sending the temperature down to 19 degrees below zero in Owosso. Winter, Jim said, was his favorite time of year.

The Danger Trail was translated into Swedish and French. The prestige was more important than the small amount of money from such translations.

One of the illustrations for Jim's story "The Strength of Men" appeared on the cover of *Collier's* February 17, 1912, issue. *Collier's* was now so anxious to publish his stories he was offered five cents a word for an article, "The Lost Eskimo Village." The letter accepting the story was full of praise.

Jim, in Detroit, wrote a long dedication to his story "Fort O'God," now retitled *Flower of the North* and published by Harper & Bros. in March 1912.

It read, "To my comrades of the great northern wilderness, those faithful companions with whom I have shared the joys and hardships of the 'long silent trail' and especially to that 'Jeanne D'Arcambal,' who will find in herself the heroine of this story, the writer gratefully dedicates this volume...."

Chapter 14

The characters in Jim's books and stories were nearly always based on people he met in real life. Jeanne Fisher of his Ohio boyhood had been his prototype for heroines in many of his stories, Leon and Ethel in many others. "Jeanne D'Arcambal" was a beautiful part-French woman who had lived in the Canadian north country a hundred years before. She was his romantic notion of what northern women were like, and now this type of woman supplanted the others in his stories. She was Me-Lee in "Me-Lee of the North" (*Red Book Magazine*, June 1912), Meleese in "Flower of the North," Isobel in "Ice-Bound Hearts," Jacqueline in his story of that title (*Good Housekeeping*, August 1918).

These women were dainty, beautiful, with long flowing tresses, of course. They were very feminine but brave and hardy.

On the other hand, he began to portray women who were mean-spirited or corrupt. They were lesser characters, of course, sometimes the wife or ex-wife of the hero. His heroes, too, were undergoing change. In more and more of his stories, they were disillusioned, often ill, usually rich or professional men— doctors, lawyers, engineers, writers—who went north to escape their pasts or to find themselves, and who became healthy, stalwart heroes. Jim, too, found good health in the north, and he was, of course, disillusioned and often depressed.

Jim added movie scenarios to all his other writing. There had been that little one-reeler in 1910. In 1911, Vitagraph filmed "Prejudice of Pierre Marie," starring Anita Stewart and Tefft Johnson. Now in 1912 he sold "Beulah of the 'Sun' " as a story to *Red Book Magazine* and a film scenario to Essanay Studios in Chicago. Ideas could be turned into both stories for the magazines and scenarios for the booming new moving picture industry. "Philip Steele" found its way to the movie theatres, too. Reliance Studios made a two-reeler of it, although he had originally sold the story idea to Selig in Chicago.

There were only two or three more films from Jim's stories in 1912, but in 1913 Jim wrote nearly thirty scenarios, most of which were filmed and most of which were original stories, although a few were from stories already published.

He was also still writing light fiction. *Red Book* published "The Laugh Maker" in April, a story about a fat, good-natured young man named Bobby McTabb who resembled Billy Smoke a great deal. He drew upon his newspaper days for "Beulah of the 'Sun,' " a story of a young woman reporter who got the story when her male counterpart could not. *Red Book* published it in July. "The Rhododendron Girl," which appeared in *Leslie's* on July 4, was a sweet love story about an old couple.

Leslie's Magazine was giving him a big buildup now, listing some of his coming stories in little sidebar items with his current story or article. Accompanying "The Elusive Umbrella," an amusing little story, was a boxed announcement about "A Gifted Writer's Notable Stories," attributing Jim's "rapid rise" to "exceptional merit. His work is substantial as well as brilliant, and he is forging to the front as the most popular of American writers....

"Already he has won a lasting place in American literature. The day is surely coming, many believe, when he will stand foremost among American men of letters." It was good publicity.

In July *Leslie's* also published one of his rare Western stories, "The Fight at Red Fork Creek."

Jim's rooms in Detroit gave him peace and quiet to write, and his six years of hunting and traveling which had taken him to almost all of Canada gave him an endless supply of material. If he got lonely, there were always friends.

He went often to Elwood and Golda's. They were parents now, too; their daughter Dorothea was born in 1910. Times at the Stretches were always fun. Golda was high-strung and exuberant, whether over her house, a cause or having a good time. She was smart and articulate, hardly an average housewife, and was soon doing some of Jim's research. Elwood, too, was an intelligent and interesting companion, a writer of poetry, and like Jack and Ralph, a pioneer in the automobile industry.

Sometimes the two men went out on the town. They were not drinking men but they did like to flirt a little—though Elwood was a married man, but then, so was Jim. Elwood and Golda knew Jim's situation at home.

Viola spent the 1911 Christmas holidays in Owosso. They had a family picture taken. In the spring, when the *Detroit Free Press* did an article about Jim's rising star as an author and Owosso's claim to him "for her very own," he gave them the photo to use as an illustration. It depicted a serene family: Jim, lean, dressed in a dark suit and with the white streak in his hair showing prominently, leaned against the mantel, looking fondly down upon Ethel and the children arranged artfully on the floor about the Christmas tree.

By 1912 Ray Long had become editor of a trio of magazines, *Red Book*, *Green Book* and *Blue Book*. *Red Book* published several of Jim's stories that year—"The Blind God," "The Laugh Maker," "Me-Lee of the North" and others. It was the beginning of a long and prosperous relationship for them both.

Ray Long was an astute and experienced editor and writer. He saw a potential in Jim's writing that prompted him to take the train to Owosso to meet Jim in person. That was all it took to cement a friendship as well as a business relationship that would last through everything that was to come and could withstand Jim's mercurial character.

Jim sent Ray a story about a dog named Kazan. It's the "best dog story"

I've ever read, Ray said. Jim set out to write more stories about Kazan, in spite of Ray's warning that *Red Book* was opposed to serials. But even Ray was enthused now, and urged him to continue. Six of them would be enough, he said. But once underway, Jim found them no problem to write. He wrote 11 and *Red Book* published them all.

With Kazan, Jim at last could write of the creatures of the wild. People were only secondary to the fierce quarter-wolf sled dog Jim created, an embodiment of those savage and stalwart dogs he'd seen and admired in the North. And with Gray Wolf, Kazan's slim and loyal mate, he wove a love story as great as any human story without giving the two animals anything other than animal characteristics. Jim, in fact, deplored writers who tried to "humanize" wild animals, giving them "reasoning" powers beyond what was believable. He had only disdain for those writers who attempted to write "true" stories without ever having experienced it themselves, notwithstanding that he'd done this same thing so many years before.

His years in the out-of-doors, and the lore and stories related by the men and women he met there, had given Jim a keen understanding of animal life. He was, at times, contemptuous of those who failed to see what he knew, and, on the other hand, eager to help them learn the truth.

Jim and Ethel were off in June on another eastern trip, via Toronto and Ottawa. In Montreal they called in at Grand Trunk Pacific and got a promise of $500 worth of transportation in exchange for Jim mentioning the railroad in his articles. Jim planned a hunting trip to British Columbia, after which he would go north into unexplored country and up as far as the Yukon.

Not all of Jim's stories that year were light fiction. *Munsey's* published "The Code of Bucky Severn" in January and "The Other Man's Wife" in May, *Collier's* had "The Strength of Men" in February, *Red Book* published "The Blind God" in February and "Me-Lee of the North" in June, *Illustrated Sunday Magazine* published "The Last Moment" in November, a story originally published in *The Reader Magazine* in March 1907. These were all dramatic short stories about the men and women of the North.

He wrote a lot of non-fiction as well. *Saturday Evening Post* published "The Trappers" in January, *Leslie's* had "A Florence Nightingale of the Wilderness" in April and "The Tragic Story of the Wilderness Mail" in November. He repaid some of his debts to Grand Trunk Railroad—for passes over its lines and introductions to people who smoothed the way for his trips into the wilds—with articles like "A Builder of Empire," about the railroad's president, and then when that man went down on the Titanic, "The Clock and the Knight," about the railroad's new president.

He turned his hand to detective stories with "Only a Trifle," which appeared in *Leslie's* in January, and took a dip into the Kentucky hills for "The System," a humorous short, short story which *Leslie's* also published in

January.

His old friend Annesley Burrowes collaborated with Jim on "The Flint Skinners: Learning Economy in Little Things," about recycling waste products and turning them into money. "The Poor Man at College," a reminder of his own college days, and those articles for American Boy on how boys could make money, were his way of showing others how to get ahead with simple things. Always thrifty—he made notes and lists on the backs of old envelopes and letters—Jim never quite forgot how it was to be poor.

Leslie's new humor magazine, *Judge*, opened another market for short humor—"Bill for a Bald-Faced Horse" was a brief non-fiction story told him by one of his Canadian friends, and "Bill" was a story about a reporter who kissed a girl.

During that summer he also wrote a short story entitled "Oko-Kan, the Bull Moose," in which his heroine, with long, beautiful hair, of course, and the hero, another rich, formerly ill and disillusioned young man who had gone north for a new life, were on the side of a majestic and brave bull moose who was wantonly killed anyway. He drew from memory of his early moose hunting trips into Ontario for this story, and of the daughter of a prominent American who had killed a moose in just such a fashion. He did not, of course, reveal her name.

On a quick trip to Detroit in June, Jim was elected to the board of governors of the new Michigan Author's Association.

In July, Ralph and Vera had a son, named Jack for his grandfather.

Also in July, Jim took a trip to Ohio and to Indianapolis. He also tried to get *Collier's* to pay more for his and Annesley's article, but had to settle for $200, although the magazine had just paid him $350 for his story "The Match." *Philip Steele*, first a series of stories, then a book and now a movie, was gaining him some controversial publicity. In August the movie was banned in Canada. "I expected this," he told the *Evening Argus*, because he had "told the true story of Bucky Nome—a story that is largely a part of history, and which the Royal Mounted wishes to be forgotten." Bucky Nome was a Mountie gone bad, and the incidents in his story were true, he declared.

Munsey's rushed a check for $600 by special delivery in payment for "The Blue Flower" ("Ice-Bound Hearts") so that Jim and Ethel could start north in late August. Ethel, however, didn't go. She and Carlotta took the train to Sarnia, Ontario to meet Jim who had been in Detroit. They traveled together by boat up Lake Huron, through the new locks at Sault Ste. Marie and across Lake Superior as far as Port Arthur. There they separated. Ethel and Carlotta went home and Jim went west. He was going to hunt grizzly bears in British Columbia, then head north. He would be gone two months.

Even with transportation furnished and the check from *Munsey's*, Jim needed help in raising the rest of the $2,000 he figured his trip would cost. He appealed to his old friends at Bobbs-Merrill for an advance on his royalties, who promptly sent him the money he needed.

It would be a dangerous trip, he told reporters—of course he publicized his trip—with only two Indians as guides. He'd like to have at least one white man along, he said, but it was difficult "to get a white-skin to risk himself on such a jaunt unless he is drawn by the lure of gold hidden in the mountains. Occasional prospectors go up and down the rivers for a distance, where canoe navigation on them is possible, but few of them undertake even the beginning of the 'cross-country' trip." All this was reported in the *Detroit Free Press*, and re-reported in the *Evening Argus*.

It was his first real big game hunting trip in western Canada. The guide was Jack Otto, a "white-skin."

And, in fact, he was, for much of the trip, with a party of other American hunters in British Columbia. Jim bagged a near trophy mountain sheep, an exploit he wrote about for *Outdoor Life*, published in April, 1913, as "Pursuit of the Elusive Forty."

Besides the mountain sheep, Jim brought back the hides of three bears, shot within an hour or so one afternoon. He figured the bears totaled about a hundred years of wild life, but it was not for another two years, during his encounter with the grizzly he named Thor, that he would seriously question the rightness of such wanton destruction.

Jim and Jack Otto did head north after leaving the hunt, to explore the northern British Columbia mountains. And they discovered gold. Jim considered returning with a mining expert, but the gold was not easily mined and neither he nor Jack had time or means to work the claim themselves. They sold their interests in it to some men in Alberta for a reported $40,000. Jim's living style didn't change, however, and the Otto brothers continued to guide hunters.

Even finding gold aroused little envy among his publishing friends, hard at work back at their desks while he tramped around the mountains, enjoying his wild, free life.

"You've got a hell of a gall discovering gold fields without sticking some claim spikes down for your Uncle Dudley," Bob Davis of *Munsey's* wrote him, because, of course, the gold strike made its way into the newspapers.

Everyone at Bobbs-Merrill is "rejoicing in your lucky strike," Howland wrote. And, the door is always open for you to return when you want to come back. They deeply appreciated his loyalty and friendly attitude. "It was more or less of a misunderstanding that caused the separation. We felt you were not satisfied so we suggested a change. When you have a story we can get behind, send it to us and we will start afresh."

In addition to hunting, finding gold, and exploring the vast, wild country of British Columbia, Jim kept up with his business life. He stopped off in Saskatoon and Port Arthur to confer about his property. A vacation was never just a vacation but always a working trip.

And even though he was no longer on the payroll of the Canadian government, he continued to publicize Canada's western lands in his stories and articles.

He suffered an injury on this trip when one of the pack horses slipped, causing Jim's horse to also stumble. Jim's right leg was injured in the mishap, troubling him at times thereafter.

With such good relations still at Bobbs-Merrill, Jim sounded them out about publishing *Isobel*, which Harper's was dragging their heels about. Bobbs-Merrill had promised him nothing except an open mind about future books, and he quickly noted that he was not acting in an unfair manner to *Harper's*. In the end, though, *Harper's* published *Isobel* in 1913.

Isobel, of course, was "Ice-Bound Hearts," published in December, 1912, in Cavalier, one of *Munsey's* magazines. It was prefaced with an explanation that 15,000 words of this 60,000-word story had been previously published in *Success Magazine*, which had since folded, under the title "Little Mystery." It is an editor's obligation to be honest with its readers, the editor wrote, and added, "To secure James Oliver Curwood's best novel of the North is more than a feather in the cap of *The Cavalier*. It is an aurora borealis."

Thus Jim had stretched a short story to a novelette to a book. Later on, it would be filmed—twice.

Jim submitted an idea to *Red Book* for a long story, a novelette of 15,000 words. *Red Book* never runs stories of that length, Ray told him, it is "absolutely against our rules." But he might bend the rules for Jim if the story was as good as Jim said. "I don't mind telling you that if it were from any other writer in the country," we wouldn't consider it, Ray said, but if it would make a bigger hit than Kazan, "I think it worthwhile to violate any rule."

"We got a raft of letters about Kazan," Ray added.

Munsey's scheduled "Soldiers of Chance" as a four-part story in *Cavalier*, and in November Jim was hurrying to finish it and get it ready for book publication. It was an exciting tale he had written a couple of years before under the title "Billy Mountain, Revolutionist," and was of a revolution in Honduras planned and executed by two Americans. It had not one but two love stories. It was a direct departure from stories of the North and a return to writing about places he'd never been. This time, however, he wrote with authority, his readers unsuspecting that he'd gleaned his facts from the books, magazines and newspapers he read. "Soldiers of Chance" was never published in book form.

In December, James and Abby celebrated their fiftieth wedding anniversary. Jim came home from Detroit for the event. He'd consulted his Detroit attorneys about a divorce. But now, looking at his parents' happy faces, he put the idea aside. How could he disgrace his family again? He would just have to get along as best he could.

Chapter 15

The old days of worrying about money were over. In April 1913, Essanay sent a check for $1,025 to cover payment for ten photoplays. *Red Book* was paying $300 apiece for his Kazan stories, and a British publisher was buying them at 15 pounds each.

He was catching up—and passing—London, Stewart Edward White, Zane Grey and all of the other popular authors of the time.

Still he couldn't slow down. The only respite was to get out into the wilds again. Since that wasn't possible more than once a year, he found relaxation in fish picnics. The entire family liked these excursions, and he invited others, local and publishing friends alike, to join these outings.

Movie scenarios were still taking up much of his time. His photoplays were playing in theatres everywhere. He had a London agent now, Curtis Brown, who was taking nearly all of his stories as soon as they were submitted to American publishers, and urging Jim to have them published in both countries simultaneously.

"Our people have been keen on your work," he added.

British publishers bought not only the rights to his stories in England, but in the colonies as well, including Canada. His books and some of his stories were now published in French, German, Italian, the Scandinavian languages, and in Dutch. The latter were mostly pirated and he was having problems over this.

Translation rights brought only a few dollars, but Brown assured Jim it was worth it, because "it all helps in a general way."

When Jim and Ethel went to New York, they stayed at the best hotels, ate at the best restaurants, dined with movie producers as well as publishers. Albert Smith of Vitagraph invited them to stay at his Oyster Bay home. It was all good for business, but Jim hated New York and was always eager to get back home.

Jack quit Reliance Truck Company and Jim bought him a garage on South Washington Street. The garage also became a dealership for Ford Motor Company, with Ed Hoffman as agent. Ralph, still with Reliance, transferred from New York to Boston.

In spite of the poor royalty report from Bobbs-Merrill— $100.73 for the first six months of 1913, mostly for the British rights to *Philip Steele*—he went back to them for *Kazan* the next year, 1914, in a one-time deal. *Harper's* royalty check, for *Isobel* and *Flower of the North*, was even worse, only $72, not to be paid until fall.

Jim's next publisher would be Doubleday, Page and Company, an association which would continue through six books.

Grand Trunk agreed to furnish $500 worth of transportation again for Jim's planned 1913 trip to British Columbia, with transportation on the lakes furnished by the "boat people" from Detroit to Port Arthur. The latest information about British Columbia was to be provided and gun permits would be waiting for them in Winnipeg.

On this trip, Jim and Ethel saw first hand the building of the "Yellowhead Highway," the new rail line across the Rocky Mountains from Jasper to Tete Jaune Cache. The rail line and Tete Jaune Cache was so named for a trapper who had first explored these mountains, a blond or "yellowhead" adventurer named John who had opened the route across the mountains and cached his furs on the west side of the pass.

Tete Jaune Cache was a wide open boom town, grown from nothing to a roaring, raucous place overnight, a town that would fade quickly once the construction was finished. It fascinated Jim. The construction crews and the people the building of the railroad drew—including the Otto Brothers and their wives—were an endless source of material for him. The "horde," he called them, and used that term as the tentative title for the book he began about them. The book later became *The Hunted Woman*. It's characters were based on the real people he met there, including the woman who rode a bear through the streets of the town, and on stories told him about the area.

The hero was John Aldous, a writer, and the fact that he was based on Jim himself was easy to see.

In mid-September, Jim and Ethel were home again. As usual, they made the usual stops along the way, checking on their property and talking with the people who helped make their trips possible and showing appreciation for that help. Once home, Jim ordered a rifle for Frank Edwards of Lac Seul Fish Company, which Edwards replied would be "an ever present reminder of your kind self and wife." Jim had also left money with Edwards to grubstake several Indians to trap fox and mink for furs for Ethel and others in the family.

He sent autographed copies of his books to everyone.

Ray met Jim and Ethel at Thunder Bay for the journey down the lakes on the way home to discuss Jim's plans for his next work.

"I feel Kazan has been especially powerful because it was a series of short stories instead of a serial," Ray wrote once he'd returned home. He wanted to follow with another connected series of stories, also bringing in animal life. They should follow right after the *Kazan* stories finish. "That means we must work very quickly. If you have a short story plot in mind, better get it out of your system and let me use it the first month after the Kazan stories as that will give us a little more time."

Jim had no such story idea in mind and considered reviving *Kazan*, but

Ray said no. You've carried the dog through 11 stories "with wonderful success" and left him with a "happy ever after finish," Ray pointed out. The dog in the new series should be a "new dog."

Grasping for ideas, Jim settled on the next best thing, one of Kazan and Gray Wolf's pups. A son of Kazan; in fact, "Baree, Son of Kazan."

There was no way of satisfying all the demands for his work.

Robert Davis of *Munsey's* wanted to see some stories. "I know you are the busiest moving picture scenario man on earth, but your first and highest ideals are literature and the great American novel. When are you going to write us that 100,000 word novel?"

The scenarios were quick and profitable, but Jim knew that his real fame and fortune was in the printed word. Script writing, while it paid well, was too draining of his time and energies to continue at the pace necessary to keep it up. By the end of 1914, he had given it up, at least for the time being.

Ray, too, thought it wise to drop the photoplays and get back to fiction for awhile.

"I am tremendously anxious to get another series immediately. If you can send me a story right away ..." Ray also wanted a story for *Green Book Magazine* about where Jim got his photoplay ideas, illustrated with photographs, "including you and Mrs. Curwood." All of the nine photographs appearing with the article, though, were of Jim and his hunting companions and none of Ethel. The article, written about him but from material he supplied, attributed his photoplay success to "experience, adventure of the real sort, and living the life of which he writes."

Gaylord Garage might have a Ford dealership, but Jim bought a Cadillac that fall, a seven-passenger sedan.

His women's suffragette photoplay, "When Women Go on the Warpath," was playing at the Colonial Theatre in November.

Bobbs-Merrill sold the movie rights to all of Jim's books to Selig-Polyscope for $100 each, with Jim to have the right to do the scenarios for not less than $50 each. He wrote immediately to Howland saying he hoped that sale had not included *Philip Steele*, since he'd already sold two or three scenarios from that book, and Howland replied that the agreement with Selig had included all but that book.

Harper's royalty statements for the end of the year were up, mainly due to the sales of his books as serials to newspapers like the *Utica Press*, *Grit* and the *Chicago Record Herald*. Bookstore sales were still poor, though he was still near the top in the best seller lists in most parts of the country.

Ray and Pearl Long came for a visit in early January 1914. Jim gave Ray the first 50,000 words of his new novel, and left him alone to read it. "Curwood, you've written the big novel of 1914," Ray exclaimed when Jim returned. He offered Jim $5,000 for serial rights to the unfinished story, and wrote a check for $1,000 to seal the bargain. The agreement called for Jim to get the final 20,000 words to Ray quickly, and to immediately begin another story which he'd outlined for Ray.

Jim couldn't resist writing to his old friend Howland at Bobbs-Merrill about his good fortune. "I am just sufficiently woke up," he wrote as soon as Ray had left. "Kazan" had added 10,000 to *Red Book's* circulation, Ray had told him. Giving the details of the new offer, he asked, as usual, for Howland's opinion. "I don't know much about serial prices.... Perhaps I've written something here that I ought to treat as confidential, but as you will probably handle the book...," he wrote.

"There is just one point on which I am going to be a little insistent—and that is the title of the story. I want to like this title MYSELF." He liked "God's Country—And the Woman."

"It seems to me that title is a corker, and carries in it almost every virtue a title can. Surely it looks tremendous, and rouses curiosity to the limit."

God's Country. Whether Jim was the first to use the term or not, that was how he thought of the untraveled places in northern and western Canada.

Red Book went all out publicizing the new story, to begin in the June issue. May's circulation was expected to be tremendous because it contained the last chapter of Rupert Hughes's novel. June was usually a slow month in the magazine business, but color inserts were being put in the May issues of *Red Book*, *Blue Book* and *Green Book* advertising Jim's new story.

Billboards along the major railways between New York and Chicago also announced Jim's coming story.

Ray hadn't wanted Bobbs-Merrill to publish *Kazan*. He had urged Jim to talk to Russell Doubleday, and now Jim and Ethel went to Detroit to meet the publisher and struck a deal to publish all of his books from then on, beginning with *God's Country and the Woman*. He met Doubleday again in Buffalo later to finalize the arrangement.

Jim planned some fish trips with Ray for the spring, but Ray couldn't get away. "We would feel so much better if you folks would run down here sometime, and give us a chance to pay back some of your wonderful hospitality," Ray wrote. But the spring and summer were busy for them both and there was little time for play.

They toyed with the possibility of forming a partnership in the photo-play business. They figured they could probably net pretty close to $20,000 a year each over the next five years. Compared to what other writers were getting, "there isn't anyone in the country who is getting out of it anywhere near the gross that you are," Ray wrote Jim. With the two of them together, there would be no limit to what they could make. But they were both committed to their present arrangements and put the plan aside.

In London, Curtis Brown was reading *Kazan*. "(H)ardened as I am with years of novel-reading for business rather than pleasure," he wrote Jim, he had enjoyed *Kazan*. The book was scheduled for publication in England in February and in the United States on March 11, the first time one of Jim's books was published in England ahead of the States.

Brown sold the English serial rights to *God's Country—And the Woman* for $2,000, retaining the book, dramatic, second serial and photoplay rights. Jim was learning to protect himself and not end up in such disputes as he was having over some of his work, especially those old stories that had appeared in now-defunct publications.

Ralph was back in Owosso, working in Gaylord's Auto Company, and had charge of its new day and night livery service. A relative of Jack's, 22-year-old Claude Smith, worked there also. The day before the Fourth of July, Claude was welding iron with a large blowtorch when the stopper came out of the big gasoline tank and there was an explosion. Enveloped in flames, Claude nevertheless grabbed up a rope, threw it around the gas tank and hauled it out of the building. Ralph, working with him that Sunday afternoon, grabbed a hose and turned it on Claude as he dragged the tank outdoors. Claude was taken to the doctor and although he was burned about his hands and face, the burns weren't serious and he wasn't even confined to home.

Bob Davis of *Munsey's*, still desirous of getting something from Jim's pen, wrote, "I hear that you are raising hell in the moving picture business and make more money with less work than any other man on the job." He wanted to see Jim's new novel, *The Hunted Woman*, and he would give it his immediate attention. But this story, variously titled "Joanne of Fair Play," "The Horde," and "The Valley of Gold," had already been promised to *Red Book*.

During the summer of 1914 Jim planned his next trip to British Columbia and invited Ray to go with him. "Your letter set me on fire to go," Ray wrote, "but I will have to go next year."

Ethel went instead.

There was so much to do before they left—minor changes to *God's Country and the Woman*, a business trip to Detroit, correspondence to be answered. Jim made his list of things to do or take on the back of an envelope: Teeth, telephone service, comb, press clothes, boots, hair cut, cigar and tobacco and razor, camera and tripod, weigh baby, pipes, union suits, socks, etc., and crossed them out as they were taken care of. He figured his finances: $1,400 in the bank, $800 in the box, $100 coming from *Kazan*, and so on, and amounts he had to pay or could not use.

They left on Wednesday, August 12, 1914, for a two-month trip across Canada, up through British Columbia to the Yukon Valley and into Alaska.

When they got home, Jim brought with him an exciting new story which he would talk over with Ray when he came in December and which would begin a new direction and purpose to his life.

Chapter 16

The theatre billboard in Saskatoon, Saskatchewan that morning in early October, 1914 read, "In Defiance of the Law." It was another thrilling movie from a story by that famous author, James Oliver Curwood. The brown and fit-looking, medium-sized man with the white streak in his hair and a bundle of magazines under his arm paused to look it over.

"Let's go around and see this, my dear," he said to the beautiful woman holding to his arm, and they set out for the theatre where the movie was being shown.

Theater manager Frank Miley was out front as the couple strolled up and asked about the possibility of seeing the movie.

"I'm sorry, but this show doesn't open until two o'clock," Miley said, a bit annoyed that they should think they could get into the theater before the announced time.

"That's too bad," the man replied. "You see, I've been big game hunting for sometime and I've never seen this picture and I would like to see it. I may never have the opportunity again."

Miley muttered his regrets. The couple did seem to have an air about them, but no, he simply couldn't run the movie for just two people, no matter what.

But the man was adding one more persuasion. "You see, I'm Curwood. James Oliver Curwood," he said. Within half an hour, Miley had found a movie projector operator and Jim and Ethel were watching Selig's film made from Jim's book *Isobel*.

Saskatoon, Saskatchewan was one of the last stops on Jim and Ethel's journey home. After British Columbia they'd gone on up into Alaska, then turned homeward by way of Peace River in northern Alberta where Jim had been touted and quoted by the newspaper there—and called John Oliver Curwood. Jim looked in on his property in North Battleford and Saskatoon, watched the movie, and then they boarded the train for home.

If Jim and Ethel seemed a devoted couple to the theater manager in Saskatoon, it was an appearance that soon faded. Ethel went home to Owosso and Jim continued on to Conneaut for a stay at Ed's and where a long letter from Ray awaited him.

"We (himself and Mrs. Long) are anxious to see you folks," Ray wrote, and to hear about the trip.

Red Book readers were still asking for more animal stories from Jim, Ray wrote, and he'd like Jim to do another series of either hunting or animal stories. He also wanted a novel for *The Blue Book*. "If you can write these two features at the same time, we can handle them, and I will make it just as profitable as I can afford." He wanted to build up *Blue Book*. I want some of your work in it, he wrote.

Jim already had a story, "In the Tentacles of the North," which had been turned down by McClure's as too sexy. "Of course, your story had sex in it," Ray said, "it is pretty nearly impossible to write a story without sex in it—but without having seen it, I'll bet your story was as clean as a story could be." The cleanness of his stories was a point of pride with Jim. Sometimes he hinted at sex, in a discreet sort of way, some of his characters were fallen women, and he let his readers know that his characters were red-blooded men and women, but he never wrote explicitly of such things and even kisses were done with chaste passion.

Jim had not yet given up writing movie scripts. You're spending too much time and energy on movie writing, Ray complained. "My own feeling is that you would be very foolish to tie yourself up to any sort of absolute contract on moving pictures." Cut down instead, and you will find "the demand for them is going to increase at such a rate that you can dictate prices which would amaze any of the other writers." Jim was already getting as much or more than any other movie playwright.

"In the long run, fiction is more satisfactory and more enduring. I know this writing business pretty well, and I know that you are making more money out of it, and getting more satisfaction out of life than practically any writer I know.

"I am very anxious to see you keep your independence of action so that at any time you want to you can tell any of them to go to the dickens."

Jim knew Ray was right, of course, but writing for the movies was easy and profitable.

"In the Tentacles of the North" was waiting for Ray when he got back from a business trip to New York. He was disappointed. It was not, he wrote Jim, "in your best vein." He offered "a quick $250 for it, just to get it out of the way so you can get on to other things." It appeared in *Blue Book* in January 1915.

"God's Country—And the Woman" was already running in *Red Book* and wouldn't finish until July 1915. Ray wanted "The Hunted Woman" to follow. But after the trip to Owosso in December, it was decided to begin "The Hunted Woman" in *Blue Book* in May, letting the two stories overlap in the two publications. Ray would wait for Jim's story of the bear for *Red Book*.

In London, Curtis Brown had a number of Jim's stories and articles on the market, and he conferred with Jim about them by letter. Everett & Co. was thinking of holding off publication of *Ice Bound Hearts* (*Isobel*) because of the war situation in Europe. He had *God's Country and the Woman* in hand and was looking forward to getting *Joanne of Fair Play*, which, of course, was *The Hunted Woman*. Would Jim also consider trying some of his best movie scripts on the English market?

Brown had opened a New York office, with the same agent who had handled much of Jim's work in England and who would help with marketing of his stories in the U.S. if Jim wanted help.

Jim was still writing his Canadian articles and considering a bit of travel writing about the British Columbia mountains, especially about Jasper and Mt. Robson parks.

He took time to arrange for the Otto brothers to have transportation over the Grand Trunk Pacific lines whenever they wanted it, and for his movie, *Ye Vengeful Vagabond*, to be shown as a benefit for his niece Marguerite's junior class at Owosso High School.

Then the second week of December, Ray and Pearl came for a weekend. The two men sat up talking, Jim recounting his experience with the bear and the novel he wanted to write of it, and of his new feelings about wild life.

Ray went back to Chicago in excitement and conferred with numerous people on his staff to get their thinking. "They are so enthused over that bear story we are going to agree to your suggestion that you send the new novel to the East and let us count on the bear story."

"We appreciate your need of a breathing spell after your orgy of work, in view of your assurance you will put the bear story ahead of other fiction work."

"Honestly, Jim," Ray wrote, "it is going to prove the best piece of work you ever have done, or I'm the worst guesser in the world....This new novel (*The Hunted Woman*) is the best you have done, but I don't believe it is anywhere near as good as the bear story will be, and that is what we are gambling on."

Jim offered *The Hunted Woman* to Doubleday and other book publishers in the Eastern markets but, of course, with all his other commitments and works in progress, there was plenty of time for Long to publish all three of Jim's latest novels as serials, overlapping them only slightly. "God's Country and the Woman" ended in the July issue of *Red Book*, "The Hunted Woman" began in May in *Blue Book*—Jim got only $3,000 for it, less than he'd asked for—and ran through February 1916, "The Grizzly King" began in January 1916 in *Red Book*.

The manuscript of "The Hunted Woman" had arrived in London, still titled "The Horde," and Curtis Brown was hard at work selling it to Cassell's. Double the current price for a serial and a goodly increase in royalties for the book was suggested, providing Cassell's liked the story as much as they expected they would. Norman Flower, editor at Cassell's, was sure they could put through the deal. *God's Country and the Woman* was just coming out there and Cassell's also wanted the next book after this new story. The firm had a publishing house in Canada and could make as good an offer as any other Canadian publisher.

When you have another book in sight, hold out the Canadian rights, Brown urged, and give Cassell's a chance to bid on it.

Jim sent him the manuscript of the bear story, "Tyr, King of the Mountains." This, of course, was "The Grizzly King," which Jim had sent to Ray under the title "Thor." It was hastily written and shorter than most of his other novels, Ray was able to offer only $1,500 for it, with the money divided into five installments to begin in the fall.

By June Jim had another short novel, "Peter God," underway. He sent it to Brown in London who got twenty pounds for it. It was not published in the States.

Flower of the North was now out in a cheap edition and selling well. This was a new source of income for Jim. Once his books had about exhausted their sales in the regular edition, they could be reprinted in cheap editions, usually by Grosset & Dunlap, and put back on the market.

Some of his old stories were being reprinted in magazines too. "The Wolf Hunters" began in *The Boy's Magazine* in October 1915, to be followed by "The Gold Hunters." "Kazan" was running in *Gentlewoman*, and "Flower of the North" in *Famous Story Magazine*. It kept his name before the public, which was clamoring for his stories, and it kept money coming in. It should have given him a bit of breathing space, but there were always commitments for new stories.

During the spring and summer of 1915 it was work, work, work. There was so much to do and so little time for anything else. The summer's trip to British Columbia was cancelled, made more disappointing with the news that the Otto brothers had guided another hunter in a successful bear hunt in the spring, bagging four grizzlies, the largest one nine-and-a-half feet, breaking a record for a single hunt. The story was being written up for *Field and Stream Magazine*.

It was hard just to find time for fish picnics.

Jimmy, not quite four, had been ill off and on for months. Two days before Christmas he underwent minor surgery and got along nicely after that.

In January 1916, Granny Smith died suddenly at Jack and Amy's. And a baby girl born to Ralph and Vee lived only five days. A sad winter for the family.

Ed and Stella's son, Guy, came to visit his grandparents and other relatives for a couple of weeks.

Jim and Ethel went to Detroit for a few days. He went alone the end of March.

Ed and Stella came from Conneaut for a visit.

Owosso's unpaved streets, and there were still many of them, were a mire from the thawing snow and spring rains.

In April, Jim was in Detroit to give a talk to the Author's League of Michigan about how he got the material for his books and stories.

There was another fire in Gaylord's Garage, this time just a chimney burning out.

Among Jim's many Detroit friends was Fred Zeigan, a banker and a writer of poetry. He was a principal founder of Banker's Land and Investment Company, in which Jim was thinking of putting some money, and invited Jim and Ethel to a dinner at his country home, Twin Towers Villa, at Ypsilanti.

Jim and Ethel did the entertaining, by recounting some of their adventures on the Canadian trails.

Two of Jim's films were shown in Owosso that spring. *Thou Shalt Not Covet* starred a handsome new actor named Tyrone Power. *The Hunted Woman*, filmed by Vitagraph, starred S. Rankin Drew, nephew of the noted actor John Drew, as the hero, John Aldous. Drew also directed the film.

The exciting scenes were real. Shot at the falls at Au Sable Chasm in upstate New York, Drew and the villain staged a fight scene in the water. They went over the falls—one take only, of course—to land in a safety net fifteen feet from the top, and continued their fight in the raging rapids below.

In April, Jim went to Detroit for the screening of *God's Country and the Woman*, a Vitagraph "Blue Ribbon Feature." The star was Nell Shipman. Jim liked her looks and her style, and her wealth of long, dark hair. She was just right for his spunky heroine Josephine. Her co-star was William Duncan. The film came to Owosso in May, and was brought back again in December.

Jack and Amy moved to one of the new apartments in a row house on Oliver Street. The street alongside Jim's house was finally renamed North Shiawassee, since a bridge had long ago linked Mulberry Street with Shiawassee on the south side of the river.

In May, *God's Country and the Woman* was rated number one on the book list in Memphis, and from second to sixth elsewhere in the country.

The Grizzly King was finished by the first of May. He dedicated it "To My Boy."

On May 10 Jim left, alone, for a spring bear hunting trip with Bruce Otto. He was back in June.

By now Jim had hunted nearly every North American big game—moose, black, grizzly and polar bears, mountain sheep, even walrus and seals along Hudson Bay. The walls of his house were lined with his trophies.

But it was no longer a thrill. For many years he had been developing his own unique type of religion. He wrote often of priests and admired the Catholic faith, but he was not a Catholic. Neither was he any avowed sect of Protestant. He believed that no matter what religion one chose to follow—Christianity,

Bhuddism, Islamic, or whatever—there was a God, a Supreme Arbiter, a Master who was concerned with every living thing down to the smallest blade of grass.

Everything has a soul, he said. The trees and the flowers were his friends, and he talked to them and of them as his soulmates. Now that he had come to see the error of his wanton killing, he respected other creatures as equal to himself, not to be destroyed for the sake of killing.

Getting away into the mountains was a balm to his harried mind and soul, but he no longer felt the need to bolster his self-esteem with trophies to hang on his walls.

Viola came when school was out. When it was time for her to leave, James and Abby took her and Carlotta as far as Ed's in Ohio. Leon met them there. Carlotta was excited to see her mother again, after so many years, but Leon was cool. Tucking the girls into bed that night, she bent and kissed Viola but she didn't kiss Carlotta. It devastated the 13-year-old girl. "My mother never wanted me," Carlotta said many years later. It drove her even closer to her father.

While the girls were gone, Jim, Ethel and Jimmy spent a couple of weeks visiting Ethel's family in Hamilton, Indiana.

Vera Haskell was now playing her violin to accompany the films shown at the Strand Theatre, including the five-reel drama by Jim, *The Destroyers*, starring Lucile Lee Stewart and an all-star cast, adapted by Vitagraph from Jim's story "Peter God."

Jim was a guest again of Fred Zeigan at Twin Towers and the Zeigans were guests of the Curwoods in August.

The old indoor baseball teams were resurrected and scheduled to play in the Armory by permission of the National Guard.

The Last Man was premiered at the Strand Theatre in October before Jim, Ethel, members of the Owosso Elks Club and their guests from Saginaw, and a reporter from the *Evening Argus*. Its showing in Detroit some days before had "aroused great enthusiam among the critics."

Money was being raised around the country to light the Statue of Liberty.

Jack London died of uremic poisoning.

Abby, James and Cora left for another winter in Florida.

Christmas night, 1916, Jim left on a business trip to New York to confer with his editors on several stories. He spent some time at the Vitagraph studios in Brooklyn selecting casts for several new movies. It was a privilege few screen writers were allowed, to have a say in who played in his movies. One of his requirements was that the women must all have long hair.

He picked long-haired and beautiful Nell Shipman to star in *Baree, Son of Kazan*, his latest novel which was to begin serially as "A Son of Kazan" in the March 1917 *Red Book* and was being filmed by Vitagraph.

Jim sounded out his old friends at Bobbs-Merrill, who had published

Kazan, about book publication. " 'A Son of Kazan'...is the greatest story I have ever written," he wrote Howland.

"Now here is a plain letter if you ever got one in your life," he went on. He'd gotten "the rawest sort of a deal from the Bobbs-Merrill people in *Kazan*," he said. They had promised to push the book and they had not. "I'm on earth for the same thing you people are, and that's money...How much money can you people see in 'A Son of Kazan'?" Doubleday is doing splendidly with my books, he said, but Bobbs-Merrill was the father of *Kazan*, "but confoundedly poor Dads, you must admit.

"Now I'm almost brutally frank in this letter because I don't want to put off a lemon on you. I want you to look at 'A Son of Kazan' with a business eye, if you're interested in it at all." Doubleday would bring him in $10,000, could Bobbs-Merrill do as well? He wanted them to publish the book because they'd published *Kazan*, "but I can't make a sacrifice for that." He'd be sacrificing Doubleday's good will as it was.

Bobbs-Merrill had not split fairly with him on *Kazan*, which Jim credited to "business acumen on your part, and lack of it on mine." But at last, he said, "I've descended from the clouds, and I'm after money...."

They were unable to come to terms, however, and Doubleday published the book late in 1917.

On April 6, 1917, war was declared. A new 8,000-acre army training camp, Fort Custer, was opened in Battle Creek, Michigan. The first influenza case of the 1918 epidemic was reported there in March of that year. In all, 647 men died of influenza out of the 10,000 who entered Fort Custer's hospital during the next year.

Jim applied as a war correspondent but failed to get credentials, although he wrote to everyone he knew from Congressman Joseph W. Forney to John Sleicher at *Leslie's*.

The Junction Hotel closed in May, leaving only the Miller House, still owned by Charles Preece, oldest hotel in West Town, to serve the dwindling number of train passengers. The automobile industry was taking over in spite of the lack of good roads—the one east to Flint was 25 miles of mud and mire, nearly impassable in places.

On June 12, 1917, Jim wrote a long preface for *Baree, Son of Kazan*, expressing his new ideas on the killing of wildlife. "I have always disliked the preaching of sermons in the pages of romance," he wrote. "It is like placing a halter about an unsuspecting reader's neck and dragging him into paths for which he may have no liking. But if fact and truth produce in the reader's mind a message for himself, then a work has been done.

"That is what I hope for in my nature books."

And what right, his readers might ask, "has a confessed slaughterer of wild life such as I have been to complain? None at all..." He had 27 guns in his house and he'd used them all, he admitted. He'd done more than his share of extermination. But if people could only be brought into the homes of the birds and animals, "we would understand at last that wherever a heart beats it is very much like our own in the final analysis of things."

What a long way he'd come, and what a long way still to go in his efforts to convince men and women, boys and girls that everything has a soul, and that wild animals were not there for wanton killing. *Kazan, The Grizzly King* and now *Baree, Son of Kazan*, he hoped, would go a long way toward helping people think of animals as living beings. Not like humans, of course—"It is not my desire to humanize them"—but with hearts that sang with joy and wept with sorrow much as a human's heart might do.

Birthplace of James Oliver Curwood in WestTown Owosso, Michigan. Photo courtesy of Ivan Conger.

Abigail Griffin Curwood and Jim's sister, Cora Curwood. Photo courtesy of Ivan Conger.

James Moran Curwood. Photo courtesy of Ivan Conger.

Cora Leon Johnson, Jim's first wife. Photo courtesy of Ivan Conger.

The young hunter with head of moose he shot in Ontario. Photo courtesy of Ivan Conger.

Ethel May Greenwood, Jim's second wife. Photo courtesy of Ivan Conger.

James Oliver Curwood's home shortly after it had been remodeled from a two-family dwelling to one-family. Photo courtesy of Ivan Conger.

Roughing it. Photo courtesy of Ivan Conger.

Ethel Curwood on snowshoes on their honeymoon in Ontario,1909-1910. Photo courtesy of Ivan Conger.

Five generations (left to right): Virginia Gaylord, her father Ralph Gaylord, his mother Amy Curwood Gaylord, her mother Abby Griffin Curwood, and her father Richard Griffin. Photo courtesy of Ivan Conger.

Looking for grizzlies; Jim and his guide, Jack Otto, on their 1913 trip to British Columbia. Photo courtesy of Bentley Historical Collections, University of Michigan.

Ethel Curwood at home by the fireplace. Photo courtesy of Ivan Conger.

James Oliver Curwood in January, 1907, as Editor of the Illustrated Section of the Detroit News-Tribune.

Jack Otto, one of Jim's guides in the Canadian West, with head of Caribou Jim shot on 1913 trip.

Jim with Northern Pike caught in Houghton Lake. Photo courtesy of Ivan Conger.

Viola Curwood. Photo courtesy of Ivan Conger.

James Oliver Curwood, Jr. Photo courtesy of Ivan Conger.

The Curwood Veterans (Curwood in back row at left). Photo courtesy of Ivan Conger.

James Oliver Curwood.

Curwood Castle, the author's writing studio in Owosso, built in 1923. Photo by the author.

Curwood's lodge at Roscommon, Michigan; he handpicked the stones for the huge fireplace. Photo courtesy of Ivan Conger.

Chapter 17

On the walls of Jim's study and in other rooms from top to bottom of his house were the heads of some of the animals he had killed with his 27 guns. The women in the family wore furs.

Looking at those mounted heads now he felt neither shame nor regret. They had been killed before he had come to his new understanding. Rather, he considered these slain animals martyrs who helped him to see the wantoness of his former "murders," and reminded him of what he had come to learn in the wilds, that everything has a soul in the eyes of God.

Jim Curwood was not a religious man in the formal sense of the word. He called himself a "pantheist" in the years that followed his confrontation with the wounded bear, one who believes that everything is a manifestation of God, that there is a Maker who has endowed everything with a "soul" and a right to live.

He also said he was an "iconoclast," for he believed that he was breaking new ground in the understanding of nature.

When war was declared in Europe, Jim viewed it as a horror, even as he applied for credentials as a war correspondent, but he believed that the war would make pantheists of others. "War is hell, physically speaking," he said, but "spiritually it is a great iconoclast, breaking down untrue things and rearing up in their places things that are true."

Some months after the beginning of the entry of American soldiers into the fighting in France, he received a letter from a man in the trenches. He and his comrades had been reading *Kazan*, the soldier wrote, reading it aloud in groups until the book was "worn to a rag." Thanking Jim for the pleasure it had brought them, the soldier told of a pair of birds nesting amid the firing and how they sang even in the tumult of death, unafraid "as though possessed of souls stronger than our own, or sent there by this great spirit which you describe to give courage and cheer."

If Jim had doubted his own beliefs, it was letters like this, and the one from a war widow in England thanking him for the comfort she found in reading his books, that reinforced him.

In the spring Jim and Ethel moved into a house on Ball Street near downtown while their house was being remodeled into a one-family home. Gone were the renters. Jim bought a strip of land from a neighbor to expand the back yard. When Jim and Ethel moved back home it was into a stately well-furnished brick house with a lovely garden in the back.

Jim's books were selling well now all over the country. Most of them were printed in as many as seven languages. His latest novel, *Baree, Son of Kazan*, was running serially in *Red Book*. His early book, *The Wolf Hunters*, was serialized in *Chums*, an English magazine for boys, to be followed, of course, by *The Gold Hunters*. *God's Country and the Woman* was in *Cassell's*, another English magazine, and he had short stories and articles in a variety of magazines in the States and abroad.

Theatres everywhere were showing his films.

President Theodore Roosevelt, a writer of outdoor stuff himself, asked Jim to swap some stories with him.

Jim spent a lot of time in New York, Detroit, Chicago, sometimes with Ethel along, sometimes alone, on pleasure as well as business. In November they were in Chicago as guests of Ray and Pearl for a few days. The Longs hosted a party of literary friends in their honor.

At home there were always family gatherings. Jim had changed, grown beyond the limits of Owosso, but with his family he was still the same. And they were the same, too, loving good times and pranks as much as ever. Vee was famous for her white cake frosted with whipped cream, and her apple pie. Young Jack and Abby, feeling prankish at one family get-together, snitched the walnuts Vee had decorated her cake with, then played the innocents when it was discovered, and were a little ashamed when they saw Vee's crestfallen face.

When Abby "got going" too strong with her fun, James toned her down. "Now, Abby, that's enough," was all it took. She was uninhibited in talking about sex, considering it a normal thing, but she sometimes went too far to suit her conservative husband.

There were still fish picnics, of course, but fewer trips to the marshes. Some of the family were getting on. They mostly reminisced now, reminding each other of good hunting times and telling tales on each other, like the time Jim set out the duck decoys and near-sighted Ralph thought they were real and shot at them.

All the family at times went to Conneaut to visit Ed and Stella. Jim and Ethel went that summer. Stella smoked smelly cubibs, for her asthma, she said, though the family suspected it was mostly an excuse for smoking, but no one minded anyway.

A couple in Kentucky named their son after Jim. It was only one of many James Olivers around the country and in Canada, named expressly for him.

War restrictions were on, but Jim and Ethel were living well. They drove the finest of cars and traveled widely. They were on a first name basis with the literati of screen and printed page. Money was of no concern.

The shabby flat on Elm Street in Detroit was far in the past. Doors slammed in his face were hardly remembered. Rejection slips were souvenirs to be kept as reminders of long ago days before editors begged for his stories.

They were welcomed everywhere, a picture of married bliss.

Life, it would seem, was at its peak.

Ed and Stella came for Christmas and then they, James, Abby and Cora all went to Florida for the winter. But winter was one of Jim's best times, he didn't mind the cold and he had no desire to go south and sit in the sun. He was too busy.

The royalty check from Harper & Bros. for *Flower of the North* and *Isobel* was $154.12 for the last six months of 1917. A mere pittance, a drop in the bucket in Jim's income. He had surpassed the late Jack London, and White, Zane Grey and others of his peers.

But the reading public was never satisfied, the critics hovered always on the fringes, complaining that his stories were beginning to have a sameness, nothing new, and Jim worked harder than ever.

With James and Abby away for the winter, the click of Jim's typewriter keys sounded again at all hours from his old bedroom upstairs in the house on John Street.

He turned to the new subject that had lately become close to his heart—his conversion from a killer of wild life to an advocate for the creatures of the forests.

"Why I Write Nature Stories," published in *Good Housekeeping Magazine* in July 1918, included eight photographs, all of them taken on hunting trips. Prominent was the one of him with three huge bear skins stretched out on a rack behind him when he had, he admitted, destroyed at least 120 years of life in half an hour. But now, he said, "I am no longer their enemy."

"An editorial request for me to tell something of what I have found in my adventuring in the heart of the wild places finds me in a rather embarrassing position," he wrote.

"It is hard for one to confess oneself a murderer, and it is still harder to explain one's regeneration. Yet to be genuine I must at least make the confession, though it is less the fact of murder than the fact of regeneration that I have the inclination to emphasize, now that I have the opportunity."

All of his twenty-seven guns had been used, he said, some with notches in their stocks to mark his kills. Mounted animal heads hung from top to bottom of his home. But I am now a pantheist, he declared. All the universe is one with God, all things have a soul.

Man has emptied the world of "much that is beautiful," meaning wild life. "Most of them are still on the job.

"But I have quit." He promised never again to kill for sport. It was his new philosophy of conservation.

I write nature stories, he told his readers, "(B)ecause I know they will do the world no harm, and may do some good."

In the back yard of the house on Williams Street was a huge old tree. It was Jim's favorite tree, and he often stopped beneath it, laying his hand on its bark and, as he called it, "communing" with it. The tree, however, began to die, and in spite of his efforts, nothing saved it. It had to be cut down. Jim felt he had lost a close friend and cried over its loss.

More and more now his thoughts turned to nature, and more and more he urged others to think about what they were doing to the world around them. If this kind of teaching could only begin with the child, at home and in kindergarten, he felt, children would grow up with this same love of nature. People were searching for religion, not only in the churches but elsewhere, through the spirits and in seances and by mediums. Why couldn't they find God in the world around them, in the flowers and trees and birds and animals? Everything, every blade of grass, the smallest creature, has a soul. If only he could convince others of that.

Jim's next novel, *The Golden Snare*, to be published by Doubleday Bros., was sought as a movie script even before publication. Jim sought Russell Doubleday's approval. Go ahead and collect the $2,500 offered for it, by all means, Doubleday said. This book, however, was far from his best writing. Not only did the deal for its filming fall through, Doubleday did not publish it. It was eventually published in England but not in the U.S. until 1921 when Cosmopolitan Book Corporation had it printed by Grossett & Dunlap, who published most of his reprints, mainly because it was Jim's and they wanted it out of the way. It did not sell well. The story was finally filmed in 1921 by David Hartford Productions, a company in which Jim had an interest.

But that was not for another three years.

Now, his new animal series, "Nomads of the North," was coming along nicely. Stories were going out in all directions, movie plots popping out of his head and reeling off his typewriter roller. It was a good time, good to be working in his old room, free of distractions.

In February 1918 Ray and Pearl Long came for a weekend, and Arthur Henry Bings, a widely known hunter of African big game, and his friend, Lord Northcliffe. They talked of Jim going with them on an African safari; Jim in turn invited them on a trip to British Columbia. He expected to go again this year.

The royalty check from Bobbs-Merrill for the last half of 1917 was ridiculously small, but the one from Doubleday made up for it—more than a thousand dollars on the four books they'd now published for him.

Then he was sick again. He prided himself on taking care of his body, with exercise and care in his diet, but he constantly overworked his mind, and consequently, his body suffered for it. Thinking of this as he wrote his article for *Good Housekeeping* on why he wrote nature stories, he admitted that "After all, it is our nerves that kill us in the long run; our over-restless minds, our worrying brains. Nature whispers its great peace to these things even in the rustling leaves of a corn-field—if one will only get acquainted with nature."

Jim Curwood was certainly acquainted with nature, he had by now been to nearly every part of the Canadian wilds, from Hudson Bay to the Yukon, except those remote parts that took months to reach, and he went as often as he could to nearer places in Michigan where he could get out into the peace and quiet of the countryside, even corn fields. He and Ethel and the children now spent several weeks each summer up at Houghton Lake, a large resort lake about a hundred miles north of Owosso, where Jim wrote, and where they fished and swam and got away from the heat of the city.

In spite of liking desserts, Jim took care in his diet. He ate sparingly of meat except on his Canadian treks, and exercised each morning in front of an open window before getting at his writing. He rode horseback as often as possible, and took long walks, especially to a favorite place along the river north of town where he sat with his back against his "own" particular tree and thought out problems with plots or characters.

It was his mind he couldn't control, and his mind wore him down.

In March the river overflowed and flooded basements along its banks, including James and Abby's. Jim pondered what could be done and wrote a letter to the *Evening Argus* about river improvement. Others in town also thought something should be done. Jim proposed some improvements at the August meeting of the Owosso City Commission, and an informal meeting was held to discuss Jim's plans for three dams along the river.

Jim was never one to do things halfway, nor to make suggestions and not follow through. He went to the State Board of Health in Lansing and asked the state engineer to come to Owosso and look the situation over. Together with City Engineer E. S. Brewer and members of the City Commission, they made a survey along the river and estimated the cost to install the dams.

Still, nothing much was done.

Jack retired, the garage was sold, and Ralph went to work as a jitney (taxi) driver.

The war was still on and Jim was credentialed at last as a war correspondent but he didn't go. The war was affecting sales of his work, especially on the Continent.

He gave the Northern Navigation Company of Canada permission to reprint "The Grizzly King" in its magazine, *By-Water*, with Russell Doubleday's okay. "Thank you (for this and) for your many courtesies of the past," the company replied.

In July, Nell Shipman was appearing at the Lincoln Theatre in *Baree, Son of Kazan*, and getting good reviews.

That summer of 1918 he worked on a new novel, *The River's End*, set in northern Alberta and the Northwest Territories.

He also wrote a long story, "Wapi, the Walrus," about an heroic huge black dog and a desperate woman, both at the mercy of one of Jim's most black-hearted villains. He sold it to *Good Housekeeping Magazine* as a two-part story for its November and December 1918 issues.

What a wonderful movie it would make. A beautiful woman trying to save her husband, a scoundrel of a ship captain, the howling wintertime along Hudson Bay, and this strong-hearted dog who helps the heroine and her husband to safety.

The movie business was growing in all directions. Everyone was still learning. A person might be an actor in one picture, the director on the next, the writer on another, perhaps the photographer on still another. Stars became producers and went into business for themselves.

An Author's League was formed to protect writers' work from unscrupulous abuse by production companies. Author Rex Beach was chairman. Would Jim be interested? He joined and for a time served on the board of directors.

It all looked so interesting and profitable that in late 1918 Jim decided to go into the movie production business himself. He had not been happy with the production of some of his stories. He would do it himself.

Besides, Nell Shipman and her promoter husband, Ernie, were offering an unbeatable deal—stories by James Oliver Curwood starring Nell Shipman, filmed by their own company.

"Following close on his five-year contract with the *Cosmopolitan, Good Housekeeping* and *Hearst Magazines*, which places him among the five highest paid fiction writers in America, James Oliver Curwood has scored another success of national interest in the organization of the Shipman-Curwood Feature Production company, with three quarters of a million dollars in capital behind it," the *Evening Argus* reported on February 13, 1919.

Movie companies were all moving west, but Jim's stories were set in Canada and that was where they were to be filmed. Of course, Vitagraph of southern California had taken the cast and crew of *God's Country and the Woman* to northern Alberta for filming, but this new company would be a Canadian one, financed by a group of businessmen in Calgary.

The moving force behind this company was Nell Shipman's husband, Ernest. "Ten-percent Ernie," as he was known in the trade, was a hustler and a native Canadian. Nell, too, was Canadian, born in Vancouver but brought up in Seattle, who'd gone on tour with a stock company when she was only fifteen. Nell and Ernie met on her eighteenth birthday in Seattle where he was managing a stock company and she was looking for work. They'd married shortly after and had gone on tour together.

Now Nell was working for Vitagraph. She'd starred in *God's Country and the Woman* in 1916 and was now in *Baree, Son of Kazan*. She had also written a number of scripts.

It seemed like a winning combination— Nell to star in Jim's stories, and

Ernie to promote them. Jim gave his okay to Ernie setting it up.

Jim's banking friend from Detroit, Fred Ziegen, wrote from his winter home in Florida, "I'm pleased Nell Shipman is in on it with you. She has a good personality and is fetching in her manner. It looks like she has lots of brains to back her work."

Why don't you come down here, Fred asked. He planned to spend every winter in Florida now, and Jim could come down and stay. He could write every morning, hunt and fish every afternoon, or play golf or tennis. In the meantime, Fred's office in Detroit was open to Jim while he was gone. "Remember us to that good wife of yours."

Jim, of course, wasn't interested in going to Florida, even to write.

That October, Viola was very ill with influenza. She and Leon now lived in Erie, Pennsylvania. There were no nurses available, so Leon took care of her, but, worn out, she fell ill herself and they were both finally sent to the hospital. With the flu epidemic raging, Jim hadn't been allowed to visit, but he kept in close touch and sent them money. By mid-December, Viola was getting better but she still was not allowed visitors. Leon was still quite sick.

In November, William Colvin of Calgary, writing on Nell Shipman stationary which proclaimed that she was "starring in stories by James Oliver Curwood, offices in New York and Los Angeles," sent Jim a small reel of film showing how Nell looked in a blond wig.

Nell, too, had been having the flu, but Colvin said he was glad to report "she is greatly improved since I wired you, and is now out of danger." Ernie had also been having the flu but was much better and Jim would probably hear from him in a few days. One thing Jim was not told was that following her high fever, all of Nell's beautiful long dark hair had fallen out. With his passion for long hair and his insistence that any woman playing in any movie made from one of his stories must have long hair, Nell's loss was something Jim was never to find out, even after it had grown back to its old luxurious length.

Jim turned down Fred Ziegan's urging to come down to Florida, but he did express his concern about his investment in Bankers Land and Investment Company. It wouldn't give him two or three dollars return for every dollar he'd invested, as a movie company might do, Fred replied, but his investment was guaranteed against loss. He'd send Jim stock worth the $11,000 he'd put in, plus interest to date, and if Jim wasn't satisfied at the end of a year he could get his $11,000 back. I'm only offering this deal to you, Fred told him. Jim's concerns were quieted for the time being.

The River's End began in *Good Housekeeping* in January and Jim was working on his third series of animal stories, scheduled to begin in Cosmopolitan in April. This was the story of two dogs, one of them named Swift Lightning.

Ray had gone from *Red Book* to the Hearst publications—*Cosmopolitan,*

Good Housekeeping, Harper's Bazaar and various newspapers. He went to California to confer with William Randolph Hearst. Hearst had big plans for Jim's stories. Serials like his current animal stories would run in *Cosmopolitan,* his novels would run in *Good Housekeeping* before book publication, and his short stories in *Cosmopolitan* or in H*arper's.* "The River's End" was due to conclude in the June 1919 issue of *Good Housekeeping* and already the editor was clamoring for another to follow as soon as Jim could write it.

"It amazed me how much you had written without rest," Ray wrote, "yet you are writing better today than ever before. Branson, the artist, considers your stories the best he has ever illustrated, and has turned down other work to give time and attention to yours." The Longs were going to Florida about the first of March for two weeks.

Jim must turn his attention to another novel, in spite of his business interests, movie scripts, home life, and his new involvement in movie production. He began work on *The Valley of Silent Men,* to follow *The River's End* in what would become a trilogy about the "Three Rivers County." He must have it ready to begin in *Good Housekeeping* by September.

First, though, he must go to Calgary to see about his new movie venture, and on up to Lesser Slave Lake where the picture was to be filmed. First choice for the new film company was his story, "The Yellowback," but this was postponed in favor of "Wapi, the Walrus." Nell was writing the movie script.

Jim and Ethel left for Calgary February 14, 1919.

Chapter 18

The air was tense in the Pelliser Hotel in Calgary on this day in late February 1919. In one of the rooms, actress and author were closeted in a battle of wills. Who would win?

Nell Shipman at 26 was a noted screen star and scriptwriter. James Oliver Curwood was a world-famous author of adventure stories. Both were talented and temperamental, volatile and domineering.

Nell had taken a lot of liberties with Jim's story in writing the script for *Back to God's Country*. Half of the movie would be over before it got to Wapi, who was still a hero but now only a supporting character. The main character had become the girl, and of course the girl was to be played by Nell. She had even written in a nude scene, to be tastefully done, of course.

Jim was furious. And Nell, though of some stature in the movie industry, was still awed by the author whose work she admired so much.

Waiting fearfully for the outcome were Nell's husband, Ernie, and the film's director, David Hartford. When star and author emerged from their conference practically arm in arm, everyone breathed a sigh of relief.

Now they could get down to work. Camera, crew and equipment had already been shipped north by train to Lesser Slave Lake where the story was to be filmed. Now Nell took the train north. Ernie stayed behind to wrap up the deal, Jim to tend to other business.

Back to God's Country was filmed under extremely difficult conditions. The cold was the worst of it.

Jim had insisted the film should be done in northern Canada in order to get the "realism" he thought important. When he and Ethel arrived at the fishing village of Faust on Lesser Slave Lake, they found the crew and cast putting up with the drafty cabins abandoned by the regular inhabitants for the winter. But they were hard at work in spite of primitive conditions. A profile set of a sailing vessel was being built on the lake to similate a ship frozen in the ice, to be burned later—in a one-shot filming, of course.

Temperatures dropped to as low as sixty degrees below zero at night. Filming went on anyway. Leading man Roland Byrum, a handsome actor from Australia, frosted his lungs, and the company manager, Bert Van Tuyle, froze his foot. They were sent down to a hospital in Calgary where Byrum later died. Cameramen Dal Clawson and Joe Walker kept their cameras outside at night to prevent the static that would build up with extreme temperature changes. Whiskers were coated with rimes of ice.

133

The local Siwash Indians thought the newcomers crazy, but they helped out, and Royal Northwest Mounted policemen stopped by for visits now and then.

Jim and Ethel's visit was brief. His writing was falling behind and it was a long trip home.

Jim was in his element in the far north again, and bragged to Carlotta, in a letter written just before he and Ethel left, that he was the camp hunter as well as overseeing the shooting of the picture. Hartford was due to arrive after Jim had left. In reality, Jim and Ethel were there only a few days.

On the last day there, Jim and Nell were to pose for publicity photographs. Ethel waited impatiently. "I don't think you should be photographed with her," she complained. To Nell, this was enough to prompt her to refuse. Besides, she was at least as tall as Jim.

There was one last brief conference in her cabin. Nell was to hand over a urine speciman in a bottle, taken at the insistence of the insurance company. And Jim had a last request. He'd only seen Nell's hair pinned up under a winter cap. He wanted to see it unbound.

How could she tell him that the fever from the double pneumonia she'd had in November had caused most of her hair to fall out, and that what he thought was her hair was really a wig? And the wigs were packed in a box. There was nothing under the fur cap she'd worn outside but the meager strands of her own hair trying to grow back. Still wearing the cap and stalling as best she could, Nell was saved by the appearance of a disapproving Ethel. "James," she cried, "the train!"

There was no time for anything more. The train was making an unscheduled stop to pick them up. They flung their gear aboard and chugged away for home.

The film company was probably glad to see them go. Jim, in his immaculate and stylish clothes and strutting imperious style, probably hampered their work. Ethel was jealous of Nell. They could work better without them.

Shooting continued through March. William Oakman replaced Byrum, whose scenes luckily had not yet been shot. The crew packed up their gear and their exposed film—it could not be developed in such extreme cold—and took the train down to San Francisco to shoot some more ship scenes. There were delays here while a whaler was readied. They didn't learn of Byrum's death until they were back in Los Angeles the middle of April, and then Nell was too distraught to work. There were more delays. All this Hartford reported to Jim in a day-by-day report.

Jim arrived home to face a new problem. Curtis Brown cabled from London that he'd had a showdown with Cassell's. It meant a complete break with them for both books and stories. He'd gone over to Hodder & Stoughton, however, as Jim had suggested, and they would take over Cassell's contracts and guarantee the same terms. English returns were less than the American, of course, but only Charles G. D. Roberts, the noted nature writer, now did better than Curwood as far as nature stories went. "It takes the English a long time to make up their minds," Brown said.

In the meantime, Jim was ill again. Plans for an early May trip to New York to confer with Ray and the advertising men at *Good Housekeeping*—"we very much wanted them to see you and know you and to get the inspiration which your presence would lend"—had to be scrapped. I won't urge a sick man to travel, Ray said, but "we do want to urge the sick man to write another novel." There was to be no respite.

"The River's End" was ending in June and he wanted the new novel to begin in July. Readers forget quickly, Ray said. "I don't mean that there is danger of their forgetting you—not by a dickens of a sight..." but they could forget to buy *Good Housekeeping* if they couldn't announce that a new story by Jim was beginning right away.

"You always have a great number of half-formed plots stirring around in your consciousness and it has been my experience with you that all that was necessary to get one of them to jell was for you and myself to sit around and talk for two or three days."

If Jim couldn't come to New York, then he'd come to Owosso, Ray said, "and we will see what we can do by some walks and talks and so on."

It was all that Jim needed to effect a turnaround. Jim wrote Ray his idea for a new story and Ray wrote by return mail, "I knew that out of your illness and depression would come a burst of strength and inspiration. That's the way you work. I have watched you do it time after time."

The film company of *Back to God's Country* had gone to Kernville, in the mountains above Bakersfield, California, to finish the outdoor scenes, but there were constant delays due to bad weather or because things were not ready for shooting. Finally, the end of May, they ran out of film. In all, they'd been able to work only forty-one days since Jim had left them at Lesser Slave Lake on March 9.

Jim may have been doubtful of his investment in Bankers Land and Investment, but he continued to buy stock. In addition to an order already placed, he placed two more small orders in April, one for 100 shares, the other for 50, "to be gifts to two people. Inasmuch as these will be my personal property," he told Ziegan, he wanted them dated back to June 1 of the previous year as his other stocks had been.

Jimmy, eight in January, wrote a hunting "storyette," which the *Argus* obligingly printed. It was a simple one-paragraph story about a man hunting a bear.

Nomads of the North was selling so fast the printers couldn't keep up and were 15,000 copies behind in printing. Nearly 100,000 copies of Jim's books were sold in three months.

Russell Doubleday was a guest of Jim and Ethel the first of May.

Ray and Pearl Long came in mid-May. The "Swift Lightening" stories had begun in *Cosmopolitan* in April. "The River's End" was due to end in *Good Housekeeping* in June. Jim's story had increased circulation in that magazine by 125,000 copies a month, Ray said. What had Jim done about another novel?

The deal the Hearst publications was giving Jim was one "no publishing house has ever done before," Ray told him. There were to be advance royalties, advance sales, "advertising beyond your dreams."

Cosmopolitan now also had its own book publishing house. Harold Kinsey was its head and one of the reasons Ray had wanted Jim to come to New York was so the two could meet. *Cosmopolitan* would pay Jim $5,000 upon publication plus 20 percent royalty and a guarantee of 40,000 copies in the regular edition. They were going to publish no more than six novels a year. Five writers only, Jim among them, had been selected to author these books.

The River's End had not yet been published in book form and Jim had signed no contract. Don't sign with Doubleday until you've considered what Cosmopolitan has to offer, Ray urged.

"I am not trying to spoil his game," Ray said of Russell Doubleday, because they had long been friends, "or to disturb his relations with any writer, but you are one of the five writers whom we consider capable of big development and it would not be fair to you to let my friendship for any one stand in the way of putting the proposition before you."

Ray's visit, as always, was the boost Jim needed. True there'd been no time for even one fish picnic, but Ray's enthusiasm was always a tonic. He signed a contract for Cosmopolitan to publish *The River's End*. It was this new arrangement with Cosmopolitan which delayed the publishing of *The Golden Snare* for such a long time. Jim was warned that allowing Doubleday to publish the book would "interfere" with the plans the Hearst organization was making for his books.

With *Back to God's Country* filmed, the new Shipman-Curwood production company ran into trouble. H. P. Carver of Canadian Photoplays, Ltd., the Calgary office behind the pictures, came to see Jim in June. They were to meet Nell, Hartford and the cutting crew and cameramen in Chicago to do the final editing. Jim was to have the final say. The company's second production, *The Yellow-Back*, from Jim's story which appeared in Hearst's Magazine in March, would start soon.

Things were not going smoothly, however, with Shipman-Curwood Productions. When Ray got home he pondered Jim's dilemma over the Shipmans. William Randolph Hearst was also putting together a filming company, mainly to accommodate his mistress, actress Marian Davies. He wanted to film Jim's stories. Would Hearst take over his organization with the Shipmans, Jim asked. This Hearst wouldn't do, Ray said, not Ernie nor the company, but he might take over the production of those pictures as Jim had planned them, and Nell Shipman, too, "since you seem to think that Miss Shipman would be the best person to act in those pictures..."

But it was too late. Nell, believing that Canadian Photoplay was doing her out of her pay, and that Jim was part of it, angrily withdrew from their contract. Jim accepted her resignation reluctantly. "I cannot but regret that you have chosen another road to travel. On that road I wish you only the greatest success."

Life at home went on as usual. Ethel had taken to the social life of the city, but Jim had little time for such things. There were a few men with whom he had become good friends—Fred Woodard, president of Woodard Manufacturing Company and a pillar of the community, and John McDonald of Connor's, and others whose bond with Jim was hunting and fishing.

Connors still made those Hoky Poky ice cream bars that had made such a hit at the fairs back at the turn of the century. Now they began construction of artificial ice making facilities at the Exchange and Ball streets plant, and were replacing two of the ice cream freezers with larger ones and remodeling an old brewery down in Ann Arbor for a branch plant in addition to the Lansing plant. That all took a lot of money, and Jim bought stock in the company.

How better to be certain of getting the kind of ice cream you like?

Martha Woodard, Fred's wife, was among the closest of Ethel's friends. Jim enjoyed a quiet evening at home with friends, and the Curwoods and Woodards spent many such evenings together. They played mah jong and a competition developed, Jim and Martha versus Ethel and Fred. Points were accumulated for a month, then the losers treated the winners to a dinner downtown. Sometimes Jim read chapters from whatever book he was working on.

Not everything Jim wrote was snapped up. A few stories and scripts he couldn't get published or filmed at all. "Little Miss Tired-of-it-All" was one. This script had been bouncing around now for more than a year. Vitagraph had turned it down and so had Famous Players.

Jim went over his old stories and books, looking for film possibilities. He wrote Bobbs-Merrill about the books they'd published for him, but they'd already sold *Kazan* to Selig Polyscope for $500 back in April of 1914. "Chambers talked the matter over with you when you were in his office on one of your too infrequent visits," Howland reminded him. *Honor of the Big Snows* had been sold to Selig in 1913.

Some Dutch publishers were pirating Jim's books, and Curtis Brown appealed to Jim for information on where they might have gotten the rights to do so. They won't tell our representatives, Brown said, and "you realize the danger of negotiations being in the hands of more than one person." But Jim didn't know any more about it than Brown did.

"As I go along with my present work," Jim wrote Ray in June, "which is coming on splendidly, I have hours in which my mind rests itself in planning that farm dog nature series." This would be a series about a farm girl who becomes friends with a "crank" naturalist living in a log cabin in a nearby woods who would teach her much of the "nature lore we are going to get into our story." Of course there would be a love interest, a young man "a little 'nicked' by tuberculosis, but who grows strong quickly in the open air." It was his old theme of nature's restoration to health of ailing human beings. He visualized it as not only a series of stories, but also as a book and "one of the biggest and best heart-throb and comedy dramas ever thrown on the screen."

The morning after he'd dictated the letter to Ray he had another "corking" idea. "To me trees are very lifelike and human things. I love trees of all kinds, and have studied them." Few people know the fight they have to make against "insects, ants, and vermin of various kinds," he said. He would have his naturalist love trees.

It was a story never written, however.

The moving picture industry was growing at a tremendous rate. Stars as well as writers were forming their own companies, like Mary Pickford and author Rex Beach. New and elaborate theatres were going up all around the country. Canadian Aero Film Co. of Toronto used an airplane in one of its movies. Some companies were making industrial and news films. The industry was fighting the Sunday law which prohibited showing films on Sunday. Some states had turned to censorship as films became more and more sexually explicit, but for the most part, film companies had cleaned up their acts themselves.

A lot of the original movie studios had moved West, most to Hollywood and nearby places in Southern California, but there were new companies forming all of the time and half of the studios were still in the East.

The final editing of *Back to God's Country* was done in New York the end of July. Jim and David Hartford went over the 45,000 feet of film and held a screening attended by New York critics.

The film threw the "cut-and-dried moving picture precedent to the four winds," one of the critics wrote. Overall, they declared it to be the best, most unusual picture ever. Nell's nude scene, with her romping in a pool below a small waterfall —she was actually in a skin-tight, flesh-colored suit—was applauded. The treatment used to show a scene within a scene, of the heroine in Montreal dreaming of her woodland home, also drew praise.

The film was widely advertised, with teaser ads showing simply a series of paw prints and the slogan "The nude is rude" running for weeks in trade magazines before revealing even the name of the film being advertised.

Jim demanded that the film should open in Owosso at the same time it was released in other theatres, and went home to prepare for his hometown's viewing of his masterpiece.

Chapter 19

There was standing room only September 16, 1919, as movie-goers jammed the Strand Theatre in Owosso to overflowing for the premier showing of *Back to God's Country*. An even larger crowd, nearly 3,000, thronged the theatre the next night, prompting the management to run the film for an unscheduled third performance.

Admission prices were kept to the regular 15 and 25 cents charge, at Jim's request, so that youngsters could see the "animal stuff"; the New York theatre where it was also shown raised its prices to 50 cents and a dollar and a half.

Simultaneous premiers were held in September in Ottawa, Canada and Sandringham, England, because it was the first really big picture to be made in Canada.

Critics invited to the openings gave it rave reviews for its animal scenes, its photography and its story.

People around the country were humming the new song, "Back to God's Country."

The rest of the country waited until October to see the film. It captured the honor of opening the new Capitol Theatre at Fifty-first Street and Broadway in New York, to the chagrin of other film distributors vying for that privilege for their films.

Jim, not resting on his laurels, was already hard at work on his next film—plus another book, of course, some short stories, and his myriad business affairs.

He signed contracts for the French editions of *Ice Bound Hearts* ( ) and *The Grizzly King*, and agreed to German rights to his books. A Danish publishing firm wanted to translate them. Curtis Brown asked if there were any other books not yet published in England that could be sold now in cheaper editions. Hodder & Stoughton, Jim's new English publishers, paid him 150£ in royalties for *Nomads of the North*. That Dutch firm was still pirating his books and stories, but Brown said it wasn't worth the time and trouble to pursue them.

Work went forward in preparation for filming *The Yellow-Back*. This was to be a Carver-Curwood Production, with H.P. Carver replacing the Shipmans. Canadian Photoplays was still backing the film and David Hartford was again director.

Nell may have been out but Ernie Shipman was still in. He was a vigorous promoter and this was an area in which Jim felt he needed someone. He hired Ernie as his agent, a move which would bring Jim a lot of headaches later on.

Most of the outdoor scenes were to be filmed near Spokane, Washington, using the facilities of the Minnehaha Studios. This studio was an enterprise of an actor, D. Wellington Playter, who had appeared in one of Jim's early movie stories, *Queen of Jungleland.*

Why the Spokane studio was chosen for the filming is hard to understand. It was more than 2,500 miles north of Los Angeles over questionable roads, had variable weather, and was already in receivership due to its financial troubles.

Canadian Photoplays finally came across with Jim's money for *Back to God's Country* in October, paying his royalty, $500 for the continuity he'd written for *The Yellow-Back,* payment of a loan he'd advanced Carver, and reimbursement of his expenses for five weeks spent in New York finishing the film. It was not all that Canadian Photoplays owed him, but Jim was lucky. Others, like Nell, were never paid at all.

The advertising manager at Cosmopolitan asked Jim for an interview, with photographs. "You write a better interview than anyone else," and if he didn't have time to write it, someone could be sent to his house.

Jim was getting high praise from the New York critics for *The River's End,* and Jim's move to Cosmopolitan books was proving to be a wise one. The advertising they put out was tremendous. Twenty thousand copies had been sold in its first month on the market. Besides, other publishing houses, like Doubleday, were having trouble with striking workers and couldn't keep up with orders.

Credit for the success was not all due to advertising. In spite of pressures to produce a new story, Jim had brought a new dimension to his writing in this book. It was the same old story, of course, of the beautiful girl, the Mountie turned against the law, the dastardly villain and a fight for survival against insurmountable odds—the critics got after him for sameness, yet when he tried to write about something other than the northern wilderness, he couldn't sell it—but there was more depth to his writing. *The River's End* would prove to be one of his most successful books.

As soon as he could get away after the movie premiere, Jim went north on a duck hunting trip. He spent three weeks resting and recuperating, reviving his spirits in the way he knew best—getting out-of-doors.

If Jim Curwood was misunderstood by the people of Owosso, it was not only that he was difficult to know but also because his work was so different from everyone else's. There were a few other writers in town, but no one else made their entire living by their pen. Writing created a different pressure than that of running a grocery store or putting out a newspaper. His friends like Fred Woodard, who owned a factory, John McDonald of Connor's, and George Campbell of the *Evening Argus* had men to keep the wheels of commerce turning. Businessmen like his father's friend Merrick Blair could also hire others to do the labor. If any of these men took a vacation or got sick, the business went on, the newspaper got printed, the factory kept on producing whatever it was it made. Others did the work.

When Jim got sick or took time out, the flow of words stopped. Everything he did was created out of his own head, like an artist whose brush needs a human hand to put the paint on canvas.

It set him somewhat apart from his fellow townsmen, and it also created a pressure they could not comprehend.

Even a duck hunting trip was only partly a vacation. Two days after he returned home he had turned out a many-paged "Important Memoranda for Messrs. Carver, Hartford, etc." for *The Yellow-Back*, full of details and suggestions for the scenes that were already clear in his mind.

Ray was just back from a vacation, too. He learned that First National, the film distributor handling *Back to God's Country*, had put out some advertising that might be detrimental to Cosmopolitan's plans for filming *The River's End*. "If you have control over this," he wrote Jim, "we suggest you see that this isn't done any more." Marshall Neilan would direct their films and they'd be released through Famous Players as Comopolitan didn't think First National seemed "to be clear just yet."

"I returned feeling better than I have in years," Ray wrote, but Pearl had suffered some food poisoning on the boat and was still not in good shape.

By the end of October Ray was again inquiring about the farm series he'd urged Jim to write for the Hearst publications. If you don't feel the inspiration to do that one, it would be a mistake. "Is there another series you prefer?"

As for writing the continuity for their filming of *The River's End*, "I, too, would prefer to have you do River's for us, but it simply can't be worked out." Neilan is doing a magnificent job, not hurrying. "You may well get real prominence."

No problem was too small for Jim's concern. When an order of 50 copies of *The River's End* for Gute's Drug Store in Owosso went astray, he found out what had happened to it and appealed to Harold Kinsey at Cosmopolitan to send 50 more. The first printing of 50,000 copies is nearly sold out, Kinsey reported, and a second printing of 20,000 is coming off the presses.

On the West Coast, Betty Blythe had been hired to play the heroine in *The Yellow-Back*. She was another beautiful brunette actress, though not the outdoor woman Nell Shipman had been. Carlotta had seen her in a film and come home raving about her to her father. "You should have her in your pictures," she had said.

Betty, David Hartford and some of the crew left Los Angeles by train for Spokane. Carver, leading man Richard Bloomer, and several others went by auto in a more adventuresome trip—they had to lay over in Medford, Oregon because of snow.

Before he left Los Angeles, Hartford viewed some of the scenes Marshall

Neilan had filmed for *The River's End*. "They are wonderful," Hartford said. The double exposures of the two men in the cabin in the north country are the best ever made. "Lewis Stone is ideal in both parts and I feel sure this picture will do you a world of good." A stage production, also in the making, won't be hurt if the picture is shown first, he said.

Best wishes to Mrs. Curwood and the children, Hartford said in closing. Over the next two or three years, Jim and David Hartford would exchange hundreds of letters and messages. News of, and greetings to, members of their families would close most of them. In fact, while Jim seldom met the families of any of his literary or movie acquaintances, except for Ray Long, of course, most of them met Ethel for she went with Jim on most of his business trips, especially to New York, and a greeting to "your good wife" closed many of their letters.

Disaster struck the family in November, and everything—film-making, writing, business—was put aside. James died on an autumn afternoon in the family home on John Street. The short, stern, English father whom Jim had revered was gone. His heart had been weak for a long time, and arteriosclerosis and kidney problems had kept him in poor health. Nevertheless, death had come fairly swift. Leaving his rocker in the kitchen for his ritual afternoon nap one afternoon, he had not gotten up again, even on Jim's urging. "C'mon," he told his father, "get up. Let's go fishing. Or hunting." But James had not risen. He had, instead, died peacefully in his bed. He was 84.

The first gap in the fabric of the family had occurred.

"When you finish *The Valley of Silent Men*," Ray wrote, "you will have written two long series of short stories and two novels practically without taking a breath between. Don't you think it would be wise to avoid a formal series for a time? If the idea of individual short stories appeals to you, let's talk it over. No hurry on the story I asked you to rewrite."

The idea was tempting. With the loss of his father, it seemed hard to stay enthusiastic over his work and the many problems involved.

Then came depressing news from Spokane.

After nearly two weeks of silence, Hartford wrote that he'd not written because "there was nothing to say. Spokane is anything but the place to make a picture this time of year; no snow, no sunlight." Playter had misrepresented conditions. They were getting ready to go out on location and, in spite of the bad situation, he wouldn't let conditions "interfere with the getting of a great big picture."

Nevertheless, he wired two weeks later that they were suspending operations temporarily. They'd been able to photograph only two days out of two weeks and there was no relief in sight. Part of the ground in the mountains was covered with snow, part of it bare, so that it was neither summer nor winter conditions. To continue paying salaries while waiting for the weather is a waste of time, he said.

Jim hastily wired Carver, now back in Los Angeles, to cut all expenses to the limit for six weeks while they considered the situation. A conference, between Hartford and Jim at least, was necessary to decide what to do now, but Hartford's wife was ill and he would not be able to come to Owosso until after Christmas.

In the meantime, Jim was dealing with Chambers at Bobbs-Merrill for the rights to *Kazan* and the book plates they'd made for *Honor of the Big Snows* and *Phillip Steele*. They were asking $854.52 and $694.69, respectively. "I'm willing to buy them, but not at that price," Jim said. "You have made a very serious mistake here when you tell me the cost of making the plates of these two books amounts to that sum. I do not believe the cost...in excess of $300." I want them, he told Chambers, not for reprints, but to experiment in the matter of a stage drama. Bobbs-Merrill had already disposed of the picture rights. "Quote me a price within reason," he asked.

Nevertheless, Kinsey at Cosmopolitan, having learned that the price included the cost of illustrations, sent Jim a check to cover the cost. "It seems wise to make a clean sweep, take everything, so send them your check and tell them to deliver the plates to us," and they'd divide the cost 50-50, with Jim's share deducted from royalties.

Don't do anything that might hurt the sales of *The River's End* until Cosmopolitan has exploited every means of its advertisement, Ray cautioned. Cosmopolitan will do even more for *Valley of Silent Men*. Sales of the new book are expected to reach 150,000 copies, maybe even 200,000, he said.

"If you get a hunch on a short story, for Heaven's sake, send it along."

By Christmas, though, Jim was hard at work on *The Flaming Forest*, to follow *Valley of Silent Men* as the third book in the Three Rivers Country trilogy.

These were all minor problems, however, compared to those he faced with the film company out West. He complained to Hartford that he'd lost $50,000 dollars in royalties over the past year because the Canadian Photoplay and Shipman-Curwood contracts had not been lived up to. His attorneys could prove that both contracts had been broken.

Alarmed at Jim's dissatisfaction, Hartford quickly wrote Carver, now in Calgary, that *The Yellow-Back* must be completed immediately or Jim would sever his relations with the organization at once. He had a location closer by where he could finish the film. Calgary must act quickly or they'd lose Jim, who knew nothing of this letter.

Hartford arrived in Owosso after Christmas, and he and Jim discussed the situation at length. They decided at last to free themselves from the Calgary organization entirely, the Calgary people were "small men" for what Jim and Hartford wanted to do, and they would form their own organization. Of course they would have to drop *The Yellow-Back*. They chose instead "Nomads of the North" for their first film. Hartford would direct it and film it at Little Bear Lake in the California mountains. Filming could begin by April. They chose Lon Chaney, Betty Blythe and Lewis Stone for the cast, provided they could get them. And they would ask Cosmopolitan to back them instead of First National.

In early January 1920, Jim went to New York, wiring ahead to Ernie Shipman to disregard anything Carver said until he got there. Meet him at the Algonquin Hotel, he said.

Ernie Shipman had established himself in New York with an office and secretary, for which Jim had agreed to pay in exchange for Ernie's promotion of Jim's movie interests. It was, at best, an aggravating arrangement. "Ten Percent Ernie" was a promoter, and a good one, but he consistently overstepped his bounds.

Before Jim could get his new organization in line, another problem arose. *Valley of Silent Men* was running serially in *Good Housekeeping* and would not finish until June. The book was scheduled for publication after that. Now an old short story, which he'd also titled "Valley of Silent Men" and which *Success Magazine* had printed long ago, threatened to upset all of Cosmopolitan's plans for promotion of the book.

Alton Play Bureau, which had marketed some of Jim's early movie scripts, bought out the rights to that early story and several others from the receiver of the bankrupt *Success Magazine* and were offering it for sale, giving the impression that it was the rights to the new novel they were selling. Jim threatened to sue but Hearst's legal department was already working on the problem and expected to ask for a restraining injunction.

As for second serial rights, "you do own them, don't sell them," Ray advised. Write a series of short stories instead of a novel now. It would be a mistake not to be in *Cosmopolitan*. The book end of the business will publish the series of dog stories under the title of "Swift Lightning" next year, or, if Jim preferred, they would make a book of the series he was asking Jim to write now. Make the locale the Hudson Bay country rather than Alaska, and the lead character another dog, or another bear like Thor.

Ray was coming to Owosso, and wrote Jim in advance, "I am feeling pretty well but, of course, this period is one of extreme nervous strain. I can't tell you what all it's going to mean to me to have a few days with you." The strain was an impending divorce from Pearl.

As if all this weren't enough, Ernie Shipman now took it upon himself to speak for Jim without authority, as Jim angrily wrote Louis B. Mayer in Hollywood. Shipman "did not in the slightest way speak the truth when he said his company had exclusive rights to my services. Never at any time have my contracts held a stipulation that I should not cooperate with people who have already purchased my stories." He wrote Shipman in New York to keep his hands off Mayer.

If Mayer filmed *Isobel* and he wrote the continuity, Jim told Mayer, he'd take a month or more to make it into a big picture. As for Selig, he didn't sell him the rights to the story, he merely wrote him a three-reeler based on *Isobel* long ago. If Mayer filmed it, he'd like to use the English title, "In Defiance of the Law."

A Hudson's Bay Post was under construction at the film site. Jim wrote a working synopsis, and told Hartford he wanted to get together with him. As soon as the corporation is formed, Jim said, Hartford would get his contract. It would give him thirty percent of the net profits of *Nomads* and all other pictures he made for the corporation, granting, of course, that *Nomads* was a success.

"If it is a failure we all die an ignoble death. So live this story, dream it, think it night and day."

"Shipman is persistently a thorn in my side with his constant talky-talk and his penchant for digging his fingers into all sorts of pies," Jim complained to Hartford. He wrote to all of the trade journals saying Shipman was not his agent.

James Oliver Curwood Productions, Inc. was formed in January 1920, with Jim's old friend, Byron P. Hicks, an Owosso lawyer and Michigan State Senator, as secretary. The new company's stationary bore Jim's name and a paw print as its logo. Ed was vice president.

All of the old properties of the former organization with the Calgary people had been turned over to Hartford, and Carver sent the necessary papers for Jim's signature for transfer of title to these items.

Don't hire any "little blonde namby-pamby girls," Jim warned Hartford. They wanted Betty Blythe, a "crackerjack girl," for the heroine. If Blythe shows a real love for animals, as Nell had, they should get an option on her and the other actors' services so that they'd have them when they needed them in April. Lon Chaney had starred the year before in Jim's story, *Paid in Advance*, and they sought him to play the lead in *Nomads*. Hartford was looking for a good writer to do the continuity.

Hartford chided Jim for having sent a copy of his synopsis to New York. Remember the conversation we had in our hotel room, he asked, when I asked you not to divulge all the secrets to the story? You don't understand that actors and actresses talk shop. There are "certain angles to this game" that you don't know, he said. "Leave the directing to me."

In spite of Hartford's request for more money to get things rolling, things were looking good at last. Jim put his synopsis, the "most wonderful story I have ever written," in the mail and suggested they shoot for a million gross.

Chapter 20

Jim was ill again in February 1920, this time with influenza. He had Ethel write to Hartford that he was still too ill to write himself. As soon as he was able to dictate again—he had, by now, a secretary, a woman named Helen Heling—letters between himself and Hartford flew back and forth, long letters full of suggestions and ideas. Jim apologized for some of his more testy letters written while he was sick. "I had a fever of 103 when I dictated that stuff and Mrs. Curwood told me I was foolish for trying to write anything then, but I was so darn nervous I couldn't sleep a wink for 36 hours."

"As I wired you last night, no matter what you say from now on I will know just how to take it—in a good spirit. You the same from me."

Lon Chaney, the lead in *Nomads*, was the best actor on the screen, Jim felt. Robert McKim, who was to play the villain, refused to work with Betty Blythe because his wife was jealous of her. If it comes to a choice, Jim said, take Blythe. McKim was dropped and Lewis Stone, who had just completed *The River's End*, was hired in his place.

First National, in advancing the money for the film, cautioned against extravagance. It didn't matter who wrote the continuity, the result was what was important. They wanted the actors under contract but not to start until May 1, and everything ready before they began so as not to waste time or money. Since Jim, who was always careful about money, had been going down into his own pockets "until they are worn out" to meet Hartford's constant requests for money—nearly every letter asked for more money: 2,000, 3,000, 7,000—agreed that care should be taken not to spend unnecessarily.

The Flaming Forest, on which Jim was working diligently between relapses of the flu, was still only a working title. Kinsey and Long preferred *The Last Domain*, but in the end kept the original title.

Concerned that Jim not be out of the pages of *Cosmopolitan* too long, Ray however admitted that if the novel was going well, it would be a mistake to break off to do some short stories. He was working on a scheme for promotion of the film version of *Valley of Silent Men*. "Of course, the only way to combine the book with the film would be through your own company."

"Another thing, Jim," he added, "I didn't ask for details to your arrangement with First National when you were here. Are you tied up there in such a way it would prevent our organizing a company for you?" They could share the profits and they would take the financial details off Jim's shoulders and he could still supervise the project.

146

By mid-February the strain of the film, his writing commitments, and the business details of both, the troubles over Ernie Shipman's meddling, the possibility of suing Mayer over the filming of *Isobel*, the pirating of his work by other film-makers and by publishers abroad, the shaky looks of his investment with his friend Fred Ziegen's firm, and the numerous other problems besetting him, coupled with the aftermath of the flu, left him with tearing headaches. "It hurts with every word I dictate," he wrote Hartford. "I must close and get rid of this headache."

On top of it all his mother was ill again, and this time she did not have the comfort of James but instead the pain of his loss.

Lying abed fighting the flu, Jim thought a great deal about getting out of film-making entirely. He was expending energy that should be spent in what he was best at—writing. But they were too far advanced into the making of *Nomads of the North* to quit now.

Ray's permission to skip the series of stories he wanted for *Cosmopolitan* lifted some of the burden, and Jim wrote to Kinsey on a "beautiful sunshiny morning" towards the last of February that "I feel myself growing stronger." Come to Owosso, he urged. "I feel that our personal chin fests do me a lot of good..." He might even do a fourth novel of the Three Rivers country, to follow *The Flaming Forest*. "I am sure I am doing far better work since the crush and worry of 'too much work' was taken from me (by skipping the series)...if I had kept on under that pressure I would have gone under within another six months."

Cosmopolitan put together thirteen of Jim's stories and contracted with Grosset & Dunlap to publish them in a book titled *Back to God's Country*. The first story was, of course, "Wapi, the Walrus," now retitled "Back to God's Country" in keeping with the movie and the book. Among the stories they used was "The Yellow-Back," which had appeared in *Hearst's Magazine* the year before, and some old stories from magazines such as *McClure's*, *Munsey's* and *Collier's*. It was issued in a popular edition with an initial printing of 10,000 copies, scheduled for release in June.

Jim wrote to Harold Kinsey, but not content to wait for his letter to get there, he wired him the same day, congratulating him on the arrangements he'd made for the book of short stories, and added, "You bet I am happy. Am writing."

Jim was always happy to be writing. For some time he and Ray discussed Jim writing some articles about himself and his personal creed. Now Jim laid aside the novel and put his thoughts on life and nature and his change from killer to a friend of wildlife on paper. He sent off his first article, "My Secret of Happiness," and got a quick and pleased response from Ray.

Jim turned the matter of Bankers Land and Investments over to his attorneys to handle, and wrote Ziegen, wintering in Florida, that he wanted to let him know this and that he wanted the facts about dividends, when and how much, so he could tell his attorney. "I've had a hard winter," he said.

You ought to come down to Florida and bring your mother, Fred replied. "It's the best place for her in the winter. I'm glad to hear you're busy, it's good for what ails you. See what fame is thrusting on you." He'd been to see *The River's End* and liked it, especially the double photo so the same man could take both parts. Maybe you'll explain it to me sometime, he said.

Jim approached the Hearst organization, through Ray, about taking over the filming of *The Yellow-Back*. Other producers want it, Jim said, but he'd like to see Hearst make it.

Hartford had a lot of Jim's stories with him in Southern California in the hopes of selling them to producers there. Harry Garson of Garson Studios wanted the film rights to *Valley of Silent Men*, but Hearst, of course, already owned that. See Hartford for some of my other stories that are available, he told Garson.

There were still plenty of problems left to deal with. *Hearst's* had a new policy that they only wanted Jim to write serials and short stories they could turn into films. It would be profitable for him and the two or three other authors they were offering such film deals. Go ahead and finish *Nomads* but don't get tied up in any other such deals, Ray wrote him, at least until they could get together and talk it over. And no, Hearst couldn't take over Jim's production company.

"Kinsey and I think you made a mistake in giving any of your time to producing pictures, for the next five years are sure to be the most important in your career as a novelist."

Some things went well. Jim's books and stories were selling well abroad. Curtis Brown was continuing to market both new and old stories in England and elsewhere. Royalties came in regularly, some large and some small, but his name was becoming well known in most of the European countries and in Australia.

Hartford's contract for making *Nomads* was devised by Jim to give the director everything Jim thought he might want. His salary was to be $1,000 a week for 15 weeks. Jim's, as manager of James Oliver Curwood Productions and therefore liaison between Los Angeles and New York—and the provider of funds whenever First National didn't come through fast enough—was $200 a week, to be held until the picture was complete.

Pleased with "My Secret of Happiness" and *Cosmopolitan*'s praise of it, Jim began work on a second article, "I Become a Killer." He recounted his experiences as a wanton killer of wildlife, and his pride in it, beginning with the newspaper story from his boyhood days in Ohio when he had killed two squirrels with one shot, and carrying him through to the day he'd killed the three bears on the mountainside, and fired a beautiful little valley in order to drive out game. He painted himself black and evil, for a third article was already planned to tell of his transformation into a respecter of wildlife.

There was no way he could tell the straight truth, even though the articles were billed in *Cosmopolitan* as Jim's own stories. He was first and foremost a storyteller. "My Secret of Happiness," he said, was written in a cabin he'd built himself 1,500 miles north of Owosso, but in fact he'd not been in Canada since his last hunting trip four years before.

To stretch the truth was Jim's way of creating a more interesting story. The end result, he felt, was more important than adhering strictly to the truth.

Jim's love of nature, though, was true and heartfelt.

"Nature is my religion. And my desire—my ambition—the great goal I wish to achieve is to take my readers with me into the heart of this Nature. I love it, and I feel that they must love it—if I can only get the two acquainted."

Certainly he was contented with the money he got for the article. It was the highest Hearst had paid for any except Teddy Roosevelt's articles on South Africa.

Jim and Hartford were already looking ahead to their second production. They still had the rights to Jim's old story "The Golden Snare," which had been published in *Cassell's Magazine* in England in 1918 and was being published by the English book company this year, but had yet to appear in the States. It had been on the market as a film story but had never been sold.

Now Kinsey at *Cosmopolitan* took up the matter of publication with Grosset & Dunlap, with the idea of tying together book and film. He wanted to know when the film would be ready as they'd like to publish the book in the fall. In the meantime, Hartford was working on a deal with Sam Rork, general manager of Katherine McDonald Studios, for the screen rights at a price of $30,000. Rork offered to buy the film, with a 30-day option price of $2,000 and a price of $25,000, plus Hartford's commission, when he exercised his option.

Wire a quick okay, Hartford wired Jim, and don't mention the price, just say at "terms quoted."

Jim wired his okay but Hartford wired the next day that some changes had had to be made, the option was for 60 instead of 30 days, but it was okay. And wire him some money. He was leaving for Yosemite Valley immediately and would write fully at the first opportunity. Melborn MacDowell had been hired as the factor and Francis McDonald as Bucky and the cast was now 100 percent complete. He kept $1,000 of the option money and sent Jim the other $1,000, and Jim could keep back $1,000 from his salary. "I am very close to the cushion" on money, Hartford said.

Ethel, Carlotta and Jimmy went to Indiana to visit her family for a few days and Jim soon went down to join them. The night before he left, Jim was guest at a showing of *The River's End* at the Regent Theatre, Flint's newest movie house which seated 1,800 people. The mezzanine was reserved for

Owosso people only, and Jim was introduced to the audience. He was disappointed in the film. It wasn't half what *Back to God's Country* was, and the only reason they were cashing in on it, he believed, was the publicity.

"It's going to make seven hundred thousand dollars," he wrote Hartford, "so we ought to make a million." Stone was "splendid" but poorly directed. He could tell a lot with his face, so "I hope you can get a lot of that quiet powerful stuff. I am rushing for the train so won't gossip any more..."

Before Jim left, though, he wrote a quick letter to Ray thanking him for the "dandy" check for his "nature" article. "I appreciate it mightily, it makes me feel like putting real ginger in my stuff." He told Ray he'd gotten $35,000 for "The Golden Snare." This is confidential, he warned. He wanted no publicity, just to let them know how cheaply they were getting his stuff. "I am tickled to death to do it, feeling very deeply that I am getting my reward from you people in other ways. Only, consarn it, I want you and Mr. Hearst to appreciate the fact that they ARE valuable..."

By the middle of April, though, things were not going well. His headaches had not gone away and his doctor advised him to see a brain specialist at the University Hospital in Ann Arbor who advised Jim that it was dangerous for him to rush as he'd been doing for the past years. He must take it easy.

His solution was to invite Ray for a fishing trip. "This visit...will do me a pile of good," he wrote his old friend upon whom he relied so heavily. "I am in rather bad shape, and I want to have a long talk with you regarding the best way for me to get back into my old condition again."

If they didn't rush the nature articles, he could afford to take off for awhile. He would spend all spring and summer in the woods, "and I will be my old self by the time autumn comes."

Now, he wrote Ray, "I am going to write one or two unpleasant things, but you will know what to do with my letters when they are unpleasant."

International had made a very bad movie and he worried that might happen to his. "Don't ever make a bad movie of my stories."

The other thing of concern was H.P. Carver, of the old Canadian Photoplays organizations and Jim's brief film-making partner in the unfinished *The Yellow-Back*. Jim had recommended Carver for a position with Hearst's organization and he'd proved to be disloyal. Now Jim was sorry he'd suggested him. "I have too much sympathy in my makeup," he said. "Just as I will willingly die for a friend whom I care for, just so I will willingly give up my life and sacrifice everything I possess to get even with a man who does me a dirty turn."

Can you come in May? The only thing Ray needed to bring was old togs. Jim ordered cords of wood cut for the fireplace. They would plan a long trip for the fall.

Fifty thousand words were already done on the novel, not scheduled until fall, and he could take off. "I've kept plugging away; too much, the doctors say."

Ray, however, couldn't get away and Jim stayed home, fretting over things.

The news from California was seldom encouraging, and always included requests for money. Hartford was necessarily on location most of the time, and Joseph Montrose handled things in Los Angeles. First National kept asking for information on the filming, and still photographs to use for publicity. Jim asked Montrose repeatedly for more and better ones.

In the meantime, Jim himself took part in the advance publicity, writing a personal letter to 40 franchise holders and sending them each an autographed copy of the book.

A hurried conference was called, and Jim wrote to Hartford that he was leaving the next morning for New York. Hartford's delay in getting himself insured was causing Jim great embarrassment with First National. Be sure the sale of *The Golden Snare* doesn't boomerang, he urged Hartford. Be sure the contract stipulates that it is not to be made until after we make *The Yellow-Back*, and that no publicity gets out until "Nomads" is on the market.

"It's vitally important to us," he said.

A new problem arose before he could leave and he delayed his trip. First National wired that *Cosmopolitan* had announced they were producing *Valley of Silent Men* immediately. He called Ray.

The announcement, Ray explained, was that they had signed Jim to give Cosmopolitan Productions exclusive motion picture rights to any and all of his stories published in any of the Hearst magazines. They didn't intend to do anything toward filming *Valley* until fall when they would shoot both summer and winter scenes, and not release it until after the first of the year.

"Come down next week," he asked, "and bring Mrs. Curwood with you. I will have the car meet your train and take you right up to the house."

Reissues of *Phillip Steele* and *Honor of the Big Snow* were being planned, but so far, Kinsey informed Jim, it was estimated they could sell almost twice of the latter over the former. Maybe it's the name, Kinsey suggested. How about *The Scarlet Rider*, Jim suggested, or *Steele of the Royal Mounted*? They settled on the latter.

The idea of quitting motion picture production had been growing steadily in Jim's mind, and now he finally put it into action. Of course, *Nomads* still had to be finished, but he wrote Ray he was getting out. "Your game is the writing game and the closer you stick to it the better," Ray replied, adding that they could talk better in person.

Jim was beset on both sides, literally, by the picture's problems. Ernie Shipman continued to make trouble with his meddling and Jim finally told him to lie down and keep quiet until he and Hartford came to New York with the film. First National continued to demand more reports and better stills of the animal scenes, and Jim nagged Montrose and Hartford about them until tempers flared.

In the meantime, Jim had negotiated a contract for Hartford that eliminated anything of an "unreasonable and binding nature on you." Jim would leave his own salary in the treasury as it would be embarrassing if they went bankrupt just when they needed money at the end.

On the West Coast, things were looking up a little. Jim wrote Hartford, "I wish to heaven I was going to be with you during the next two months. I would just like to sit down and look on while the thing is being done, and probably I would be able to get a square meal once in a while." What price could we get to write the continuity for *Valley of Silent Men*. What do you think Hearst ought to pay us if we do it?

Montrose was sending some reports. They had managed to get 21 cabin scenes, Blythe and McDonald were excellent, and they had finally gotten Lewis Stone for the part of O'Connor.

But it was still money, money, money, and Jim nagging them for more details, better reports, and stills of the animal scenes that could be used as publicity shots.

Harrison Fischer was waiting in New York to do a portrait of Jim for Cosmopolitan. "We're eager to run it with the series," he was told. Jim would appreciate the distinction of having Fischer do it; he is the "peer of them all."

The news about *The Golden Snare* leaked out and Jim suspected Shipman. He decided to deal only with the three top men at First National from then on.

Sam Rork was already making arrangements with First National for distribution of *The Golden Snare*, and was after Hartford to direct the film, but "he knows I can't do it until after *Nomads*, Hartford assured Jim. As for the continuity, it should be worth to Hearst "anything you want to charge."

"Just count on me to the finish," he promised. "All looks fine now." As for Shipman, "I know just one man in this transaction and that man is James Oliver Curwood."

Nomads of the North called for a tremendous forest fire scene. It could only be shot one time, of course, and a battery of cameras was used to film every possible aspect. The smoke and flame could easily be seen from 20 miles away. The last interior was to be shot May 6. Don't stop the money, Hartford pleaded.

With Jim's trip to New York delayed—Jim was ill again, his headaches had scarcely abated—and Harrison Fischer scheduled elsewhere shortly, the artist came instead to Owosso to do Jim's portrait, a side view which the Hearst organization used liberally in its advertising campaign.

Jim apologized to Kinsey for not coming to New York. "You know more than anyone else what tremendous responsibilities I have ahead of me in keeping high class fiction for our novels.... After three breakdowns, I was compelled to see a mental specialist. He was the third to tell me that unless I gave up work for six months to a year, I would be laid out permanently."

"I made a law for myself then and there that during the next six months I would do no literary work, and do everything possible to build up my physical and mental machinery."

Nevertheless, he was going to New York for a week. It was not the sort of rest he required. "What I need is the outdoors."

"It is simply a matter of weighing values...my health is not a matter to gamble with." At last, Jim was admitting that he could not drive himself indefinitely without paying a high price.

His business troubles did not cease. Although the picture finally seemed to be nearing completion, the costs kept rising with every communication from Hartford or Montrose. Shipman was keeping quiet, however, and Jim's attorneys were handling the Ziegen investment. At Cosmopolitan, too, they were easing up. "We will see that nothing is done to impair your health or work," they assured Jim. Ray was planning at last to come and visit.

Jim withdrew some of his stories for sale as film scripts. Hartford was coming soon with the film of *Nomads* and they would go to New York and do the editing and final wrap-up. I'll "go down into my own pockets if necessary to finish. Do not worry, help me all you can," he told Hartford. They could discuss *The Golden Snare* when Hartford got there.

Jim relaxed a bit and visited with friends. He had formed a close friendship with Probate Judge Matthew Bush over in Corunna, and he enjoyed visiting the judge and his family. As with any place where Jim became familiar, he felt free to walk into the Bush's home, check out the pantry for pie, bring his dogs along, bring vegetables from his own garden—he was especially fond of green onions and radishes and grew them each year—and to sit about and talk hunting and fishing with the judge. If he came at meal time, he ate with them, requesting, as he did at home, to have his dessert with the meal. He took little bites of it as the meal went along.

There were plenty of fish picnics now, when they loaded the picnic basket with the frying pan and the accompaniments to the meal, and depended upon catching fish for the main dish—and never went without.

Jim walked a lot, he rode horseback, he went out to the farm north of town where he kept the family cow pastured, he strolled along the riverbank and sat for long periods beneath his favorite tree to make notes and write bits of dialogue. Ray came to visit and enjoy the picnics and have long talks with Jim.

It was not enough. His "accursed headaches" continued.

Chapter 21

In June 1920 Jim was 42 years old. In 12 years he'd had 19 books published, had two more ready for publication, and was finishing still another. He'd written dozens of stories of varying lengths, hundreds of movie scenarios, and been actively involved in the filming of two huge movies, plus a third that was just being completed.

His business interests ranged from property in Saskatchewan and Ontario to varied investments to sitting on the boards of four companies. Some of his investments had gone sour, some had prospered, but they were all problems that must be dealt with. He'd sued, or threatened to sue, unscrupulous interests who had stolen, or had tried to steal, his work.

Life at home had settled into a stormy arrangement with a strong-willed wife, an equally strong-willed teenage daughter and an undisciplined son. He felt the loss of his father keenly, regretted the circumstances that absented his second daughter, and worried over his increasingly frail mother.

The once yearly trips into the Canadian wilds were a thing of the past. He was fortunate to get into the Michigan woods now and then for the comfort their solitude brought him and which he sorely needed. Trips to New York, which he disliked intensely, were frequent and only intensified his need to get away from things once in awhile.

Twice now his health had broken down completely.

And although his friends—Ray Long, Harold Kinsey, David Hartford, Fred Ziegen—urged him to relax, to take it easy, they continued to make demands that increased rather than decreased his workload.

Jim took his family north for a fishing, working vacation. They spent a month at Houghton Lake where they could swim, fish and boat. Jimmy, now nine, caught a huge walleye pike and posed proudly with his trophy. While he was at the lake, Jim wrote in the mornings and spent the rest of the time with his family. But he spent a good deal of the month going back and forth between the lake and Owosso.

Just before leaving for the lake, Jim had received a box from Montrose containing statements, vouchers, progress and camera reports and more stills. He thought he'd already sent enough stills to satisfy First National, Montrose complained. Hartford had gone up to Lake Tahoe after still more pictures.

"Your wire was the first inkling I had that First National was going to publish *Nomads* as a purely animal picture," he complained, although Jim had been urging for weeks that they send more and better animal stills. "When I first

154

read the book," Montrose wrote, "I couldn't figure out how a motion picture could be made of it," and then he learned that the animals were to be made subsidiary to the human interest.

Jim answered by night letter that Montrose's letter was filled with "meat and good cheer." The human story is tremendous, he said, but "I want to emphasize (that) the animal action in the publicity places us in a field outside all competition." The entire ad campaign is based on having good animal pictures, he said. Get pictures of all the animals in the picture.

First National continued to ask for more animal pictures, however, and suggested a photograph of the man and woman and the two animals with packs on their backs silhouetted against the sky. If they couldn't get them from California, First National would hire some actors and take them out to the zoo and get the pictures themselves.

On Jim's first trip back to Owosso, after getting Ethel and the children settled at the lake, he sent Montrose a night letter. "No word of your (money) requirements this week, or are we fortunate in having none?"

Requests for money were not finished, however, and Jim dug even deeper into his pockets to keep them going in California. Since Hartford was to share the profits, Jim thought it only fair he dig into his pockets, too, but he didn't volunteer to do so.

The Courage of Marge O'Doone, filmed by Vitagraph from Jim's book, played at a theatre in Lansing and Jim went to see it. Fred Ziegen's idea of having a live bear at the theatre to advertise the animal scenes had been carried out in some of the theatres, and Jim reported to him it had turned out successful. He wrote Albert Smith at Vitagraph that he liked the picture but was dissatisfied with the returns he'd gotten from the pictures Vitagraph had filmed of his stories. *God's Country and the Woman* was being reissued and perhaps they'd do better from that.

Selig had *The Wolf Hunters* and *The Gold Hunters*, but those were stories for boys, and an adventure yarn for boys, with few exceptions, would be a sorry thing on the screen. Selig also owned rights to *The Courage of Captain Plum*, *Honor of the Big Snows* and *The Danger Trail*, but to date he'd only filmed the latter. It was so bad, Jim told Ray, that he'd been ashamed for weeks after it had been shown in Owosso.

Now they were doing *Kazan*. I'm sorry they didn't come to me for cooperation, he said.

Towards the end of June Jim wrote Hartford a long letter about a "few matters I think you should understand in order that you cooperate with me in straightening them out."

"The cost of producing *Nomads* has gone far beyond the figures anticipated, bringing about problems that you out there have not worried about..... First National will not make an advance beyond $75,000 so every dollar I send now, including the $5,000 last Friday, is borrowed money and not to be counted as our cost of production when it comes to profits. That's why I asked you to stop drawing your $1,000 week until the picture is finished and you come to Owosso."

Hartford had drawn $9,750 to the end of June, and Jim had not drawn a penny. Jim had anticipated that $75,000 would not only make this picture but carry them over into the next one.

As for *The Golden Snare*, Sam Rork had paid an $8,000 advance but was hedging over paying the rest, which had been due the first of June. He offered to provide Hartford with $125,000 to produce the picture and wanted to pay Jim $25,000 from the first money received after the cost of production had been paid. Jim declined. Such a deal would be no advantage. It would be more profitable to make the picture themselves. These and many other things they could discuss when Hartford came.

With *Valley of Silent Men* out to the trade and doing well, and *The Golden Snare* published in England and due to be published by Grosset & Dunlap in 1921, Rork will then see how "idiotic" he was to turn down the latter, Jim said.

First National was scheduling the release of *Nomads* for November. It was imperative that Hartford come east with the film as soon as possible.

"I've much to discuss with you, so get here even if you have to work overtime," Jim told Hartford.

In the meantime, a new problem arose. Salisbury's movie company was taking pictures at the set created for *Nomads* at Little Bear Lake. Montrose wrote Salisbury's that this set had been built exclusively for James Oliver Curwood Productions at a cost of $10,000, that 75 percent of the film *Nomads of the North* had been shot there, and that they would use every legal recourse to prevent Salisbury from exhibiting for public consumption any part of the film they had taken there.

"We'd like to be as courteous as possible," he told them. "We would like our representative to look at your film, which would probably preclude legal procedures."

Jim spent the last week of June at the lake and returned to find stacks of mail awaiting him. He was tremendously anxious to see the picture and the delays kept him agitated almost beyond endurance, not because of the money the delays cost but in anticipation of what the final picture would be like. He had put his trust in Hartford to produce a good picture and now he was about to see if he had placed that trust well.

But Hartford's trip to Owosso was repeatedly postponed, and Jim fretted over the delay. He wired the last of his $15,000 loan to the picture. "Try your damnedest to make this finish, and leave something for our New York expenses. As a partner, can't you arrange to finance the rest if more is needed?"

Each day's delay wore on Jim's nerves and furthered his suspicions of what was going on in California. "Have Montrose write me what condition you plan to have the picture in when you reach Owosso," he asked Hartford. "Also an explanation of the purchase of the Cadillac car."

If Jim had seen what was going on in California, he probably would have been even more agitated. Little Bear Lake (now Lake Arrowhead) was still rather remote but it was fast becoming a playground for movie people, and a Cadillac was probably a minimum necessity to keep up appearances.

Carver was giving Jim trouble, too, over their defunct movie project. Carver-Curwood Productions had been formed to film *The Yellow-Back*, and the agreement was to be null if the picture was not made according to plans. The contracts as they existed between Carver and Canadian Photoplay and Jim had not been cancelled, though they were dead and void as far as Jim was concerned. He wrote all this to Ray, who was caught in the middle, and sent a copy of the contract.

"So Carver has no case," Jim said.

Some things went right. Kinsey reported that his salesmen had taken advance orders for 6,000 copies of *The Valley of Silent Men* in Michigan alone. Advance sales in all might go to 100,000. A first printing was planned for 140,000 copies, 110,000 to be bound as first editions. "Best wishes to you and Mrs. Curwood," he added.

Jim's efforts to get the rights to *Isobel* and *Honor of the Big Snow* from Harper's were successful, though this didn't solve his problems with Selig who was working from the old two-reeler Jim had written for him as "In Defiance of the Law" in 1913.

And the photographs taken when Fischer was in Owosso to do Jim's portrait had turned out beautifully, "especially those of you and your mother," Ray wrote, so well that he'd had copies made for his own office and an enlargement for Jim.

Waiting impatiently for Hartford to finish in California and come east, Jim was stunned and angry to learn that Hartford had been offered a deal to direct another picture which was to start in two weeks. This would interfere with his plans to come east with "Nomads." "If you feel my presence is necessary in New York, wire immediately."

Jim wired back. "This corporation must insist you live up to your part of the contract with First National. Take no other work until you have personally delivered the finished product in New York."

And Montrose asked for another $6,000 in mid-July, which would "clean up everything," including salaries to July 31, "when the picture will be ready for delivery to you, subject to the usual conditions of motion picture production, which business is one of thrills and surprises."

Jim, however, had had his fill of such thrills and surprises. He was determined this would be his last venture into movie-making. As if this were not enough, Ray went to a private showing of Louis B. Mayer's remake of *Isobel* and called it the "punkest piece of screen work I've ever seen." The photography was good, but the story was unintelligible, they had done foolish, outlandish things, and changed the title to *The Trail's End*, which would surely affect *The River's End*, which was being made into a stage play. If a person were to see this film, then saw an advertisement for *The River's End*, "you couldn't get him into the theatre," Ray said.

Jim was furious. He asked First National to back him in his fight to stop this film and asked them to write Mayer that "he is up against the biggest fight of his life." Of course, Jim confided to Ray, this was mostly bluff. "I can't afford the time or money for a legal fight right now." Would Hearst take it up for him? "For six months I have fought like the devil to keep him (Mayer) from making this picture..."

"I am much wrought up over this."

Jim's third essay, "My Brotherhood," Ray thought the best yet of the series. The fourth would be the last, and then they would expand them later for the book.

Banker's Land and Investment's stockholder's letter made it look like the company was "wobbly on its legs," Jim complained to Fred Ziegen. The other three companies of which he was a director are making money "hand over fist," and if Banker's Land and Investment can't do it now, they never can. He was putting out his ideas as sometimes another's ideas helped. If he could sell his stock he could surely use his $20,000 elsewhere.

He was losing faith in the business only, though, not in Fred. "I would rather lose $20,000 than a friendship as strong as ours.... The frying pan is polished up and waiting for your visit."

In spite of Jim's avowal of friendship, Ziegen answered Jim's "sad and lonely little wail over dividends" with little sympathy. "Sorry, old boy, that it is giving you any worry but the times are just as they are."

Now there was a strike by film laboratory workers in the east to blame for the delay in preparing *Nomads*, but he'd have a printout soon, Hartford said, and would leave for Owosso immediately when he got it. He still gave no indication of what shape the picture was in nor how it had turned out.

First National continued to breathe down Jim's neck for news of the film and a date when it could be expected in New York.

In spite of their failure to come to terms over *The Golden Snare*, Sam Rork, his wife and daughter visited the Curwoods while Jim was waiting impatiently for Hartford.

First National was demanding the film be delivered in New York by August 15, and Hartford wired Jim that he'd explained the delay. Most of the trouble was still originating with Shipman, he said, who was urging a September release in a race to beat *Isobel* to the general movie houses.

"Sit tight," he told Jim. Don't let them pressure you. "We will bring home the bacon with Nomads."

Jim decided to buy up the rights to all his old stories to save future trouble. He wrote Reuben Sleicher, who had succeeded his father at *Leslie's*.

"I wonder if you remember a certain James Oliver Curwood who wrote for you in the old prehistoric days.... My hair is somewhat gray now, but I'm still pegging along.... I don't think I need tell you the dishonesty of some people, so I'm trying to buy up the rights to all my old stories. Can you write me a letter saying you only bought the magazine rights?" Sleicher returned the rights to 41 of the stories *Leslie's* had printed, and sent Jim copies of the magazines they'd been in.

Thanking Sleicher for sending the stories, Jim recommended a young woman writer. "I feel Miss Duff does splendid work," he said, and asked, "Is your father improving?" Jim never forgot all the help he'd gotten in the beginning and was quick to help other aspiring writers.

A similar appeal for story rights to *Munsey's* found them not quite so eager. He'd sold them a variety of rights, they said. Eventually, however, he was able to gain back the rights to most of these stories, too.

In the end, it was necessary for Hartford to go straight to New York with the film. Ethel and Jim met him there and the film was finally finished. Hartford was morose and unhappy in New York, and Jim blamed it on his dislike of the place. That place "gets his goat," Jim told Ray, "just as it does mine. I would be tickled to death to know I never had to go there again."

Advance reviews of the film called it one of the two greatest pictures ever made. Jim announced plans to have it shown at the Strand Theatre in Owosso, the proceeds to go to the Dorcas Home, Owosso's home for orphaned children.

On the train coming home from New York, Jim and Ethel were ill and blamed it on their last dinner in New York. Ethel recovered quickly, but Jim was in bed for several days after they got home. "I tell you, Ray, I think it is all the reaction. I have been under such a strain during the past two years, that now, being free of it, Nature just gave me a tunk on the end of the jaw..." I'm looking forward to a fishing trip to Houghton Lake, and the trip we're planning for the fall. And could Ray send him the name and address of the man with those good cigars, and Jim would get in touch with him personally.

The cost of the picture had left Jim's bank account severely depleted. He wrote Kinsey for an advance, although it had been agreed he wouldn't get any more money until after the first of the year. *Cosmopolitan* would have to borrow it, but Kinsey said he'd arrange it if November would be soon enough.

Jim got away for a few days of fishing in late September, and came back feeling somewhat better. There was a letter from Montrose explaining about the Cadillac. The Hudson, he said, was always out of order, rented cars cost $35 a day, and they were able to buy the Cadillac for only $1,550 and could sell it for

$1,000 when finished. Jim went back to work on his novel.

"Here is what looks like a pretty kettle of fish to me," Jim wrote Ray. In 1913 he'd written a little two-reel scenario of his short story "Valley of Silent Men" and sold it to George Spoor at Essanay Films. Now Spoor was trying to capitalize on the new novel of that name by bringing out a film, padding the old script into a five-reeler.

"I simply do not know what to do." He'd written Spoor three times about it. "I have offered to build the story up into a big feature for him if he'll release the title to me. There's no similarity between the scenario and the novel.

"Is it true that you CANNOT COPYRIGHT A TITLE?"

Jim considered taking out some trade journal ads to clear up the matter. He wrote Shipman and Williams and enclosed a copy to Hartford. "I don't say behind their back what I wouldn't say and more to their face. I think it a good idea to let the whole damn organization down there know how I feel in this matter."

You and Montrose can make a "nice bunch of money," Jim wired Hartford, and he'd explain it all when Hartford got to Owosso for the showing of *Nomads*. "I've sold all rights to *The Golden Snare* for $20,000 spot cash plus $15,000 from First National. I'll also sell "Bride of the Long Night" for the same price of $35,000 if you care to take it." This was a story Jim had written nearly ten years before, published by *Leslie's* as a two-part story in 1913.

Jim wrote his third version of the continuity for *The Yellow-Back* and sent it on to Ray. "I'm making *The Golden Snare* for First National but I'm not tied up for any more pictures. I'm not making any more pictures. That's why I'm sending *The Yellow-Back* to you." He was also offering *Little Miss Tired-of-it-All*, which he'd written specifically as a movie scenario and had been trying to sell for some time.

Hartford chose Leadville, Colorado as the location for shooting *The Golden Snare*. Montrose wrote from there in early November. "In another two weeks we'll have all the cabins and the stockade complete." He was happy to learn that Hartford and Jim had patched things up. "I felt pretty rotten when I realized there might be a split."

The cast for *The Golden Snare* would have not only Noah Beery Sr. as the father but his three sons to play the boys. Lewis Stone would play Phillip, Wellington Playter the villain, Ruth Renick the female lead, and Boris Karloff would play Pierre, and they'd gotten "a splendid baby," Hartford reported. Reindeer were being shipped down from Alaska and they had 75 dogs lined up, and might get a hundred.

Jim's four "nature" articles were now scheduled for publication in book form in the spring, under the title *God's Country, the Trail to Happiness*. There would be only a picture of Jim by one of his wilderness cabins on the book jacket and no illustrations in the book itself.

The problem with Essanay about rights to the title *Valley of Silent Men* continued to drag on, a "confounded tangle," as Ray called it. Their fall hunting trip had to be called off, and Ray was disappointed. "I am so confounded anxious to get out into the woods..." Ray faced another trip to the West Coast and they planned to meet in Chicago if he did so. "I don't think anything that could come up, Jim, could change my feeling towards you."

Jim, however, did go north for a few days. It did him a world of good. Hartford was brimming with eagerness over the new picture and the Colorado location, sure that Jim would like the background. *Nomads* was grossing well and meeting their expectations. Reports from Curtis Brown in London were fine.

Several people were interested in doing *The Yellow-Back* but Jim still wanted Hearst to do it, and he lowered his price to $25,000. "I'm a little ashamed to press," he told Ray. But they wanted neither that story nor *Little Miss Tired-of-it-All*. They were going to concentrate on "Valley of Silent Men."

The year was not to end with all problems solved, however, and a new one reared its head in December. Alton Play Bureau, which had marketed some of Jim's early stories to the movies, announced that it was the agent for several of Jim's properties. And E.P. Hermann released the news that he'd gotten the rights to four Curwood books. The vultures were about to strike again.

But before they could, the grippe struck instead.

Chapter 22

This time Jim was sick only a few days.

Still groggy from the flu and excusing the briefness of his letter, he wrote Hartford. I wish you were coming to visit, he said, adding that Hartford, too, would soon be doing work for Hearst. "And let me tell you," Jim said, "that when all is said and done, that man, whom more people curse at than any other man alive, is the finest man in the world to do business with."

"I've not smoked a cigar in two days," he added, "and you know I have to be pretty bad off to cut that out."

The Golden Snare was now Jim's only story being filmed, and that by what had become David Hartford Productions, with Jim strictly on the sidelines. Interior shots were being done in Los Angeles, but the shooting of outdoor scenes in Colorado was held up because there wasn't enough snow to cover the "damned sagebrush" that persisted in sticking through, Montrose said.

Finally, the entire outdoor production was moved to Truckee, California, near Donner Pass in the Sierra Nevada Mountains. An entire duplicate of the fort had to be built. "It's a dandy spot," Montrose wrote, with eight feet of snow. "We'll try not to waste a minute."

Ray came for a visit the week after Jim was able to be up again. His visit was a boon to Jim's ailing mind and body. Julian Johnson, who had handled the stage production of *The River's End* for the Hearst interests, came too, and the three men spent the week hunting rabbits, talking and playing cards. They went north to West Branch and stayed at Struble's. There were many people who opened their private homes to hunters and fishermen like Jim and his friends, and Struble's was Jim's favorite.

Jim no longer had the press of the movie business, other than his communications with Hartford and Montrose over the filming of "The Golden Snare." He was not directly involved and it was a great relief.

His attorneys were handling most of the problems with Spoor, Mayer and others who were producing such bad films from his work, and Alton Play Bureau, Hermann and others who claimed they were representing him.

Jim still had a little picture material on hand but he was determined to use great discretion in disposing of it and then only to the biggest producers. Selig's picturization of *Kazan* was "so rotten that positively nothing could be done with it." The owner of the picture had sailed for England and left it in cold storage in New York.

"Any writer who has achieved any reputation at all has the same sort of trouble with the cheap blood-suckers who are trying to get something for nothing," Jim wrote Montrose. "I had a talk with Rex Beach a while ago, and he is constantly in the same mess."

Bob Davis, Jim's old friend from *Munsey's*, opened an author's agency in New York, and Jim hired him to take over the marketing of his material.

The royalty check from Cosmopolitan, covering the previous six months, was for $26,977.13. Those paltry royalty checks he'd received from his first 10 or 12 books were far in the past. Harold Kinsey patted them all on the back, "you for writing such splendid books and ourselves for the distribution."

Jim suggested to Kinsey that Cosmopolitan use the "Swift Lightning" dog stories for his next book, instead of a novel. Kinsey agreed. It would give Jim a different line of work for awhile as he'd done two or three novels since his last animal series. "Of course," Kinsey warned, "a book of animal stories will not sell like a novel, but I can see how it would help you to have a break in your train of thought. If it's best to publish *Swift Lightning* after *The Flaming Forest*, we will do so."

Actually Jim, "in harness and going strong" again, was working on a new series that would have both a dog story and a love story as well as adventure and excitement.

The motion picture business had been going through a depression during the winter but *Nomads* had survived the general calamity because it was an unusual picture. Jim was "happily disappointed" in "Nomads." Independent bookings had brought in only $54,000, plus the $325,000 guarantee from First National, but the picture had cost $105,000—the initial $75,000 from First National, then an added $15,000, and Jim's $15,000 loan.

Letters were pouring in from readers across the country about *God's Country, the Trail to Happiness* and all of the reviews were good.

Jim was enthused about his new series. They would be individual stories, and Ray pondered the problem of payment. Think as you would for a novel and make the divisions naturally, Ray advised. Ten thousand words are okay for the first story, but then make some short chapters because of the paper shortage. But how can we pay like a novel when we don't know how many installments there will be? Let each story be an installment and each could be paid for as though it were an installment of a book. That way, Jim could write as many as came naturally and "we all can work comfortably on this." Eventually, though, there were only four.

If there had been too little snow in Colorado, there was now too much at Truckee, 12 feet of it on the level. The light was bad, there was a storm, but "don't worry," Hartford said, writing on his new letterhead proclaiming "David Hartford Productions, Producing Stories of James Oliver Curwood." It was shaping up nicely, with the best staff and inspiring teamwork. He wouldn't venture a guess as to what the picture would cost but we "will do our damnedest" to keep expenses down. "Beyond that we are in the hands of the weather man and at the mercy of the usual run of good and bad luck that seems to invariably attend motion picture making."

The "good and bad luck" of picture-making was no longer of much concern to Jim, for which he was thankful.

Carl Milligan was handling Jim's stories for Bob Davis. Joe Schenk wanted some of Jim's big stories, he reported, and several other producers and directors "are clamoring for your stories." George Walsh was considering "A Nice Quiet Time" for Douglas Fairbanks, and the Griffith studios were looking at "Little Miss Tired-of-it-All" for Dorothy Gish. He had "The Yellow-Back" in the vault and wouldn't let it out even though Louis B. Mayer, Irvin Willat, Harry Garson, Monroe Salisbury and others wanted to see it.

The weather at Truckee was finally clearing up and shooting was almost half-way through, but the hardest part was yet to come. Hartford had been sick but was better. He wanted to open the picture with a shot of the "great North," then have about 50 words from Jim as a forward. I thought about stealing something from "My Brotherhood," in the November *Cosmopolitan*, but didn't think that would be the right thing to do.

Would you write something for the film, he asked Jim. "You know what I want." Jim struggled for days with this, but finally sent the following:

Down through the infinities since Life began, painting for us its age-old message of the mightiness of God and the littleness of the pigmy-thing called Man, the Great White Northland whispers 'to him who will hear and understand.' If this is not God, what is God? And who, in your smallness and your egoism, are YOU?"

Ray's article, "James Oliver Curwood and His Far North," appeared in *Bookman Magazine*. *God's Country and the Woman* was reported number five on the list of "most asked for" books in libraries across the country. Two months later, *Valley of Silent Men* was number one in the Western states, and number five overall in the country.

Swift Lightning was published in England at Christmas time, and there was nothing that could be done about keeping it out of Canada. Cosmopolitan had no immediate plans for it after all and, in fact, didn't publish it until 1926.

The weather still spelled trouble in the mountains near Truckee. Snow, wind and fickle light played havoc. Black Dawson's stronghold, built on a beautiful spot at Hobart Flats, had to be moved to a new location on Van Arden Lake because of the rotting snow. "Don't worry," Hartford said. "Everything is lovely."

With his involvement with the film only from the sidelines, with his books selling well and the problems with Selig, Mayer and the others nearly settled, his new series going well, his health improved, and life in general much better, there was more time for trips up north.

Relaxed and less pressured, he began to take more interest in what was going on in the Michigan woods. He found forests burning in unchecked fires, wildlife being slaughtered, the entire situation apparently under poor control. His recent articles about his own personal creed of the wild and his ideas on conservation, plus his novels of the Canadian northland, had not only whetted his interest, but brought him to the attention of men who were concerned about these things too. Among Jim's stacks of mail were letters from many people also taking an interest in wildlife conservation.

Having given up movie production and putting his troubles in the hands of others, Jim was about to enter a new field of interest that would drain him even more than any of his past endeavors.

It was as though trouble and controversy followed him.

In late February, Jimmy had his tonsils and adenoids out in the hopes this would improve his health. Carlotta, just turning 18, was away at school, and Jimmy, recovering from his tonsillectomy, wrote her, "I hope you are feeling well. I am sorry with influenza and the doctor says it may develop in to amonia. P.S. Send me my dime in case I get well." He drew her a picture.

Abby continued in frail health that winter, but Jim was feeling fine, full of energy. He had eliminated most of his worries. Or so he thought.

Jim met Hartford in New York with the film of *The Golden Snare*. He wanted to see it first, before it was shown to First National. He was deeply disappointed. There were no long friendly discussions about future plans, and, in fact, Hartford and Montrose avoided him as much as possible. Jim began to guess the truth, that Hartford intended going on without him.

Another of Jim's close friendships had been betrayed.

Red Book Magazine, unlike *Leslie's* and some of the others in which Jim's early stories had appeared, was not as gracious in returning Jim's rights to his stories and refused to enter into any controversy by correspondence. "In view of the position you take, there is nothing we can say to you except we are maintaining our rights and hold you to a strict account with full understanding of these rights. We shall proceed, under advice of our counsel, as we may deem it expedient for protection of these rights."

Doubleday, Page also refused to discuss return of the rights of his books to Jim. They were making good money on reprints without expense to themselves. Kinsey had better luck with Bobbs-Merrill. He paid much more than he'd wanted to but less than the original price of $20,000 for the plates for five books they'd published. Bobbs-Merrill's contract with Grosset & Dunlap for reprint rights was still in force and Kinsey agreed to let that continue along with the royalties. "It broke my heart to pay so much," Kinsey wrote Jim, but it seemed wise for the long pull, "and I thought it would please you."

Where were all the good will and friendship he'd known for so many years? They hadn't seemed to begrudge him success at the time he left them and had, in fact, passed him on with good wishes. It saddened Jim, especially coming on top of so much trouble.

God's Country, the Trail to Happiness, a slim little volume of Jim's four essays, was published March 19, 1921, with an advance sale of nearly 5,000 copies.

In the beginning there'd been a problem getting animals for *The Golden Snare.* Now there was the problem of what to do with them now that the picture was finished. It cost $210 a month for their keep, which had been charged off to First National but would have to change, Montrose explained. What shall we do with them?

"Hartford and I had a good talk while in New York regarding the properties owned by the Curwood Corporation in Los Angeles," Jim replied. "He should know what to do with them. They should be sold and the money turned into the corporation...I wish you and Dave would clean this up...."

"I am very sorry that you and Dave thought fit to make private plans as you did without first advising me in advance and I think you have made a mistake.

"The fact that you made a failure of *The Golden Snare* did not discourage me, these things occasionally happen, but I was ready to go on with further production. Now I have made other plans, and shall continue productions for First National through other channels. My one regret is that you did not break with Curwood Productions in more open, courteous manner."

In spite of his hurt and anger, Jim could not help closing in his usual manner, "With all best wishes and the sincere hope that you will have the best of success."

With Jim's involvement in the actual process of movie-making now at an end, he had time to think about his new interest—wildlife conservation. State Game Warden John Baird wrote him that he hated to see politics in conservation. He accused Governor Groesbeck of such political maneuvering and pledged to help Jim in a fight for a clean conservation department. "Wild life and forest conservation is not a trivial thing," he wrote. It wasn't just the numbers saved, it meant health, pleasure, beauty, building up for children.

These two men, both advocates of protection of Michigan's natural resources, were, in the beginning at least, on the same side of the fence. They would soon be bitter adversaries on how to accomplish their common goal.

In mid-April Jim sent a wire to the governor protesting his political organization.

At least one magazine editor was not out to capitalize on Jim's rising fame as a writer. Griffith Odgen Ellis, editor of *American Boy Magazine,* wrote Jim that someone wanted the film rights to his old story, "James McGregor Billings' Moose Hunt" and would divide the profits 50-50 with the magazine. This story had appeared before the days of giving film rights, so it was probable that *American Boy* had the right to sell them, Ellis said, but he didn't think that would be right as he didn't know if Jim wanted this story from his beginning days to represent him now. Indeed he didn't want that story sold to a film company, Jim replied.

Authors should be allowed to make more money out of it if they could, Ellis agreed, as long as it wasn't at a disadvantage to *American Boy*. They'd used their rights for protection, not profit. We won't make this picture deal, Ellis wrote, and added "I'd like to publish another Curwood story if I could."

In early May, Jim went north fishing again. This time Judge Bush and two other local friends, W.V. Robinson and William A. Rosenkrans, went along. They spent several days at Struble's. Mrs. Struble had just repapered her living room and complained about the stain left by someone's hair oil where they had leaned back their head. No one admitted to it, but she suspected Jim.

One night, sharing a bed with the Judge, Jim had a nightmare about snakes. In the morning he told the judge he'd once been in a rocky area and saw a man approaching, dodging about as he came. When Jim went on he saw rattlesnakes coming out to sun. He shot about a hundred of them, and had had nightmares about snakes since.

He came home from the fishing trip feeling better than he had in years.

Nomads of the North had grossed $232,000, but the "paid and played" money actually received was only $158,573 and approximately $170,000 must be received before the corporation could expect any dividends. The interest on the loans they'd taken out was running up fast and Jim was anxious to get them paid.

There were few Curwood stories on the market now. Jim had bought back the rights to all of his stories published at any time in the *Saturday Evening Post*, the Street & Smith publications, *Munsey's, Leslie's, Collier's, McClure's, Cosmopolitan, Good Housekeeping* and the screen rights from other sources. He was getting ready to announce that both *The Yellow-Back* and *The Bride of the Long Night* would be produced on an unusually large scale.

Four stories—"House of the Red Death," "Jacqueline," "The Case of Beauvais," and "Love and the Law"—had been sold to Pine Tree Corporation, headed by Governor Milliken of Maine, for $80,000. He would have no part in their production. It was true after all that it was better to sell outright.

Jim wrote David Hartford his usual long chatty letter. I'm sorry about the misunderstanding in New York, he said.

"I can see in several instances that I have been a pretty bum critic of pictures," he admitted, and hoped that what Hartford said about *The Golden Snare* was true, in spite of the attitude of the whole First National bunch and others who'd seen the picture. "I hope they are mistaken, too. Even if the picture is not up to snuff, it will undoubtedly gross fairly well on the strength of other Curwood-Hartford pictures." Both *Isobel* and *Kazan* have done tremendously and their success will help *The Golden Snare* when it comes out, he reasoned.

There was his usual ending, "...and along with this I wish you all good luck and the best of success in whatever ventures you may enter upon."

Charles Scribner's publishing company planned a five-volume set of Jim's books on an installment plan with a year's subscription to *Scribner's Magazine*. They wanted to use *Back to God's Country, Kazan, The Golden Snare, The River's End* and *Valley of Silent Men*. Although the royalty would be very low, perhaps two-and-one-half cents, and only 10,000 in the initial printing, Jim agreed.

Jim's new series was to have featured a dog, but it introduced a man named Jolly Roger McKay who soon evolved into the central character, along with a girl for the love interest, of course. It was scheduled to begin in the July *Cosmopolitan* under the title "The Country Beyond," and would run 12 months.

Jim's interest in wildlife conservation grew, as any interest he ever took up, by leaps and bounds. A nationwide fight was forming, led by Gifford Pinchot, the nation's first forester, and Jim decided to join. He began to speak out about his views. A number of states were moving strongly toward conservation of natural resources, and some were asking Jim's help.

On June 1, 1921, Jim left for New York on business, but from there he was going on to Maine to be a guest of former Governor Carl Milliken and Senator Hinckley for two weeks. They would discuss contracts for the movies Pine Tree Productions, in which Milliken was involved, was making from his stories. Milliken left the governorship in January 1921 to return to his former post as secretary of the movie industry's first self-censorship body, Motion Picture Producers and Distributors Association.

But the primary purpose of Jim's visit was to tour the state by automobile and see for himself what steps Maine was taking toward wildlife conservation.

"Michigan is one of the worst states in the Union when it comes to a governmental interest in wild life and forest conservation and propagation," Jim declared in an interview in the *Evening Argus*.

His efforts would be toward saving his home state, he added, and in finding a governor who was interested in wild life.

Chapter 23

Jim Curwood had been in many fights—to have his writing accepted, to gain recognition, over movie scripts and book rights, with wives, even for health. He took up his new fight with the same energy and gusto as he had all the others.

He wrote a conservation article about his trip to Maine and sent it out to 540 newspapers around the country. It was read and copied and used for advertising for his books.

"I'm going to have something to say to the tune of about 100,000 votes when the next governor (of Michigan) is elected," he declared.

He wrote to people interested in wild life conservation, and to editors and others who could get his message across. He sent autographed copies of his books—Teddy Roosevelt got a copy of *The Flaming Forest*—and invited people to visit him and Ethel or to go fishing with him.

"I have no political ambitions," he repeated over and over when people looked for some reason behind his public declarations of cleaning up the conservation department or the need for wild life preservation.

"My literary work keeps me very busy," he said. "It is my chosen work for all time."

People in other states wrote urging him to join his voice with theirs in their fight for conservation. "Michigan is the most wonderful state in the United States in the possibilities it offers in the way of natural resources," he said, and declared that he would work with anyone, man or group, regardless of politics.

Jim went north fishing again. Everywhere he went he talked conservation. He sought out people working in the field, game wardens and forest rangers, and asked their views and voiced his own ideas. Outstate, he found wholehearted support, but he was bitterly opposed by most of the politicians in Lansing and the men in the Michigan Conservation Department, including a few wardens, "crooked" ones, he claimed.

Some people, on the other hand, thought his article wasn't strong enough.

"Forest protection is a farce," W.H. Aubrey, ranger at Higgins Lake State Forest north of Houghton Lake, wrote Jim. I want to talk to you, show you around, he said, and added, "Don't let Baird know of this letter."

John Baird, like so many men Jim met in his conservation fight, had appeared to be on Jim's side but now he showed himself opposed to Jim's views after all. A bitter struggle between them began. Jim asked the *Detroit Free Press* to write an editorial about "Don't-Give-A-Damn Baird," calling him a good man to run in harness with the Governor Groesbeck policy.

Even women's clubs were getting into the fight, and invitations to speak at their meetings up and down the state poured in.

There was other business to think about, too. The first edition of *God's Country, the Trail to Happiness* was about sold out, and a second edition was being run off but there was a binder's strike on.

Jim began making notes for a book to follow. "Why are you afraid to die?" he jotted down. "Why people don't go to church," and his answer to that. "People close to nature not afraid to die," he noted.

"To die should be the most beautiful thing in the world to look forward to. When I go into the mountains I anticipate it.... Man may do almost any one thing many many many times but so great is death that it is given him only once the great and glorious privilege of dying," he wrote. "It is not the failure and the heartbroken who should look forward to dying. It is the happy and contented one."

He also believed that he had lived before, that everyone has many lives.

"There is no living thing, even an ant, that does not think itself the greatest of all created things."

And he noted that "One cannot help but have faith when one views the mortar and brick out of which this universe is made. For where there is a building there must, at some time, have been a builder." God, to him, was someone wonderful and omniscient, but also someone close with whom a person could speak.

The book was never written. As soon as he got one problem under control, other matters forced themselves upon him.

The bills for *Nomads* were cleared up at last and there was a cash balance in the bank. Hartford, after repeated requests from Jim, had still not done anything about the properties left over from the filming. "If you want it yourself, itemize it and set a fair price," Jim wrote him. "We will deduct it from your dividend."

"I am feeling ten years younger" since getting out of the picture business, he declared. The Maine people had produced two "very rotten" pictures from his stories, "but I am not worrying over them because I am not personally associated with them. I have sold my stuff outright and if they make fizzles, they are the ones who must pay the piper."

Hartford had an overnight stay in Detroit, but he made excuses to Jim why he didn't come on to Owosso to see him. "Things in the picture business are in a hell of a shape just now, so I am sitting tight," he wrote when he got back to Los Angeles.

Ernie Shipman had sent Hartford one of his "mystery letters" in which he'd said that in a couple of days he'd have a proposition for Hartford that would surprise and please him, but to date the pleasant surprise had not arrived.

First National had advised him, however, that Shipman was going to handle distribution of *The Golden Snare*, with Jim's approval. "This was a surprise," Hartford said. I'll follow your lead if it's true, but there'll have to be a "damn good reason" before I'll tie up with Shipman again, he said.

The Golden Snare was playing at all the best theatres in the Los Angeles area and getting good notices, Hartford reported. "I am satisfied the picture will do a corking business."

He would come East again soon, and if possible he'd drop off in Owosso and say hello, "for the sake of Auld Lang Syne."

By mid-August Hartford was preparing for his trip to New York, and he was taking his lawyer with him. "You know how I despise New York so you must realize I felt it necessary to go. I am not in a position to stand the expense but I'm going," he wrote. Jim's contract with Shipman was the ordinary ten percent agent's commission, but Hartford remained adamant that Shipman not represent his interests. Forget your animosity toward Shipman, Jim advised, and let him take care of the picture for us both.

It was of little interest to Jim what went on with *The Golden Snare*, other than the money end of it. Michigan's forests were burning and its wild life being slaughtered. The motion picture business had been nothing but a headache to him.

Arrow Pictures, distributing Pine Tree films, sent Jim copies of *Hearts of the Northland* and *God's Country and the Law* for private screening at an Owosso theatre, hoping Jim would study them with a view to improving future pictures. They were not good films, but Jim's temper did not rage at them as he had before. They were not his doing.

Jim's conservation opponents sought ways to tame Jim down. A citation was issued against Ovid Creamery Company, in which Jim was a stockholder and director, for pollution of the Maple River by dumping its wash waters in the stream. This was a company in which John McDonald was also involved, and he sent for an expert from Ohio to look the situation over. The company was willing to put in a filter at great expense but the report stated that "it is almost an absurdity for this company to put in a filter when only 400 feet above their sewer is the sewer of the Clinton Creamery, which empties...a wash carrying much more pollution than that of the Ovid Creamery Company." Ovid Creamery is one of the most sanitary, carefully run institutions of its kind I have ever been in, the investigator said.

And besides, Jim complained, he was only a director and had nothing to do with running the plant, so the accusations were meaningless as potshots at him.

"I have discovered a species of animal that is a distinct hope here in the timbers," Aubrey wrote Jim in August. This was R.S. Babbit of Grayling, a "good conscientious hard-working man." He also wanted Jim to meet P.J. Lovejoy, a "country gentleman, a genuine progressive forestry man, one of the best in conservation in the U.S." Lovejoy had already gained a reputation in the state for his level-headed and astute views on saving Michigan's natural resources.

But Jim fell ill again. His fever rose, his kidneys were giving him trouble, and the doctors warned him he would not get better unless he took care of himself. He continued to dictate letters while flat on his back.

Come recuperate at my house, Aubrey said, it's big and quiet, and since Jim was coming up to Houghton Lake anyway, why not come on up to Higgins Lake instead? Professor Filibert Roth of the forestry department at the University of Michigan was already there. Aubrey's letter was full of bits of information and names of people involved in conservation work that he thought Jim should meet.

Albert Stoll, nature writer for the *Detroit News*, wrote Jim the results of an inspection trip around the state and a meeting of the Conservation Commission. Your name was mentioned a number of times, he said. Will you meet me sometime at the Detroit Athletic Club for lunch?

Dictating to his secretary from his sickbed, Jim answered that he'd never seen worse conditions in all the states than found in Michigan. There are several good men on the commission, he said, but as long as Baird, Pantlind, Wallace are in there, it's hopeless. Other states are spending less money and achieving more. "What we need is a good license law and the right sort of hatcheries."

Game wardens are picked not for efficiency but as vote-getters, Jim said. During huckleberry season, people in three out of four camps eat partridge and rabbits out of season. Gunfire can be heard all around.

Ray, sympathizing with Jim's latest bout of illness—"you certainly are having a terrific time of it"—suggested that he and Kinsey come down to see Jim for a good hunting trip. The only drawback, he said, was that Kinsey didn't know the first thing about a gun and he would probably shoot the both of them instead of the birds. They decided to leave Kinsey out of it for this trip.

Jim was recovering slowly and he invited Stoll to come to Owosso. Jim's first big broadside in his campaign to rescue Michigan's wildlife from the politicians was scheduled for a meeting of the Medical Association of Genesee, Livingston and Shiawassee Counties in a few weeks. I think some of the information I have will make the hair rise off your head, he wrote Stoll.

The *Detroit News* is the first paper in the state not friendly to me, he complained. "Who is your literary critic? That person is filled with bile toward me. He openly says he has never read one of my books and yet that critic hammers hell out of them." Jim had been gone from his editor's desk there for 13 years, but the old animosity seemed to linger on.

Jim had been taken sick the middle of August. Now in mid-September he was just getting back on his feet again but was still groggy. Stoll was due to come September 20. Come by train and I'll meet you, Jim wrote him, and we'll have lunch or dinner.

Perhaps he should give up his fight against Baird and the governor, Jim thought. His latest bout of illness left him with little strength for such a fight. But when Stoll arrived he urged Jim to wait a bit before giving up even in part the planned campaign. "I think the commission will be alright, I don't question them, but I'm not yet convinced they will make progress.... Baird has more authority than the commission."

There were still problems with Hartford and the film. "I have a great suspicion Shipman is going to make trouble for you," Jim told Hartford, who had hired a new promoter. "Your letter does not explain your arrangement with Schulberg regarding me. Shipman was my personal agent and gave personal service. He attended to the royalty and collections." Would Schulberg report to him as well as Hartford? Let it remain, Jim said; Shipman would keep him in touch with everything right to the last minute. Schulberg probably wouldn't.

They were still wrangling over the properties left from filming *Nomads*, which Jim estimated were worth about $1,500. "If you want to take it at that, we will deduct this from dividends coming on *Nomads*." Citing the bad state of the movie business, Hartford claimed they weren't even worth a thousand dollars. Wait a bit, he asked, but Jim replied that if that was all he thought it worth, let it go at that price.

Governor Milliken had given Jim a dog named Joker during the trip to Maine, and it had become Jim's favorite. Walking home from Abbie's one day in late September, Jim found Joker dying at the front door. It was obvious he'd been poisoned. Heartsick, Jim immediately offered a reward of $1,000 for information that would lead to the poisoner. "I've lost the best friend I ever had on earth," he cried.

Then he upped the reward for information to $10,000, and announced he would pay it $500 at a time for bits of evidence that would lead to a conviction. He railed against the people who hated cats or dogs but hadn't the courage to do things openly. They were the "lowest types of criminals that crawl the earth."

"I would give $25,000 if that would bring him to life again." And then he found that a neighbor had put out poison meat for killing rats. Joker, roaming away from home, had gotten it. The reward was withdrawn. It was all a bit embarrassing, too, since he had told the story to the folks at Cosmopolitan and it had been used extensively in illustrating Jim's feel for animals.

Still weak from his latest illness, upset over the loss of Joker, and behind in his literary work, Jim came to a definite conclusion as to what he could and could not do in the way of physicial endeavors. His experiences in the moving picture business had nearly done him in, and he was no sooner rid of that burden than he had taken on the present one. It had grown so quickly and become so heavy that it not only threatened his literary work but also his health. He was tempted to give up the fight altogether, but finally decided to make the fight in the way he worked best—through the printed word.

He turned down all requests for speaking to groups, and there were dozens of them. "I am not a speaker because I have never trained myself to speak," he said, "and I have brains enough to know it."

The people at Cosmopolitan were worried about Jim's health, and afraid he would jump into things too quickly again. "You know, Jim," Vern Porter of Cosmopolitan's staff wrote, "you have a duty not only to yourself but to the community. Several thousand persons to some extent are dependent upon you for entertainment, inspiration and thought.

"You've got to make a long life for yourself, keep your health so you can give them the best that is in you." He'd been doing too much for years, Porter said.

"We don't want you to deliver the 8th Jolly Roger story until November, so could you dictate a few scenes to your secretary for the artist?"

Canadian Photoplay was in liquidation. Jim's ten shares of stock, for which he'd paid $4,925, now had a par value of a thousand dollars. If he wanted to dispose of them, give the lowest figure he'd take and if it wasn't too high, they'd purchase them for the final winding up. It had been a costly venture, in many ways.

"Forestry needs you and needs you very much," Professor Roth wrote Jim. I've worked since 1888 without letup to further forestry, he said, and since 1903 in Michigan, and all this time I've had practically no help. I know you're more interested in wild life, he said, but it and forestry run hand in hand.

"Hew closely to the line in the press, regardless of who you hit," he advised.

How could Jim quit now, with entreaties from such a dedicated man as Filibert Roth? Yes, Jim answered, I'll go on.

The River's End was due to come out in reprint soon. Instead of using an American reprint publisher, like Grossett & Dunlap, as before, it was decided to use the Canadian firm of Copp, Clark & Co., Ltd.

Jim went north for a few days in October and prepared for a deer hunting trip into Michigan's Upper Peninsula for the next month. It was really to be an investigatory trip, to study the hunting situation in the lightly populated northern woods. Baird, recognizing the power of Jim's investigations across the state, commissioned him a special deputy game and fish warden.

At home, he had a room built especially to house his hunting clothes and Ethel's furs. He sought advice from Professor Roth as to whether to use cedar or something else for mothproofing.

Ready to leave for the north again, Jim wrote his old friend Albert Smith of Vitagraph. Smith had offered Jim five percent royalty for two of Jim's old stories, "Law of the Lakes" and "God of Her People" and the book *Flower of the North*. Better than that, Jim replied, if you'll return the rights to the two stories, I'll give my okay to exploit the fact that I consider *Flower of the North* as one of my best novels.

"Are you interested in my one buck law investigation?" Jim asked Baird when he returned from his hunting trip. Jim had confidential reports from seventeen camps. "My experience is that the one buck law is the best piece of legislation we have yet." In his camp of 12 men, 19 does could have been shot during the week, but were not, and only five bucks were shot. With such a low kill, fewer hunters will be going north for a couple of years, he predicted, but then there'll be better shooting than ever.

"I want to talk to you (about these conditions)," he told Baird, adding that he'd traveled 8,000 miles that year on his investigation trips.

Jim had a trip to New York to make and he was revising the series of stories from *Cosmopolitan* for publication of the book, to be called *The Country Beyond*. A "Yellow Bird" calendar was being prepared to promote the book, with a picture of Jim's Indian heroine, and possibly one of her daughter, Sun Cloud.

"Then do you plan starting on a novel?" Ray asked. "I suggest you get the serial started and go leisurely. If we get the next novel by the first of April it will let us plan with the greatest comfort to start the story in September."

Sales of *The Flaming Forest* had passed 125,000, outselling Peter B. Kyne's *Pride of Palomar*. Kinsey suggested, for income tax purposes, that Jim take his share of the cost of the plates they'd bought from Bobbs-Merrill off his royalty check now. What did Jim think?

Always on the lookout for ways to invest money, Jim read with interest some brochures he received in the mail from the Peninsular Fire Insurance Company. One of its agents, Nathan Singer, called on him, and Jim bought 150 shares at $60 per share, for a total of $9,000.

The movie version of *Flower of the North* came to the Strand and Jim, taking credit, of course, for a hand in its production, praised it lavishly as he had promised Albert Smith he would. "I consider *Flower* to be the best of my picture works to date. It is one of my favorite novels and because of that we have spent $150,000 in its production and have put into it a cast of actors unexcelled by any screen production in the past five years."

Most of Jim's correspondence now dealt with conservation. He wrote copiously to other men on his side of the situation, and received more invitations to speak than it was possible to accept. He turned them all down except one; he agreed to speak at a meeting of sportsmen in Flint in December.

"My dear Albert," he wrote Stoll the first of December. "Do you want to put your shoulder to the wheel along with mine in this winter's campaign?" Come to the meeting in Flint with me, he urged. "By combining our fire...we can bring about a very great change in conditions as they now exist."

Jim talked at length—more than two hours—at the Flint meeting, before an audience of 1,200 sportsmen from around the state. There were nearly a dozen and a half reporters at the meeting.

"Our first shot certainly stirred up people of the state even to the farthest towns in the Upper Peninsula," Jim wrote Fred Keister, a newspaper publisher at Ionia, about 40 miles west of Owosso, and one of Jim's strong supporters. Letters and wires are pouring in in support, he wrote Keister, and I want to talk in Lansing next and need some "red hot NEW stuff" to give the audience. Can you and your friend Fred Green find another shot of a "startling nature?" I'd like to know what went on in Baird's and the governor's own hunting camps this deer season. This is all confidential, of course, "so light a cigar with this letter."

Pine Tree Productions in Maine produced a movie, *The Girl From Porcupine*, from Jim's scenario *The Firefly*, on which he and Hartford had collaborated. Only Jim's name had appeared in the credits, and Hartford, learning about it, wrote that they'd agreed his work on the continuity was worth $1,000. "This is not serious," he wrote Jim, but he expected a check immediately.

Jim replied that he wasn't trying to hide anything. The old price for *The Firefly* was $15,000 "in the good old days of big prices." His agent had had to let it go for a tremendously lower price and Jim had thrown the continuity in for nothing. That didn't relieve him of his responsibility of paying Hartford for his "four days' work," of course, but he hadn't been paid yet himself, and wouldn't be until February. He suggested that $750 ought to be a satisfactory price.

"On the other hand, I'd very much like to have your interest in this continuity offset all property of the Corporation which has been in your hands." If you agree, he told Hartford, we could clear the books of the matter of those leftover properties.

"I will deduct this price of $750 from what I was to receive from the company, or to make it even more fair, I will deduct $1,000 from my share in the company. This, you will remember, refers to the 10% which I gave up to Canadian Photoplay and which, according to my contract, I am to have returned to me from the earnings of Nomads.

"So it will clean up the books all round. I think this is eminently fair as you had these properties in your hands a long time and they are worth a great deal more than you will be paying for them."

With that settled, at least as far as he was concerned, Jim turned his mind back to his conservation fight. His decision to slow down, made only a few weeks before while he was sick, was forgotten. He collected affidavits from dozens of people willing to swear to what they had seen or experienced and he sought the help and support of anyone he thought might be of use. He wrote letters and newspaper articles and "interviews," sending them to papers across the state.

Baird withdrew Jim's warden commission. "I congratulate you on your broadness of mind in recalling my Deputy Game Warden Commission," Jim wrote him. "You have undoubtedly noticed that the entire state press is almost solidly condemning you for the pettishness of such an act on your part. However, I am returning the commission cheerfully."

Alaska was figuring strongly in the conservation fight now. Carl Lomen, an Alaskan experimenting with domesticating reindeer, was in New York, and Jim's friends at Cosmopolitan urged him to come and talk with Lomen, since Jim was planning to write about Alaska in his next book. In the event Jim ever planned to make another trip there, Lomen might prove worth his while.

For the present, though, Jim was merely writing something about Alaska in his conservation articles. His fight for Michigan's wild life was uppermost in his mind.

"What we wardens need is a new deck and a new deal," one game warden wrote Jim. He was out to provide them both.

Chapter 24

A matter of life and death. That's how Jim viewed the issue of preservation of forests and wild life. He jotted down some ideas for an article on conservation: Without trees, vegetation and wild life, man would become extinct. It would be like giving a huge dose of poison to the two-and-a-half billion people of the world. The world could be transformed into a mad-house of plague, starvation and death.

The seriousness of the situation, at least his view of it, drove him to devote the major portion of his time to the fight that winter of 1921-22. He challenged John Baird to sue him, as Baird had threatened to do over Jim's charges that political expediency governed the conservation commission.

A libel suit, Jim said, would serve to arouse people still more, "even down to the smallest backwoods settlement.

"In court and out I shall continue to fight the present inefficient system of wild life and forest protection," he said. There was no selfish motive or personal animosity at any time in anything he'd said or done, Jim declared. He was taking his stand "simply because I love my state."

Writing, however, had to go on. *The Country Beyond* was being readied for publication and he was getting to work on his next serial/novel, "The Alaskan," using his own experiences when he and Ethel had gone on up into Alaska several years before, and reading everything he could find on Alaska to fill in what he didn't know from his trips. He made arrangements to talk to Carl Lomen on his next New York trip.

He and Ethel were planning a trip to Canada again, but this time to the east, an expedition to the Ecorces River area of the Lac St. Jean country in northern Quebec, to the village of Peribonka. He planned it in his usual thorough fashion, making lists of everything six people would need for a three-week trip—besides Ethel and himself there would be four guides and helpers.

In the meantime, he filed suit against Peninsular Fire Insurance Company, charging fraud in the sale of those shares of stock in December.

He set aside money for his conservation fight.

He was working seven days a week again and often late into the night, the doctors' warnings about taking it easy forgotten again.

The new conservation department ordered Owosso to build an intercepting sewer and sewage disposal plant to take the sewage out of the river, claiming it was killing the fish and creating unsanitary conditions. Even though Owosso was no worse than other places, the city felt it was being "picked on" first. The cost would be prohibitive.

Invitations to speak continued to pour in but he turned almost all of them down, including one in Chicago at a meeting of the new Izaak Walton League, and prepared to leave for a long trip to New York. He hired a second secretary and left lists of things for her and Helen Heling to do while he was gone, including typing 46 copies of a five-page article to be sent to daily newspapers in the state, because he knew the "psychology of originals" sent to an editor.

Nevertheless, he ran into trouble over something he'd said at that Flint meeting in December. The Rev. Edgar Cochran claimed Jim had slandered the Virgin Mary. Jim shouldn't be allowed to speak at the Izaak Walton League meeting in Chicago, he declared, but Jim had already said he wasn't going, so Cochran's charge was merely an attempt to discredit Jim.

"It's all a damned lie," Jim told the *Argus*. "I never said 'Isn't it a fact that the mother of Christ was somewhat of a violator, too?'. He'd really meant Mary Magdalene and he'd just gotten mixed up, he explained.

His outburst at the meeting had come in defense of a member who'd been charged—unjustly, the member said—with a game law violation and against whom Baird had spoken. "There probably isn't a man in this auditorium who has not broken some law. Even the mother of Christ was human and subject to human sorrows and weaknesses. Even Christ was never happier than when one person who had gone astray came back into the fold," he'd said. "Why, if John Baird should become a good conservationist, I would welcome him back into the fold."

The controversy was overriding the real issues but if it had been meant as a means to slow Jim down and discredit him in some people's eyes, it failed. Even an attack on Jim through the pages of *Michigan Sportsman Magazine* failed to deter Jim from his conservation fight.

Jim returned from a week in New York more inundated with work than ever. He was preparing a speech for the Flint meeting of the Michigan Sportsmen's Association. P. J. Lovejoy was to speak also, and he wrote Jim that his topic would be Michigan's idle lands. If it would lend itself to wide publicity, would Jim distribute it through his "machinery" for getting things into the press? Then he took Jim somewhat to task for his fight with Baird.

I want to "pour oil" on the situation, Lovejoy said, and pave the way for advancement of our cause. I don't want to become involved in your differences. It's merely a difference in position.

Jim, he said, is "measuring ahead from where we are to where we must get, Baird is measuring from where we were to where we are; both are in a degree quite correct, no doubt." And that was not the main issue.

They talked on the telephone, and Lovejoy wrote Jim afterward. "What I am really trying to say is that I don't want to see the details of the Main Job get obscured by personalities. The Main Job, as I see it, is to get the backing for an adequate program of *doing things*."

Stoll, writing Lovejoy, said the Conservation Commission was ignoring Jim, and that talk of a liable suit was bunk. But if Jim had done nothing else, he had stirred up a lot of talk on conservation affairs.

He was continuing to receive, and turn down, requests for giving talks. He accepted only two, one February 13 at the meeting of the Shiawassee County Sportsmen's Club and the February 27 meeting in Flint of the Michigan Sportsmen's Association. In Owosso he was the main speaker.

The night before the banquet in Flint, Jim and Ethel were overnight guests of Charles S. Mott and his wife. Mott, vice president of General Motors Corporation, was an influential man in local and state affairs. There was some talk of his running for governor.

Jim was not the main speaker this time, but he was honored by the sportsmen for his work and gave a short talk on conditions as he'd been finding them in his trips around the state. "I'd like to swear a bit about that Lansing bunch and would if it wasn't for the ladies present," he said. He had several investigators out at his own expense, and "some of the things they have found would make plenty of hell and brimstone." He ended with a toast to Mott as the "next governor." He was to find that, again, he had inadvertently given the reporters something they could twist and fling back into his face.

Jim's apparent backing of Mott raised concerns by many of his conservation backers. Fred Keister of Ionia warned him that he was getting "political." Their "mutual friend" was disappointed.

"I had no intention our mutual friend should buy me," Jim replied. "My personal political tendencies have nothing to do with that...the attitude he has taken shows me quite plainly he had another scheme in mind....

"I have had many men break faith with me. It is no new thing." I've spent more than $2,200 making a thorough investigation of the north, and I'm perfectly able to "stand such a trifle," he said. Let our mutual friend read this letter. I'm sorry you two people were working me for a political end.

"I would work as hard for any other good man as I would work for Mott," Jim wrote Keister, "but in working for any man, when the time comes, the only reason shall be it is an end toward the achievement of that conservation system I want to see in Michigan."

The mutual friend, Fred Green, wrote back a tart reply. "It has always been a great wonder to me how it was possible for a man to get himself into a frame of mind where he was always right and the other fellow wrong."

With Green out in the open now, Jim eagerly replied, patching up the little difference between them and reminding Green of the pleasant visit he and Ethel had had in Green's office some time before. I'm looking forward to seeing you again, he said.

Green, too, regretted having worked previously through a third person, and the misunderstanding it had caused. A bond of friendship quickly formed between the two men.

The strain was beginning to tell on Jim again, and he fled to the woods, thick now with winter snows, to rest up, to write, and to get away from the harrassment from both sides in the conservation battle. He would talk only sparingly from now on, he declared, because his "business as a business is strictly literature or at least alleged literature."

His retreat this time was a cabin several miles from Roscommon, north and east of Houghton Lake, owned by J.A. Byerly of Owosso. It was a place of quiet and solitude, heavily wooded and with a fast flowing stream, fronting on a sandy trail down which few people ever passed, and then mostly afoot or by horse. He stayed five days, then he was home again and back in the thick of things.

While he was gone, Albert Stoll was appointed secretary to the Conservation Commission, and Jim wrote him congratulations. "It's no good to make laws without good wardens to back them up. Baird and Groesbeck think this is personal but it's not." He planned on leaving for Alaska in the spring, he said, but of course, the trip he was planning was not in that direction at all.

But now Stoll, who had always defended the members of the Commission, jumped off the fence and landed on the side of Baird.

The Izaak Walton League was gaining across the country, and the chapter formed in Owosso already had more than 50 members in mid-March. Jim, of course, was a member and an active and vocal one. Ethel, too, joined.

Jim's home was always open, and he and Ethel entertained people from around the state who came to talk conservation.

He ran up to the cabin at Roscommon whenever he could, but the pace was picking up and a planned trout fishing trip had to be cancelled. To everything else—his writing and the necessary occasional business trips to New York, his voluminous correspondence and many informal meetings in his conservation fight, his new involvement with the Izaak Walton League—was added numerous community activites. He could never just serve on a committee, he had to jump in with both feet and take on the burden of seeing the project through as though it would fail if he did not.

For some time Owosso had sought the use of the National Guard Armory as a community center and began a conscription drive to raise funds. Jim and John McDonald, among others, were appointed to the committee.

In spite of the fact that people sought Jim's opinion and advice, when he gave it honestly they often didn't agree and did their own thing anyway. He felt sometimes he was wasting his time.

Disregarding Stoll's apparent switch to the other side, Jim wrote asking him to look into a fish kill up at Beulah. What did it matter if they disagreed on most things, if it concerned what Jim was fighting for? The fish kill, however, turned out to be suckers that died due to high spring water stirring up the dirt and clogging their gills.

In early May he went north for a few days, but his trips were no longer restful as they had been in years past. There were sportsmen everywhere who wanted to talk to him and to whom he wanted to talk. It was necessary to go east again for a week, and then again to the cabin at Roscommon in late May.

In June he began a lawsuit against Affiliated Distributors, Inc., Edwin Carewe Pictures and others, for the illegal use of his name as author of a picture they had made and were marketing under the title *I Am the Law*, and for infringement on the rights to his novel, *Valley of Silent Men. Cosmopolitan Magazine* and International Film Service began a companion suit at the same time on the infringement of *Valley of Silent Men.*

Two months before, two representatives of the film company had approached Jim about a little animal story of his that had appeared in *Outing Magazine* in 1910. They had already bought the screen rights from the magazine, but they offered Jim $1,000 for his "good will." He had accepted. Now he found that the film had already been made and it had nothing to do with his story. They had merely wanted to "buy" his name. The film had also used some of the best parts of the films, *The River's End* and *Valley of Silent Men*, produced by International Film.

This type of fraud and theft of material from authors had been growing rapidly in the film industry, in spite of a "much-touted Hollywood 'clean-up'," and Jim said he would lead the fight to limit such misconduct on the part of many producers who for years had paid scant attention to the copyright laws.

He had taken out paid ads in the film trade magazines warning just such producers that he was not bluffing when he said he would sue anyone who stole from him, and now he was proving that he meant what he said. He sued for all the monies thus far earned by *I Am the Law*, all property rights in production, and for an additional $100,000.

He won his lawsuit, although not all the money he sued for, in July.

In mid-June the family went on its annual family outing at Houghton Lake. Jim planned to go on to Petoskey to speak at a meeting of sportsmen, but he was taken sick instead. He promised to come to their meeting in the fall.

Jim's northern "vacation" was hardly that. He spent his time traveling about the nearby country and talking to sportsmen and game wardens. He was upset over the number of fires that summer. Fifty percent of them, he said, were due to careless smokers. Some sort of receptacle should be provided in cars for ashes.

The family—Jim, Ethel, Carlotta, Viola, home for the summer, and Jimmy—went by automobile to Michigan's Upper Peninsula where Jim had gone deer hunting the fall before. He'd ordered a cabin built back in the woods and now he was going to bury himself there to write. They stayed five weeks.

Chapter 25

At night the wolves howled outside the little clearing and sent shivers of fear through Carlotta and Viola sleeping in the tent next to the little cabin in the Upper Peninsula wilds. The cabin James Leatherby had built for them was hardly big enough for Jim and Ethel and Jimmy, and Jimmy often slept out in the second tent with their camp boy, Rex Erickson.

During the day Jim took pad and pencil and roamed through the forest and sat for long periods along the nearby river, working on his story of Alaska. The Michigan woods and surrounding "mountains," merely hills compared to the Canadian Rockies, were nothing like the Alaskan landscape, but Jim's memories of what he'd seen and his imagination took care of that. His story was centered on the attempt to domesticate reindeer, even though he was critical of the Michigan Conservation Department's experiment with reindeer. There were, of course, a villainous opponent, the handsome hero, and the beautiful heroine around which Jim wove his inevitable love triangle.

Jim had not lost his fascination with long hair. His hero "noted that it was dark, with varying flashes of luster in it under the dinner lights" with "smooth, silky coils..." The hero admired her hair with "immense relief after looking on so many frowsy heads, bobbed and marcelled..." Jim hated the new short hairdos and forbade Ethel and the girls to cut their hair short. His admiration of women's long hair was so strong that he, at least once, drove miles just to see a woman with hair so long she could sit on it. He might even stop a woman he didn't know on the streets to compliment her on her coiffure.

Not only did he not like bobbed hair, Jim also disliked jewelry. Ethel and the girls might wear furs and the latest fashionable gowns, but they didn't wear jewels.

Neither had Jim lost his ability to write about places he'd never been. The first part of his story took his main characters up the Inside Passage, and although Jim had been to Alaska twice, he had not taken this means to get there.

In the Curwoods' wilderness camp, a romance blossomed between good-looking Rex and pretty Viola, both 15, dampened by the disapproval of Jim and Ethel. Jim was often absent from camp, and when there, spent most of his time at the typewriter, but he nevertheless noted the young romance and the handsomeness of the young couple and stored it away for later use. People often remarked, but not usually with complaint, that you had to watch yourself around Mr. Curwood or you would find yourself in one of his stories.

Before love had much chance to bloom, the family struck camp and were home again, and it was time for Viola to go back to her mother and Carlotta to head for college.

Jim was soon knee deep in conservation matters again, but the brief respite in the north woods, as any time spent in the woods always did, had revitalized him.

He received a copy of a letter Lovejoy had written to Aubrey at Higgins Lake. Lovejoy wanted to be sure that others knew he was not joining the opposition by working on a committee with Baird to draft timberland tax reform, but was rather getting associated with them and getting an inside look. In the meantime, he hoped that Curwood "bawls all hell out of the administration, but, myself, I'm going to try to get them into modern plans so deep they'll never get out,..."

Each one seemed to have his special area of interest, and with Lovejoy, it was naturally forests. "We cannot have fish and game unless we have forest," he wrote. "Every dollar that we can raise ought to be put into fire protection."

Jim worked with them all, writing letters, arguing his ideas of what ought to be done, sending his books as gifts, inviting them to visit him at home or go fishing with him. He did not write an article for just one newspaper but sent it out to dozens of them. On the other hand, others urged him to see their views, to back this candidate or that one, to go slowly or pound hell out of the opposition.

He was willing to back anyone he thought might be on the side of conservation. When the first candidate for governor he backed lost in the primary, he swung his support to the Democratic candidate, though he had himself always been Republican. The things Jim had seen in his trips around the state that year had made his heart ache, and if he blew things out of proportion because of it, it was out of eagerness to make others aware of the desperate need to make a change in Lansing.

"We must save what we already have and then look ahead to what we can achieve in the next fifty or hundred years," he wrote Lovejoy, who had just been named to the Conservation Commission. Lovejoy replied, "Probably because I've been hungry for so long, it may take less to make me happy than in your own case. Certainly things at Lansing are very much better than ever before. I'll have to insist on that. But I realize very keenly, I think, how hopelessly inadequate they still are and I do not think that anybody up there will put anything over on me."

Jim wasn't sure about that.

In October he was away to the woods again, to the cabin at Roscommon and to Aubrey's at Higgins Lake. As usual, he sent a warm letter of thanks to his host and wife and family, and said he had told Mrs. Curwood all about it and she was anxious to see that beautiful country of theirs.

From there he went up to Petoskey to keep his promise to speak at the fall meeting. He received a standing ovation and much applause. Stoll and another member of the Department from Lansing were there, but only one of them was allowed to speak and Stoll complained afterward about that.

Jim returned home in time to speak to an overflow crowd at nearby St. Johns. Nearly a thousand men and women attended. He backed his talk with an array of facts and figures.

"Conservation is not a matter simply for the hunter and fisherman," he said. "Our very lives and future prosperity depend upon it. If all wild life, forests and vegetation were to disappear from the face of the earth tomorrow, human life would cease to exist within one year."

He had critized Baird and Groesbeck two years before "and the dance has been on ever since."

Jim's accusations that conservation money had been used for boats and bathing suits was true, one reporter said, "but not all the truth." The Dodge brothers, who had made a fortune in the car industry, had given the state eleven state parks, but the titles were still not clear and they told the state to furnish those things and they would pay it back. This was irregular, of course, the reporter said, and Jim might not know all these facts for "he seemed to be well intentioned."

It was Jim's last speech for awhile. His publishers were "almost at the threatening point," he claimed in turning down efforts to get him to speak. He turned his refusals over to his secretary, Helen, and concentrated on his novel.

Jim had once told Harold Kinsey that Owosso "is the nicest place in the world. I was born there and I hope to die there. It's American and it makes you feel at home." Kinsey used that quote in his article about Jim in the November *Good Housekeeping*, "Jim Curwood of Owosso."

In November, Groesbeck was elected for another two years. For nearly two years, Jim had devoted himself to the fight to get Groesbeck and his "crowd" out of office, to the detriment of his writing, and he had lost. He went north again to work on his novel which was now sadly behind schedule.

Abbie's illness brought him home in late November. She was very ill again, and there was some talk of moving her to the hospital, but in a few days she was improved. Jim went north again, this time taking Ethel with him to Aubrey's.

They were gone only briefly. Now Jimmy was sick with flu and Jim himself was down in bed again soon after they got home.

The triumph of the Groesbeck forces downed Jim only temporarily. He wrote to the newspapers that "whom the Gods would destroy they first make mad," and he was not through yet.

On the last day of the year, 1922, he wrote the last line of his novel, "The Alaskan." It had taken him a full year to write it.

Will Dilg invited him to the January meeting of the Izaak Walton League in Chicago but Jim declined, citing the sickness in his family and because he was behind in his literary work. He sent them an article, "Fifteen Years of Tragedy," for the *Izaak Walton League Monthly* instead.

In the Izaak Walton League Jim found a new force for his fight for Michigan wild life. He embraced it quickly, as he did any other means for reaching the end he sought. In spite of his determination not to speak publicly again, he changed his mind and decided he would speak in Chicago after all. But then he was not able to go.

The Peninsular Fire Insurance case came to trial January 3, 1923. It required Jim's attention for the next ten days. At the end, the jury awarded Jim $9,472.50, plus interest from the date he purchased the stock December 1, 1921.

In the meantime, representatives of the Michigan Congress of Sportsmen's Clubs met with the governor and recommended keeping the one-buck law enacted two years before, an open season on partridge in the Upper Peninsula in October, and a fishing license to apply to all kinds of fishing. These were all ideas Jim had fostered.

Jim was toastmaster at the annual January meeting of the Sportsmen's Congress in Flint. Others did the talking this time, but Jim was the center around which everything else raged. He was, they said, the leader who had welded together the forces fighting for protection of wild life. To the accusations that he had political ambitions, Jim replied that he was fighting for a principle.

"If you have such a great value in natural resources, your first duty to yourself and your state is to get the right kind of people to care for it...," he said.

"Do not mix up conservationists with hunters and fishermen," he warned. "Conservation demands the interest of everyone. It is vital to men, women and children in its necessity to human life, and sportsmen alone are not the ones who reap its benefits."

He was in the position of being either the bat or the ball, Jim said, "and so, if I wasn't being hit I was hitting. And if the ladies weren't here, I would say it is a damn uncomfortable position to be in."

Nevertheless, the Lansing chapter of the IWL barred him from speaking there, claiming that he had descended from his role as toastmaster to arguing with members of the audience.

Abbie was very ill again and Jim put nearly everything else aside to stay close to her bedside. He and Ethel rushed home after the Flint banquet, though a blizzard was raging, because her situation was now critical. The next day they held a conference, expecting the worst, but she gradually gained until she was again out of danger.

For many years Jim had maintained his old room upstairs in his parents' house, though he had a studio in his own home where he conducted his business and did most of his writing. Now and then he escaped to the old room, seeking the peace and refuge he couldn't find elsewhere, except in the north woods.

A cracked jaw took him to the dentist's where he sat for two hours while the doctor worked on his wisdom tooth. "Ye, Gods, but it's fun," he wrote Ray. It was necessary for him to go to the University Hospital in Ann Arbor to have the piece of jaw containing the tooth sawed out.

January proved to be an unhealthy month for the entire family. In addition to Abbie's illness and the trouble with his tooth, Jim had a touch of the flu again. Then Amy and Jimmy both were down with it. It was Jimmy's third bout of flu, and Will Dilg recommended taking him south for the rest of the winter, but of course that was out of the question. Abbie continued to fail. In early February she was better, but Jim didn't believe she would get up from her bed again.

Dr. Preston A. Bradley, a well-known conservationist from Chicago, was the main speaker at the annual meeting of the Owosso IWL chapter. Jim attended but did not speak.

He was very tired, but now he took on an added responsibility, accepting the post of chairman of the local Welfare Drive. As usual, he did not do the job half-heartedly. He set about to organize the city ward by ward, not sparing anyone, rich or poor, from a request to donate money.

He was also collecting funds for the IWL. He sent his article "Fifteen Years of Tragedy" to the magazines of many organizations besides the IWL— Rotary, Canadian and American forestry magazines, and others. Since he was under contract to Hearst's, he was not allowed to sell his work anywhere else, so he gave away this and other conservation articles gladly in order to reach new and wider audiences.

Invitations to speak or to visit continued to come in from many areas now. The Wisconsin and Minnesota legislatures asked him to speak, and he was invited to visit Yellowstone, Mt. McKinley and other places. But his interest remained primarily with Michigan.

Jim and Ethel continued to attend sportsmen's banquets whether he was to speak or not, and he was honored everywhere for his conservation work. Ethel, over the years, had become his right hand, in his work as well as his other interests. He had turned the rights to many of his literary properties over to her and many of the checks that came were made out to her. When he joined an organization, like the IWL, she joined, too. She traveled nearly everywhere with him, and whenever he was ill or away from home, she carried on for him, under his instructions.

Their personal life was still stormy, but in other ways, she was more than ever his "companion on the trail."

Now it was clear that something had to be done to lighten his work load, and in March he hired a literary collaborator. Her name was Elita Sheasby. She and her young son arrived the end of the month from New York where she had been a newspaper dramatic critic.

She was happy to be in Owosso, Elita declared, and had long wanted to be associated with James Oliver Curwood and his out-of-doors novels. She spent time at the Community Center, swimming, engaging in games and calisthentics. Her three-year-old liked to wake up hearing the robins singing, she said. He'd never heard them before.

Elita Sheasby was a beautiful young woman and Jim took her with him to Judge Bush's in Corunna where she thrilled Bush's son, Homer, with her charm and femininity, but he, of course, was married. This was hardly a deterrent with other men about town, and it wasn't long before the town gossips' tongues were wagging.

Work began early that spring on a studio Jim had had in mind for some time to take the place of the one at home. He bought the land next to his mother's house and workmen began laying the foundation for a 15th-century style castle designed for him by a Lansing architect. As soon as the snow was gone, Jim began scouring the countryside for stones that would make up the walls.

He also bought an acre of land across the river and planted trees. "Twenty years from now," he said, "it will be a thing of beauty both summer and winter." He urged others to beautify along the river and opposed a plan to create a drive along the river. Keep traffic away from the river, he urged. Keep it a place of beauty where a man can take his family for a picnic and a few hours close to nature without the noise and dust of motor traffic.

In June Jim took the family to Houghton Lake for their annual outing. He was writing, of course, but he found time for fishing, too, and posed for his picture holding a northern pike nearly sixteen inches long, not a record but worth a photo nevertheless.

"The Alaskan," now running serially in *Good Housekeeping Magazine*, had been a departure from his other northern stories. In fact, a Royal Northwest Mounted policeman was a villain. For the new novel, *A Gentleman of Courage*, Jim took his readers back to the country between Lake Superior and Hudson Bay, and wove into his story a gentle love affair, with the lovers patterned after Viola and her summer romance with Rex Erickson.

Jim never went to northwest Canada again and the setting for all of his remaining books, except his very last one, was eastern Canada.

Groesbeck was firmly in the governor's office, and therefore Stoll and Baird also were firmly in place, but Jim did not abandon his conservation fight. He fired a broadside now and then and still gathered information, but he, at last, put conservation matters secondary to his work.

For the second time Jim cancelled a spring trip to Alaska. There was no literary need to go now as his book about Alaska was finished. He had sought funding for further trips there, even considering staying a year or so to write about Alaska's conservation problems, but he was unsuccessful. He'd been able to travel so widely in Canada, he said, because much of the expense had been taken up by others, but without help, he abandoned his plans for Alaska.

In August he and Ethel went to Quebec on the trip delayed from the year before. Jim took copious notes and collected material, putting it into a scrapbook, to be the basis for a new book with a new theme.

The castle studio being built beside Abbie's house was a quaint and incongruous structure for a small mid-Western city, but it fulfilled Jim's romantic notions of a place to write his stories. He had never been commonplace himself, and he wanted something unique. And he could afford whatever he wished.

The studio was of stone and stucco, with a large turret in one corner and smaller false turrets at the others. The first floor was one large room with a step-up storage cupboard at one end and glassed-fronted bookshelves at the other flanking the fireplace of Italian marble. There were three levels in the large turret. Jim's desk was in the lower of these rooms and his old typewriter on the oilcloth-covered sewing machine stand on the second. The roof was of gray slate.

Handwoven draperies were imported from Italy for the casement windows. A long black walnut table came from France. There was a full basement, with the little circular room under the turret fancifully called the "dungeon keep."

Once the castle was completed, he set up a routine for when he was in town. After a few exercises in front of an open window and a healthful breakfast, he walked to the castle for his morning's work. Ethel was mindful of appearances, and so he left home each morning dressed in his three-piece suit and proper shoes. As soon as he was out of her sight, he took off his coat and vest and hung them over his arm. He took off his shoes and put on his worn bedroom slippers, continuing his trip in comfort. Only his neighbors along the way knew of the change.

A sign was erected in front of the studio to let people know when they could come in. "Halt!" it said, "Mr. Curwood cannot be interrupted. He is doing original work." At noon he went home to lunch and a nap, then walked briskly back to the castle where the door was open for visitors, from publishers, movie producers and worldly businessmen to the folks next door.

People in town had grown accustomed to Jim's peculiarities, his stopping women on the street to admire their hair, his absentmindedness, his immaculate dress. He might stop and shake hands and talk at length one time, and pass the same friend by without a word the next, depending on whether his thoughts were free or on a story plot at the time.

One day, his mind on his novel, he drove his car downtown. Taking care of whatever business he'd been on, he walked home. Sometime later, he noticed his car missing from in front of the house where he usually parked it. He phoned the police that it was stolen. To his embarrassment, they found it downtown, right where he'd left it.

He played pool with his friends at the local poolroom, and liked to bet on the games. And though he had all the money he could wish, and gave away thousands of dollars to various local causes, he swore and carried on when he lost so much as a dime.

On a cold November morning in 1923, Abbie died. Jim was beside himself with grief. Inconsolable, he went to the funeral with a heavy heart. Ever the dramatist, he confessed to Carlotta later that he'd held a bottle of poison clutched tightly in his fist, prepared to do away with himself. But his grief was very real. Now he had neither mother nor father. How could he continue? They, and especially his mother, had been his support and mainstay in everything he'd done.

The conservation issue, however, was still present. Stoll was out as secretary to the Conservation Commission, but it was hardly a time for rejoicing. In his stead Groesbeck appointed Jim's "arch enemy," the Rev. Edgar Cochran, a Congregational minister. "This is the minute and hour for every man and woman in Michigan to rise up in mighty protest," Jim declared.

And now a new controversy was raging in Owosso, not over conservation but over the Community Center whose director was E.J. Mazurkiewicz, a "foreigner brought here to teach our children," Harvey Hinman said, speaking for those who wanted "Muzzy" fired. Jim took up the defense and the *Argus* printed his story side by side with one by Hinman. "Muzzy" stayed.

Viola and Carlotta were now both in college. They came home for the Christmas holidays as usual, but the social scene took up as much time as family doings. They held a luncheon at the Colonial Tea Rooms for eighteen of their friends, then took them to the new castle studio for bridge. Christmas was not like it had been in the old days.

At the end of 1923, Jim bought a half interest in the Roscommon property from his friend Calvin Bentley. Later he bought the other half. It was his place to escape from the troubles and stress that always plagued him at home in Owosso.

Chapter 26

Jim's handwriting "flashes across the page with bouyant gestures, fleet and forceful, as though impelled by an interior power which animates his vital thoughts." So went a handwriting analysis published in the *Detroit Free Press* in January 1924. "Here and there he stops reflectively," the analysis said, "with breaks between strokes of words, or to gather in new ideas, fresh spirits of his dreams, which he creates into living, vital realities.... Dominated by his broad ambition to create, he never ceases in the elaboration of this theme,..."

The analyst knew, of course, whose handwriting he was analyzing, but he'd never met Jim.

Jim spent a lot of time at the cabin at Roscommon that winter, hunting rabbits, snowshoeing and otherwise spending time out-of-doors in the snow. John McDonald and other friends sometimes joined him. Nevertheless, by March Jim was suffering from exhaustion again, and his doctors ordered him to cease working for at least three months. He'd been burning the candle at both ends, and now he must pay for it. The woods rejuvenated him physically, mentally and spiritually, though, and by mid-March he was allowed to dictate half an hour a day. He had a new secretary, Charlotte Quinn, a pretty and vivacious girl from Detroit.

Jim and Jimmy, now 14, and one of Jimmy's friends went up to the cabin in early April. They found someone had broken in and apparently had a party, leaving behind whiskey bottles and unwashed and broken dishes. The player piano was broken, the kitchen wood supply used up and things mussed up in general. Jim was irate but he wasn't able to find out who had done it.

Jim was invited again to speak at the annual IWL convention in Chicago in April, and this time he accepted but didn't go. Mrs. Dilg reported to Jim after the meeting, describing the large picture of him displayed in the banquet room, with "flame-tipped" words below, "Only the people with the power of the ballot can put their lakes, their streams and what wild life and forest they have left into hands capable of caring for them, perpetuating them and increasing them."

He missed a meeting of conservationists held in Owosso, with Prof. Russell Watson as speaker, where he was honored as one of three men who had done much in the conservation field, the other two being Teddy Roosevelt and Gifford Pinchot.

Watson stayed over for the dedication of the new Carnegie Library at the corner of Main and Shiawassee streets, and again Jim was honored in absentia.

Jim's new castle studio got little use that spring as Jim kept to the cottage

191

up north, following his doctor's advice to get back to nature. He was working on his newest novel, due to appear in *Hearst's Magazine* that fall.

Literary critics had been hitting him of late with the repetitiousness of his novels, and he sought to bring something new to his work. Besides, for many years he'd been writing what he thought people wanted to read, "writing for the proletariat," he said, and now he would write what he wanted. Money and fame were no longer a goal; he had them both. For more than two years he'd been gathering historical information on the Quebec area and the French and Indian War, with plans to write a historical novel. In the meantime, he wrote *The Ancient Highway*, using modern day Montreal and Quebec for its setting, and putting into the story some of his philosophy of life.

In June, as usual, the family went for their annual outing at Houghton Lake. The cabin at Roscommon was too small for them all and besides, Ethel and the children liked swimming and boating and the other activities they could have at the resort.

If his opponents in Lansing thought Jim had given up his fight for wild life in Michigan, they were sadly mistaken. He was merely gathering his strength. There would be a new election and he intended to have something to say when the time came. In the meantime, he continued to write letters and articles and to bide his time.

In late summer Jim and Ethel went to Quebec again.

But mostly Jim worked quietly, and spent as much time as he could at the little cabin in the north woods. His books and stories were being made into films, but he took no part and little interest in them. If they succeeded or failed, it was not his doing.

The girls were home for the Christmas holidays as usual, and there were family doings. Carlotta and Viola spent much of their time with friends and then they were off to school again. With his mother and father both gone, Amy and Jack growing older, and Ed and Stella no longer coming home for the holidays, it was just not the same.

The winter went as quietly as the summer. Jim and Ethel spent evenings playing mah-jong with Fred and Martha Woodard. They kept a running score for a month, the winners being treated to dinner by the losers. It didn't matter who won or lost. Jim and Martha were partners, Fred and Ethel their opponents. Their favorite restaurant was Ming Pen Lo's for Chinese food, but Jim liked a good beefsteak dinner best. Usually they took the boys, Jimmy and Dean, Fred and Martha's son, with them.

Sometimes, when the Woodards came to the Curwoods for their evening of mah-jong, Jim read them the latest chapter in the historical novel he was now working on, *The Black Hunter*.

The women were busy with their social events—Women's Club, church and other functions, and the men kept to their business, Fred as president of

Woodard Manufacturing, now makers of fine furniture as well as caskets, and Jim with his writing. Both were involved in community affairs, especially with the Community Center. Jim became a Mason and contributed generously. He gave money for the building of the new Elks Temple, and to the nurses' home where girls stayed while taking nurse's training at Memorial Hospital.

The old indoor baseball team was revived. Jim sponsored it, furnished uniforms and money for traveling to other cities to play, and played on the team as right shortstop. He was proud of his playing.

He no longer ranted over conditions in the conservation department, but that didn't mean he had given up the fight. He was tired and sometimes ill, his kidneys were giving him problems and he was being treated at Ford Hospital in Detroit for gastroenteritis and his other ailments. Amy was sick that winter, and Queen quit her job as a teacher to stay at home to nurse her. Marguerite was called home from San Francisco where her husband Lt. Ralph Tate was stationed. By mid-January, Amy was much improved.

They were all getting older and settled down.

Nomads of the North, Kazan and *Baree, Son of Kazan* were all translated into French in 1925, and the first two and *The Wolf Hunters* into Russian. Others had already been printed in Dutch, Swedish, German and other languages, and, to Jim's pride, into Braille.

Jim was elected president of the Community Center. "Muzzy" left and a new director was hired.

He took on the chairmanship of the annual Welfare Chest Drive again, and held "red hot pep rallies" in the studio for the workers. The drive went over the top by $3,000, the most ever raised in Owosso. Jim said they would put the extra away to start the next year's drive. He praised everyone for their part in making the drive a success.

Jim agreed to be a speaker at the annual meeting of the Shiawassee Sportsmen's Association, to be held in Owosso on February 3. His topic, however, was not conservation of wild life but rather the problem of liquor, and the "liquor law violators who are endangering the lives of our boys and girls in Owosso, our most prized resource of a future citizenry."

He said he had evidence of pitiful conditions, of selling liquor to young people, that fifteen kids had to be escorted out of the theatre for being drunk.

"If I ever find a person supplying my boy with liquor I am going to kill him," he declared. Jimmy, at 14, was already nearly incorrigible. Jim suspected that the violators knew his son very well.

Then he went to Ford Hospital for a week of rest and treatment. Jimmy stayed with the Woodards and Ethel went with Jim. He stayed 11 days.

The local sportsmen talked of building a clubhouse north of town, now that highway paving was to be extended out that way.

In early March Jim went north to the cabin. "These are what I call the hunger days in the deep swamps and big woods and I like to study wild life at this time and all birds and animals are thin and weak from winter's fight..." He spent his time writing and tramping the snowy woods on snowshoes and skiis. John McDonald came to visit and there were evenings in front of the fireplace with good cigars and good conversation.

Jim stayed up north a month, working on his book. It was a wonderful spring, but very dry. The trailing arbutus were about to bloom and Jim set out nearly four hundred trees. "My happiness would have been complete if I had not been compelled to miss playing in the exciting championship (indoor baseball) games which my team put up with the Studebakers," he wrote Ray. The Studebakers won in a battle that was a "scrap all the way."

But Jim was out of practice and thought he'd be a weakness to his team, so he stayed up north. Besides, the book was due to be finished soon, and he was working hard to meet his deadline.

"The winter was a fine one for all wild things," he said. There were more partridges than usual this spring. All night long they drummed in the clearing about his cabin on the bright moonlit nights. There were often as many as 16 deer in the clearing in the evening.

"This is the most beautiful time of year in the north country."

Jim attended a dinner at the American Legion home to hear Lt. Jack Harding, around-the-world flyer, and Lowell Thomas, historian of the flight. Jim invited them to the studio before and after the affair, for conversation and reminiscences of traveling to Alaska and the Yukon.

He was home a week and then headed north again. He sent Martha and others baskets of trailing arbutus, hiring a woman in Roscommon to gather the plants and prepare the baskets for mailing. There was always someone he wished to thank, or to commend for something, or simply to remember.

Visitors came to the little cabin—Ethel, Jimmy and Martha, Charles Sackrider, who had married Vera Haskell, Jim Mahaney and Judson Shattuck, and other friends from home. Ray Long, Harold Kinsey, William Randolph Hearst and William Douglas of the Scripps-McRae League joined him there for a few days.

Jim had always loved the local fair, and now it was foundering. He and Sid Dowling bought it, Jim became president and they helped set it on its feet again. Sid was a long time friend and played on the indoor baseball team. Jim sponsored an "ugly mutt" sweepstakes and other events.

The Woodards were going to Europe this summer, and Ethel prevailed upon Jim for them to go, too. He was not enthused. But Carlotta's fiance had just died, and Jim thought it would be good for her to get away from things for awhile, even her studies at the University of Michigan. Maybe a trip to Europe would be good for her. He made the necessary arrangements to sail in August.

Jimmy was 15 that year and wanted a car. Jim went to one of the local dealer's to buy him one. He picked out a used car. "But, Mr. Curwood," the salesman said, "why don't you buy him a new one?"

"He can wreck a used one as well as a new one," Jim replied. His words turned out to be prophetic. Jimmy did just that. He lost control of his Packard sedan, went into a ditch and tipped over. He had turned out to let another car pass, he told his father, and skidded on the wet pavement. Jimmy's arm was believed broken and he was taken to Memorial Hospital where it was determined he was only bruised. The three other boys in the car were also only bruised and scratched.

The summer of 1925 was very hot. Many people across the country were dying in a heat wave in early June. Along the Shiawassee River, smelly rubbish littered the banks.

A special meeting of the Shiawassee Sportsmen's Club was held. They put up $200 to begin work cleaning up the river banks. Jim was appointed to the committee and members agreed to donate their time to the project. Within two days $1,000 had been donated to the project. Jim made a generous contribution. The committee met at Jim's castle to plan the cleanup drive.

Jim had been agitating for just such a cleanup for years. Five years before he had tried to get a river cleanup going and paid to have flyers printed calling on the "Friends of the River" to vote on several amendments to the city charter, including one that would put control of the river into the hands of the city commissioners. "But above all cast your vote for the Old Shiawassee, which we all love and along whose shores of which many of us were born, and many of us will die," the flyer urged.

Nothing much had ever been done. Now Jim was asked to decide where to put the dams that were deemed necessary. They were to be of fieldstone, and high enough to raise the river level so that the current could carry away most natural refuse, and to break up and aerate the waters.

In his usual prompt fashion, Jim quickly determined what he thought to be the best location for the dams and presented his plan to the committee.

Four or five men would begin the cleanup on Monday between Main and Shiawassee streets, where the river curved around the castle, and owners along that stretch were asked to cooperate by not adding refuse and by allowing refuse taken from the river to be put on their banks until it could be hauled away by the trucks being volunteered for this task.

A flat-bottomed scow, dubbed the "Shipyards," was built by Sturtevant and Blood Lumber Co. and launched for use in the cleanup. Volunteers were signing up in good numbers.

Jim, however, was not one of them. On June 21 he left for Detroit to take care of some business. His secretary, Charlotte Quinn, had been given the summer off and she left to take a literary course at the University of Michigan summer school.

Ethel, Viola and Jimmy joined Jim in Detroit. At the last minute, Carlotta decided not to go with them, preferring, she told her father, to "fight my battle alone." The family took the train to Quebec where they boarded the ocean liner "Empress of France."

They were off to Europe, Ethel and the children eagerly looking forward and Jim looking backward, already homesick for the north woods.

Chapter 27

Jim missed his prunes in Europe. Conditions were dirty, especially the toilet facilities, he complained. English women's bobbed hair gave him a headache. Every time he left his hotel he got lost. The trees in England were falling into decay. But what he really missed was the north woods.

"I wish I were back in Michigan," he moaned as they boarded the train in Paris on their way to Rome.

"Stay at home," he advised people back home. See America instead. Europe is flea-bitten, decaying, unprogressive, and everyone is out to gyp you, he said. More than a 150,000 American "fish" were in Paris, looking for something unusual with big, fishy, foolish eyes. If Wisconsin and Michigan's lake counties were brought to Europe, people from the United States would flock to them.

Nevertheless, he enjoyed himself. In London, he was honored at a dinner given by former premier Lloyd George. He visited the Museum of Natural History, and was so impressed with a slice of California redwood on display that he wrote an article, "My 2,000-Year-Old Friend."

They went to Germany and motored to the estate of Crown Prince Wilhelm near the Polish border. The Prince had happened upon some of Jim's books while in exile in Holland some years before, and had written Jim how much he'd liked them, and inviting Jim and his family to visit him if they ever came to Europe. Jim and the Prince strolled the grounds of the Prince's country estate and had long discussions about many subjects.

In Italy they met the King, and Benito Mussolini, a growing power in that country. Jim was recognized and touted wherever he went.

The Woodards were in Europe, too—Fred, Martha and the children, Pier, Dean and Florence. The two families met in Paris. Jim and Fred enjoyed their cigars and let the women and children do most of the sightseeing together. They all visited Frederick Frieseke, the celebrated painter from Owosso who now lived in France.

Ethel loved it all, but Jim was homesick.

"How I will love that cabin," he wrote Bruce Rutledge in Roscommon. He was lonesome for it, he said. "I wouldn't trade that cabin for all of Europe."

A telegram arrived with shocking news. Carlotta had run off and married a fellow student from the University of Michigan, Anthony Jirus. The deed was done, there was nothing Jim could do about it, but he fretted to be home to see for himself if his daughter was happy.

197

It was hot when they got home the last day of August after two months away. They took up their old activities. Jim was referee at a sports program at McCurdy Park in Corunna. The mah-jong games resumed when the Woodards returned a week after the Curwoods. Carlotta brought her new husband to meet her family. Jim was still reserved about whether she had done the right thing. Ethel's sister from Indiana came to visit.

A lot had been going on while they'd been gone. The river cleanup went well, but the dams Jim had proposed had been called impractical. The sewage needed to be removed from the river before could they install dams, the head of the state health department said. And the two low dams planned would not provide the flushing of the riverbed that was needed. There was already one dam just above Oliver Street, put in by the sugar beet factory years before. The other two were to be built just above the Washington Street bridge and just below the Main Street bridge near Jim's studio.

Four trees at the corner of Main and Washington streets had been cut down, the "last remaining vestige of a village." The two catalpas and two horse chestnuts had been planted there by Andrew Patterson, owner of the old National Hotel in the early days of the city. His widow had asked for them to remain as long as she was alive and she had died two years ago.

A "mechanical cop" was being planned for the main corners.

Central Fire Station moved from its old quarters into the new station on Water Street, abandoning the old building that had housed the horses on the first floor and city offices on the second some 60 years before.

Owosso was moving up into the modern age.

Most distressing to Jim, however, was that John Baird had been named head of a committee formed to force the state legislators to fulfill their conservation promises. This was done at an IWL meeting and was backed by 20 other sportsmen's groups.

"The Black Hunter" began in the September issue of *Cosmopolitan*. It had taken him 13 months to write this latest novel.

A parody of Jim and his work, "The Rollo Boys in the Curwood," written by Corey Ford, appeared in the September *Bookman Magazine*, making Jim smart under its ridiculing satire.

The Shiawassee County Sportsmen's Club met to plan a clubhouse on the riverbank near Corunna. Jim pledged $5,000 to establish a nucleus of the building fund.

Then, taking Judge Bush with him, he fled to the cabin up north.

Ethel and Martha were in their element, telling of their adventures in Europe. They described their trip to the ladies of the Women's Club, and Martha reported that she had persuaded Frederick Frieseke to paint a picture for the Club and the City of Owosso.

Up at Roscommon, Jim had had in mind for some time to build a new cabin to replace the old and very small one. Now materials were delivered under his supervision. He envisioned a "lodge" in the style remembered from the Canadian north country and described in several of his books. It would have a huge stone fireplace and would be kept primitive, without modern facilities, to give the kind of atmosphere he wanted for writing historical novels. He wanted a real retreat where he could be comfortable but shed any vestige of the city.

He came home in early November and wrote the dedication page for *The Black Hunter* in book form, then was away to Roscommon again. A few days later Ethel and the Bushes joined him. Jim and the Judge spent much of their time outdoors, walking in the woods and talking hunting and fishing. Then on one of their walks, Judge Bush suffered a heart attack. Jim helped him to lie down on the ground and hurried back to the cabin. Luckily, Ethel and her guests had driven up—Claude Smith was now their chauffeur. He was able to drive the car near the judge and they got him back to the cabin. The attack was a mild one, but it had been an anxious time.

Steele of the Royal Mounted was playing at the Lincoln Theatre in town. *The Ancient Highway* and *The Hunted Woman* were coming soon.

In each of the past six years Jim had written a book that had sold more than 100,000 copies. No other writer had had such success. They were stories of adventure and romance. And they were clean; Jim was proud of that. "People like to read clean books," Harold Kinsey said, and the popularity of Jim's books had proved him right. They were now being published in 16 languages.

With the publication in 1925 of *The Ancient Highway* and *Swift Lightning*, his dog series put into book form, and *The Black Hunter* due for publication next year as soon as the series had finished in *Cosmopolitan*, Jim had produced 28 books in 18 years, since *The Courage of Captain Plum* in 1908. One of his books, of course, was a collection of short stories and another his four personal essays, but they had been coupled with dozens of short stories and about 200 film scenarios.

Now he began work on a 29th novel, *The Plains of Abraham*, another historical novel set in Quebec. Gone were the days of adventure stories in the Canadian northwest and the colorful Northwest Mounted Police.

One morning that fall, Jim, Ethel, Fred and Martha drove out to see where the new sportsmen's clubhouse was to be built, but the roads were too muddy to reach it. They returned to the Woodards for one of Jim's favorite lunches, mush and milk, and an afternoon of mah-jong.

Will Dilg, hospitalized in St. Louis with cancer of the larynx and taking radium treatments, wrote members of the IWL asking them to pray for his recovery. Only their prayers had saved the IWL in its dark times, he said. But Dilg was no longer in favor with the IWL, and Jim had begun to doubt his support of Dilg and shied away from him.

It was to be another quiet winter of writing, mah-jong, small suppers and dinners out with the Woodards, evenings with the Bushes, family gatherings, visits from Viola at Christmas and of Carlotta and Tony, with Jim growing worried over the latter couple. Amy worried him, too, with her continuing poor health. Jim bought her and Jack a house on North Shiawassee Street two blocks north of his own house.

But Amy was unhappy there. She missed her familiar spot on the front stoop of the old apartment where she could sit in her rocker and watch familiar people going along Oliver Street. The house was barely three blocks away, only around the corner from Oliver Street, but the people were different. Jim, eager to have her happy, moved them back to their old apartment.

The Curwood Veterans were playing baseball again this winter. Jim imported Ike Command of Grand Rapids to pitch. It was an accepted thing to hire pitchers away from other teams to come and play against their own fellow townsmen or former teammates. Jim arranged for a doubleheader for New Year's Day between the Veterans and the Detroit All-Stars for the state championship. He would play, of course. His batting average this year was .454.

Many cities in lower Michigan and in Chicago and other cities had indoor baseball teams. It was a game that filled the winter months. Owosso had had, in the early part of the century, four teams. The West Town team had been the best and had won the "world championship" from the Chicago Spaldings. When the game was resurrected all the best players, like Johnny Shotwell, the Dowling brothers, Tunny Young and others, formed one team.

They played in the National Guard Armory, which the Guard allowed the city to use as a community center, as it was the only building with a large enough space. They used a big mushy ball to prevent its being hit beyond the reach of the indoor "field," and there were two shortstops, right and left. Jim played right. It was a game he loved.

Christmas Eve that year of 1925 was cold, dropping from eight degrees down to minus six degrees during the night, with heavy snow. Many roads were blocked Christmas Day.

The Curwoods and the Woodards continued their games of mah-jong that winter. Martha made 2,100 points one game. She and Jim were usually ahead.

Whenever the weather permitted, Jim went north. He often took the train to Roscommon and arranged to be met at the station and taken out to the cabin by horse and cutter. By now he knew most of the people in the little northern town and kept track of their activities. Approached by a school girl to buy a "tag" to benefit the basketball team, he gave her five dollars. When he heard how much the team needed money, he called the girl and took his five dollars back and wrote a check for $50 instead. When the team ended their season with an 18-4 record, he wrote a letter of congratulation and pledged $100 if the team needed money. Supt. H H. Robinson thanked him and wrote that indeed, the team did need money. Jim promptly sent his promised check.

Jim often stopped in town to talk to people. He told Robinson that winter he had enough work to keep him busy until he was a hundred. He spelled abominably and his grammar was worse, but others corrected those deficiencies.

A horse was kept at the cabin when Jim was there. He still liked to ride, and he walked and ran, snowshoed and skiied.

At the cabin that winter he worked on the autobiography he'd begun the winter before.

Jim had had a secretary for several years now. When the workload was heavy, he used young men and women from the Owosso Business School to do extra typing, or sometimes hired a second secretary for awhile.

There was always a lot of gossip in town about Jim. His quarrels with Ethel were well-known. So was his admiration for pretty girls. Parents and boyfriends hesitated about letting their daughters or sweethearts work for him.

In January, Charlotte Quinn left. Jim hired a local girl, Ruth Martin, as his secretary. She and Ethel became good friends and the gossips' tongues let her alone.

The Veterans suffered a number of injuries in the New Year's series. Ed Putnam slid into home base and hurt his neck. He played the second game—the All-Stars won both—but under such excruciating pain that he was taken to the hospital where it was found he'd broken his back. Then Sid Dowling injured his hand, Jim tore a ligament in his leg and splintered a finger, Sandy Sanderhoff twisted his knee, and third baseman Tunny Young fractured an ankle.

It was the end of the Curwood Veterans. Too many injuries, but more importantly, they no longer had a place to play.

The Community Center had ceased to function.

The Michigan National Guard's Co. G reclaimed the Armory and refused to come to any agreement for further use by the public. Jim, as president of the Center, was angry and upset. That evening Jim and Ethel went to the Woodards, but Jim was all in. He had not been able to sleep the night before, worrying over the situation. He was sick about the Center closing, as was everyone else interested in the youth of the city.

On Monday a group of men and women, including Ethel and Martha, met with the board of directors, officers of Co. G and state Guard officers for a last attempt to solve the differences. Jim was spokesman. The Guard agreed the Center could resume activities, but the Armory must be under control of the Guard.

It was an unsatisfactory arrangement, temporary and shaky at best.

Fred was appointed chairman and Jim a member of a committee appointed by the Chamber of Commerce to look into the matter of a proposed new hotel. Jim was becoming more deeply involved in local affairs, draining away more of his time.

He fled to the north again, to superintend the cutting of the huge logs for the lodge. It was very cold, but it was the kind of weather Jim liked, and the bracing air, the fresh snow and the hours out-of-doors revitalized him.

He returned for the dedication of Frederick Frieseke's painting, "Lady With the Sunshade," hung in the public library. Valued at $1,000, Frieseke gave the city the painting in honor of his late grandmother, Valetta Gould Graham of Owosso, who had also been a painter.

Jim was elected president of the Chamber of Commerce. A new high school was being proposed for Owosso and Jim wrote to his old friend George Campbell, editor of the *Evening Argus*, which had combined some years before with the *Owosso Press* and was now the *Argus-Press*, "I have recently sent my own 15-year-old boy away to school in the East, not because we want to get rid of him and not because we are not terribly lonesome without him, but simply because Owosso is not anywhere near up with the times in its educational opportunities." He didn't add that Jimmy had become almost more than he or Ethel could handle.

He revived his interest in conservation matters. This was an election year again, and he renewed his determination to get Groesbeck out of office, and thereby John Baird, too. He had had to stand aside when his opponents had won, but Jim had never admitted defeat and he was eager to get back into the fray.

Someone sent him pictures of some dead fish up near Bay City, and the sewer through which the refuse from the Michigan Sugar Company factory discharged into the Saginaw River. In place of the editorial he'd been asked to write for IWL's magazine, *Outdoor America*, he sent the pictures instead and a letter saying they answered the question of what was the most important phase of national conservation. He'd been trying for years to clean up situations such as this, which existed all over the United States.

Winter weather kept him at home, working in his castle studio. Weather permitting, he spent part of the afternoon horseback riding or walking. In summer he had played tennis or golfed at the new country club, though he disliked the social aspects of his membership there and had sworn when golf was introduced at the new club that he wasn't going to spend his time chasing a "damn fool ball" around.

Evenings and weekends, of course, were shared with family and friends. He no longer worked seven days a week and long into the nights.

In March Jim and Ethel went to Detroit for a few days. When they returned Jim went to a meeting of the Sportsmen's Club. The members were still trying to decide on a location for a new clubhouse as the first site chosen by the river near Corunna had proved unsuitable. About 75 members gathered for the meeting. Jim was chairman. Some thought was given to land west of town, and to a 20-acre site north of town, but no decision was reached.

March was cold and snowy. Jim, Ethel and Jimmy went to the Woodards' on Palm Sunday to play mah-jong and eat mush before the fire. April was not much better, coming in like a lion more like March.

Margaret Lord was the daughter of Rolla Lord, an Owosso businessman and a friend of Jim and Ethel's. She was a student at the University of Michigan and had written a play, *Becky Behave*. Jim went to see it and wrote her a note, complimenting her on her work. "I won't use the word genius," he said, "I prefer four other words, 'Hard work, determination and courage.'" If I can help you, he added, I'd be happy to do so.

Jim was always on the lookout for new talent, and Margaret Lord was only one of the many writers in which he took an interest. Sometimes these new authors were people he knew, like his friend's daughter, some were referred by friends—Ray Long brought several to his attention—and some were writers who contacted Jim. He never failed to do his best to find someone who would publish their work, or to give them an encouraging word. It was not that long ago that he'd been helped along himself.

In April Jim donated $5,000 to the Masons in memory of his father, to be used for finishing the new Masonic Temple. He'd already donated $1,000. He took his second degree in the Blue Lodge that month.

In addition to working on his novel that winter, Jim had written a long story, "The Crippled Lady of Peribonka," based on his visit to that northern Quebec village two years before. It was longer than he'd intended, and he sold it to *Cosmopolitan* as a two-part story. He planned now to expand it into another book.

However, he made arrangements for First National Pictures to offer it as a screen play for $25,000.

Jim went back up to Roscommon to oversee the building of the lodge and to work on his novel. After a few days alone, Ethel joined him, bringing Ruth Martin with her. Jim's secretaries usually accompanied him north, boarding at Robinson's or Corwin's, neighbors down the road. In the evening, when work was finished for the day, Jim, and Ethel when she was up north, walked them to their lodging, taking supper at one place or the other. Jim seldom did his own cooking in the evening when he was there alone.

Ethel came to the cabin at Roscommon often. She loved the out-of-doors almost as much as Jim. She was a good marksman, good at sports, and didn't mind roughing it. Her love of nature and outdoors activities were the bond that held her and Jim together. She was a good driver and Jim a terrible one—one time, coming home by car from Detroit, Jim was driving and Ethel fell asleep. She awoke to find Jim asleep and the car bumping down a railroad track! After that, when they traveled by automobile together and Claude was not along to drive them, Ethel did the driving.

The Woodards were frequent visitors at the cabin that spring. They usually drove up, making the hundred mile trip to Roscommon in less than four hours, stopping in Roscommon for lunch before taking the sand trail out to the cabin several miles northwest of town. Fishing, driving about the countryside, looking for deer in the evening, playing mah-jong and other games, and listening to Jim read from his latest writings kept them busy and eager to retire at the end of the day.

Other people, from Flint and Detroit, were making their way into the solitude of the woods. Clifford Durant, the Flint auto magnate, had bought several hundred acres a couple of years before and opened a resort for himself and his friends on the other side of Chase Creek from Jim.

Owosso decided the city needed an airport. Flying was safer than driving, people claimed, and a 30-acre site north of town was chosen. It was level land, with a level field adjacent in case of forced landings, free of wires and trees that would interfere with "flattening out" on approaches. Bud Hammond already operated a flying school there. The land fronted on M-57, the highway that went north to Saginaw, which was due to be paved next year.

The young people in town eyed it eagerly. Owosso was really becoming a modern city.

Chapter 28

"I Shall Live To Be 100" was published in June 1926 in *Hearst's Magazine*. In it Jim gave his recipe for maintaining the good health that would give him a long life. In reality, of course, he was suffering now from severe kidney problems, complicated by stomach distress and the periodic breakdowns in health he had suffered over the years due to overwork and emotional and mental strain.

All his life he had striven to keep himself physically fit with exercise, time in the open air, sensible food habits and moderation in drink. His one vice, perhaps, was his love of a good cigar.

But even as he wrote his article on long life that winter he knew that he would never live to be a hundred himself. He would, in fact, be lucky to reach half that age. That June he was 48.

Jim planned to hold a literary workshop on a 40-acre parcel of state land next to his Roscommon retreat, and enlisted the aid of Rep. Roy Woodruff to take the matter up with the forestry department. It did not come about.

He spent most of June at the Lodge.

Jim resigned as a director of the IWL and member of the editorial staff in protest over the ouster of Will Dilg. His scathing letter to the IWL was also sent to a number of newspapers and magazines. His comments drew a lot of fire from the new IWL president and bad feeling from some of the members.

Jim backed Dilg in what he considered an unfair dismissal as president of IWL, yet when Dilg wrote Jim asking for money for his fight for reinstatement, Jim refused. He didn't want to get into the fight, he said.

"I have found that my influence is tremendously greater since I stopped talking with my mouth about conservation. My writing reaches millions where my voice reached a few hundred."

The Izaak Walton League is doomed, he prophesized. He was backed in his stand with the IWL by editors of *Wild Life* and *Northern Trails* magazines who offered free use of their columns for his writings.

Later, when word leaked out about Dilg's alleged use of League money for entertaining lady friends and other personal uses while head of the IWL, Jim didn't know what was true or not, but he was now wondering.

Jim accepted the chairmanship of the education, publicity and good literature committee of the local Boy Scouts, but he was not often on hand that summer.

The young people were all home for the summer, except Carlotta who was now in Columbus, Ohio, with her husband. Jim believed it was not a particularly happy marriage but there wasn't much he could do about it. Viola was in the local social whirl. Jimmy brought home a friend from school, Scott Russell of New York City, and the boys raced around town in Jimmy's car, getting into scrapes and having fun.

Jack and Amy's first grandchild was born to Marquerite and her husband, Lt. Ralph Tate, in Maryland where they were stationed. Jack, Amy and Queen motored down to visit.

There was much visiting with Jim at Roscommon that summer. The new lodge was still under construction and the old cabin was very small. The boys camped out.

Residents in the Roscommon area and down around Houghton Lake were soon reporting being frightened by an old car with a California top tearing along the country roads, making a lot of racket and filled with young men pointing a gun out the window and shooting aimlessly at whatever caught their eye. The citizens were up in arms over these teenage desperadoes. Jim Bennett, owner of a grocery between Roscommon and Houghton Lake, wrote the authorities. They go by every morning, he said, headed south.

When officers finally stopped the car they found a load of youngsters and a "weak-lunged" BB gun. Driver of the car was Jimmy Curwood. His passengers were Dean Woodard, Scott Russell and Jimmy Clarkson of Owosso.

No real harm had been done, and the boys were not arrested. Being Jim Curwood's son probably helped. In fact, Bennett and several others announced they were "open for treats." Anyone passing could stop in for cigars.

It was not the end of Jimmy's escapades, however. He and his cousin Jack Gaylord II, Amy's grandson, often racketed around the Owosso area in Jimmy's car, once shocking officers when they were caught riding around naked.

Viola graduated from school and came home for the summer. A beautiful blonde 20-year-old and artistically talented, Jim wrote The Illustration League Art School in New York about getting her admitted. She was, he said, determined and ambitious, and he hoped for her to become a practical illustrator. Artist and publishing friends in New York had recommended their school as the best. "With my association in the magazine and book publishing fields," Jim wrote, "my daughter will have a rather unusual opportunity for developing her ability in the illustration line, if she really has that ability, which I sincerely believe she has."

She was, of course, admitted, and left for school in July, Scott Russell accompanying her on his way home.

The local sportsmen finally settled on five acres of land north of town for their new clubhouse. It was heavily timbered, with a level spot that could be used for games and shooting. Steep banks led down to the river and a sandy sloping beach already popular with swimmers. They bought it for $2,500 from

M. L. Bittell, who promptly donated $500 of the purchase price toward building of the clubhouse. Jim was on both the building and finance committees.

Work was begun in August. All bids for the work were turned down and the members decided to build it themselves.

It had been a very hot summer so far, but towards the end of July the heat wave finally broke. Ethel was a patroness for a party at the Owosso County Club held for the young people, but Jim didn't like such social affairs and didn't attend.

He was home for a few days as Jimmy prepared to leave on a 13-state motor trip with the Beacon Institute, but Jimmy was having problems with his ear and had to have it lanced. His friends, Jimmy Clarkson and Jack Ellis, left without him. Jimmy left a few days later to join the tour at Harrisburg, Pennsylvania, but he was back in a week. Jim had gone back up north and Ethel took Jimmy up to see his father.

The Black Hunter was out in book form. One critic wrote that "Curwood has always been able to take you out of a stodgy environment into far places..." Other critics claimed that readers either greatly liked or disliked his works.

The same could be said for Jim himself; people either greatly liked or disliked him.

Jim had been dickering all summer long with First National over "The Crippled Lady of Peribonka." He was asking $35,000 for the story, since it was a novelette instead of a short story. When they hadn't seemed interested, he'd offered it to Sam Goldfish of the Goldwyn studios. Now First National agreed to film it but wanted a name change. They didn't like using the word "crippled" in a title. Ray and Jim voted to keep the name, but finally agreed to "The White Savage." And Ray decided to run the story, not as a two-parter but as a full-length novelette in one issue, unheard of for *Cosmopolitan.*

On one of Jim's trips home in August he went to Detroit to put his financial affairs completely in the hands of the Detroit Trust Company. He signed an agreement that gave him $2,000 a month and gave allowances of $100 a month to Amy and $75 a month to Carlotta. He had a lot of stock in Arctic Ice Cream, which had bought out Connor Ice Cream Co. some years before, in Union Telephone Co. of Alma, Michigan, and in Independent Stove Co. of Owosso, and bonds for various public improvements in North and South Carolina, Texas, Ohio, Virginia and in Flint.

If he should die, everything was to be transferred to the executor of his will.

The end of August Ethel and Jimmy went to Roscommon to spend a few days with Jim. About eight o'clock, Jim and Ethel left Jimmy at the cabin while they walked Ruth down to Corwin's where she was rooming. It was a lovely evening and they enjoyed the walk.

They returned to find Jimmy crouching behind the bed with a revolver in his hand. He said he'd been lying down waiting for them when he heard someone trying to come in through a bedroom window. Jim went outside to look around, roamed about in the darkness awhile and then saw three figures near the new Lodge.

"What are you doing there?" he called. The men, at least he assumed they were men, threw rocks at him and ran. Jim fired five shots at them and they fired one back as they scrambled over a wire fence into the swamp. Jim found blood spots several places and figured he'd hit at least one.

Sheriff Bobbenmeyer of nearby Grayling was called to the scene and Jim offered $1,000 for information leading to the capture and conviction of the men. No one was ever arrested.

Bobbed hair was now the rage with women across the country, and Jim railed against it. A woman's crowning glory was her hair. He'd specified in his movie contracts that all actresses in films of his work must have long hair. He had forbidden Ethel and the girls to cut their hair.

He was so incensed by the new craze that he wrote an article, "Our Feminine Brothers," published in September 1926 in *Cosmopolitan*. The article stirred up such a controversy that bobbed hair clubs and long hair clubs were formed, and Jim received a lot of mail both pro and con his views.

Leon read the story in *Cosmopolitan*, cut off her long luxurious hair and sent it to Jim in a shoebox. "Why did she do this?" Jim asked Carlotta in dismay. He locked the box away in his safe.

The sale of "The Crippled Lady of Peribonka" to First National ran into a snag when the company claimed that its agreement called for purchasing the story after publication as a *serial* and a book. The serial had now become a novelette, published in one issue, and publication of the story as a book was to be sometime in the future. He withdrew the agreement and offered the story to other film makers.

All summer Jim had stood by as Fred Green fought Groesbeck for the Republican nomination for governor. He refused to be drawn into the fight. But when Green won overwhelmingly in September, Jim threw his support behind his old conservation friend and began working on his campaign. Comstock was Green's Democratic opponent. The Democrats were looking into Green's expenses, trying to find something to use against him.

Jim issued Green his usual invitation to join him at Roscommon but, Green replied, the Republican Central Committee had not yet blocked out his time so he didn't know how much would be his own. Ring him up when Jim was at home and they'd set up a meeting. Jim wanted to talk to him about the Conservation Department director's job. There were more applicants for that position than any other. Merrick Blair of Owosso was being considered, among others around the state.

"However," Green wrote Jim, "you need not fear as I am going to be very firm in this position. I am telling all of them that I will not consider anything until after election. I had in mind that you and I could canvass the situation very carefully first and then issue invitations for a conference."

I hope to get up to your "shack" at least for a day or two, he added.

Viola was home from art school but Jimmy had gone back to St. Luke's near Philadelphia which he had attended the year before. The family was often at Roscommon when Jim was there, watching the building of the new lodge. Ruth Martin was there whenever Jim was there. There was not the heavy correspondence there'd been when he was in the film-making business, or even at the beginning of his conservation fight, but Jim relied more and more on Ruth's assistance to take some of the burden off his shoulders and give him more free time.

The Ku Klux Klan, testing its strength in Owosso, and also the anti-parade law, held a parade that fall. Unwilling to take a stand, the police chief said it was up to the prosecutor to do something, and passing the buck further, the prosecutor said the state police were there, and anyway the law excepts religious, historical and patriotic organizations and the Klan says it is historical. Nothing was done.

Cecil B. DeMille offered to buy "The Crippled Lady of Peribonka" on an advance and percentage basis. That was the way Rex Beach handled his picture stories and he got twice as much money that way. Jim was skeptical. What would the advance be and how much would the percentage be? He wanted some idea of just what he'd get out of it. He was now expecting about $40,000 in an outright sale of the screen rights and he didn't much like the chance he'd take in DeMille's offer. They could come to no agreement, and the story stayed on the market.

The Michigan Conservation Congress met in October to adopt a platform regarding resident hunting, and proposed a $1.00 license fee for fishing licenses, the money to be used to buy land for wildlife refuges, forest preserves and public hunting and fishing grounds. Closing the season on partridge for the 1927 and 1928 seasons, the prohibition of the sale of Christmas trees except under state supervision, the abandonment of the state trapping system, and a return to the bounty system were advocated. Some of these were things Jim had urged for years.

Toward the end of October, Jim and Ethel went to the cabin to prepare for the annual visit from Ray Long and others from the newspaper and magazine publishing fields in New York. These visits were "play" time for Jim, with fishing or hunting during the days and long evening talks before the fireplace with his literary friends.

Green was elected governor in November by 130,000 votes. Jim promptly wrote him complaining about illegal deer hunting. Twenty does were killed last year between Roscommon and Grayling, he said, and now, only four days before deer season was to open, eight men from Flint had been caught with shotguns, two does and a buck near his cabin. They should have to spend ten years in jail, Jim fumed. Close the season for two years on deer, partridge and trout, he said. One night he'd heard shots only half a mile from his cabin. He'd investigated the next day and found where two or three deer had been killed and a car had come right to the place and carried them off.

Jim and Ethel planned to go to Europe again in the summer of 1927. Jim decided to learn French and sent for two copies of *Methode Berlitz for Children* and wrote Doubleday for a book, *French at Sight*, asking if this was what he'd need or was it "tourist French"?

In mid-November he and Ethel went to New York for a few days, Jim to take care of business and Ethel to spend a few days with Viola, now back studying at the art school.

They spent as much time as possible that fall at the cabin up north. Jim was working on his next book, a modern novel set in Detroit and a "ghost town" not far from his cabin. It was a radical departure from all he'd written before. The story began on the seamy side of modern-day Detroit and moved to the Michigan north woods near Roscommon, and of course there were to be the usual hero, villain and long-haired heroine.

Jim was a voracious reader, sending away for books on all sorts of topics. Among those he sent for that fall was one entitled *Outwitting Middle Age*.

He also read many magazines. Nicotine was no more harmful than the telling of a good joke, he read in one article. He fired off a letter to the author, a professor of Experimental Psychology, saying he'd given up smoking some years before. For twenty-five years he'd enjoyed his pipe and tobacco, Jim said. Smoking was one of his chief enjoyments on his northern expeditions, and he'd been smoking four to six cigars a day at home and in his studio. But he'd found his endurance was not as it had been before.

So he'd quit smoking, and within ten days he could see the difference. Within six months he could run a mile without being seriously winded, and his literary work had become better.

He'd also given up meat, he said. Of course, this was all mostly poppycock. There had been that time he and Ethel had gone on a meatless diet at Carlotta's urging, and he'd sneaked downtown for steak.

The first of December the cabin was finished. A special parking place had been made for tourists who came to watch while it was being built. He'd had to hire a watchman, too, he said. But now it was finished and they could move in.

The Welfare Drive that fall had a goal of only $11,000. Jim pledged $500 until he saw that the drive might fall short. Then he threatened to withdraw his pledge unless others gave more, and the final count was $13,023. "I wish I were there to help," he'd wired Muzzy, now back in Owosso and chairman of the drive, who replied that Jim's threat had done as much as the hours of work he'd spent when he was chairman.

In early December, Governor-elect Green appointed Leigh J. Young director of the Conservation Department and Jim a member of the Conservation Commission. Now, at last, he would be able to have a real say in saving the forests and wild life of his beloved Michigan.

On December 9, 1926, the new Shiawassee Conservation Club quarters were dedicated. Jim was in New York during final preparations, but rushed home to be on hand for the dedication ceremonies. A meeting followed the banquet. Jim pledged $1,000 above what he'd already given, and offered to match dollar for dollar any amount over what others pledged. The final pledge that evening was $1,600 and he kept his word.

Governor Green was announced as the speaker scheduled for the annual meeting in February.

Ray Long had left Hearst's organization and was now editor of *McCall's Magazine*. In late December Jim agreed to sell *McCall's* his autobiography, "The Glory of Living," for $20,000, to begin as a serial in the spring of 1928. Since he'd originally sold this to *Cosmopolitan* while Ray was still there, he withdrew it from them now and repaid the $6,000 advance he'd received from them. He also got *McCall's* permission for it to appear in the *Argus-Press* a month or so after its appearance in *McCall's*.

Plans were underway for its publication by Doubleday Page in the fall of 1928. But there was a slip-up in the Curtis Brown office in London, and both this and *The Crippled Lady of Peribonka* were published in England ahead of publication in the States.

At the end of December, John Baird resigned as director of the Conservation Department, as he'd promised to do if Green was elected, and the appointment of Young and the new commissioners was announced.

It had been six years since Jim had entered the fight to save Michigan's natural resources. The battle had been long and hard but finally, victory was at hand.

Chapter 29

The members of the Conservation Commission didn't wait for the new year to get down to work. They met on Friday, the last day of December 1926 and again on New Year's Day. They were stormy sessions.

Leigh J. Young had been appointed director of the department but his appointment hadn't yet been confirmed. Baird agreed to stay on until Young's appointment could be approved by the Senate the following week.

Edgar Cochran, commission secretary, wasn't there. Baird had fired him some weeks earlier, but Cochran didn't stay fired. Among the charges made against Cochran were that he "talked too much," that he'd "faked" his expense account, that he'd approved a bill for $380 for "biological work" for a friend, the Rev. William Merrill of Hillsdale, and had hired Glen Murphy, a game warden, to drive through Clinton County with a slogan on his car that read "KKK Vote for Green." Cochran had denied it all, of course, and had threatened to take the matter to court.

At the Friday session, Baird repeated these accusations. P.J. Lovejoy, special advisor for the Conservation Department, was appointed temporary secretary. But when Cochran stalked in later, the battle began.

After a fiery session, four commissioners, W.H. Wallace, chairman, Fred Z. Pantlind, George Miller and Charles E. Lawrence, resigned. Another member, Herman Lunden, said he was quitting, too, but would wait until someone was appointed to take his place. Howard B. Bloomer and T.F. Marsten were absent but it was supposed they would also resign, unless Green wanted them to stay.

Jim hadn't received his official appointment and no announcement was made as to who he would replace. He went up to the lodge. Young and other conservationists joined him there to talk over, in an "unofficial way," the situation in the state. Jim planned to survey the northern part of the state.

January 6, Green's appointments were made public. Bloomer was the only holdover. Besides Jim, the new members were Lee J. Smits, a newspaperman from Detroit and an old friend of Jim's; Harold H. Titus, a writer from Traverse City; Phillip Schumacher, an Ann Arbor merchant; Norman Hill, editor at Sault Ste. Marie; and John Duffy of Grand Rapids. Four of the seven members, then, were writers. Green ordered Cochran to resign.

The Shiawassee Conservation Club was elated at Jim's appointment. Its members had been leaders in the fight for conservation for a long time, and now they had a strong and direct voice on the state commission. Green had lauded the Shiawassee men as having done more than any other group in pioneering the conservation movement, and the club sent Green a wire commending him for his appointments of Jim and Leigh Young.

"One thing is certain in the appointment of Mr. Curwood," the *Argus-Press* editorialized, "and that will be the absence of politics in the consideration of conservation matters. It is the habit of Mr. Curwood to express himself freely ..."

Young echoed these sentiments and avowed that the department would be run free of politics. He asked all present department officers to remain until and unless they were proved incompetent. George Hogarth of Ionia was named secretary.

Jim was back in the thick of the conservation battle again. Smits came to see Jim, and they, with Ethel, the John McDonalds and Fred and Martha, attended a meeting at the Conservation Club. Smits was the evening's speaker. Smits, Jim claimed, knew "more about bird life in America and the underworld of Detroit than any other man alive."

Smits and Jim had spent a lot of evenings together in Detroit. He knew Jim, whose income came from writing as his own did, might write personal letters of 1,800 words arguing a disputed point in conservation. He was not a trimmer, Smits knew, nor a politician.

The two men saw eye to eye on most points, and Jim counted on Smits to back him in what he was fighting for on the Commission.

It snowed heavily the night of the banquet and the roads were closed until noon the next day, then the temperature dropped to eight degrees below zero.

On January 18 Jim went to Lansing to see Governor Green. He also saw Frank Rogers, state highway commissioner, and learned that plans were underway for the extension of M-47 all the way north from Owosso to Oakley. They would only go as far as Henderson first, and a half mile north of Owosso had already been done. The new sportsmen's clubhouse was halfway between these two points, so Jim was satisfied.

He also talked to Green about conservation matters, of course, and the next day was back in Lansing for a meeting of the commission. Smits wasn't able to be there. All but W.H. Loutit of Grand Haven, appointed in place of Duffy who found he wouldn't be able to serve, took the oath of office. Schumacher declined the chairmanship due to "private interests." There had been some talk of electing Jim chairman, but instead he nominated Bloomer as temporary chairman. Hogarth was appointed secretary.

Jim was named chairman of the Game and Fish committee, with Smits the only other member, and was appointed a member of the Parks and Recreation Committee.

He wasted no time in making recommendations for new game and fish laws, suggesting reorganization of the game and fire warden departments and the use of civil service tests in hiring personnel.

Jim also took care of a personal matter the middle of January. He saw his attorney and had his will drawn up. But he didn't yet sign it.

Ticket sales to the annual sportsmen's banquet at the new clubhouse had to be cut off at 1,100, but by the time the tickets were turned in, it was found that 1,400 had been sold. Seven directors were to be elected by the general membership and these directors would elect officers. Jim was expected to be one.

Jim had hired an agent, C.W. Griffus, some time before to handle the sale of "The Crippled Lady of Peribonka." Griffus claimed Jim owed him $2,500 agent's fee for this, but the story was still not being filmed. Jim turned it all over to his attorneys.

On February 2, Groundhog's Day—the sun was shining, which, according to legend, meant that the groundhog could see his shadow and there would be six more weeks of cold weather—the second meeting of the new members of the Conservation Commission was held in Lansing. Babbitt was reinstated as District 11 warden. Walter Hastings was hired to work in the department as a lecturer, showing his moving pictures of Michigan wildlife, birds and such, at a salary of $3,600 a year. Jim and other committee heads submitted their recommendations.

The next night the gala first meeting of Shiawassee sportsmen at their new clubhouse was held. Jim was honored and lauded for his work on behalf of Michigan conservation and his generosity which enabled the clubhouse to be built.

Carlotta and Tony came for a quick visit. Tony was now interning at Henry Ford Hospital in Detroit.

On Saturday, Jim, Ethel, Ruth Martin and Jack—Amy did not feel well enough for the long ride—left by motor for Englewood, Florida. Jim would finish his novel, *The Plains of Abraham* there, and get in a lot of fishing.

Shortly after they arrived, Jim broke his glasses. He sent them back to Owosso to Dr. Madison Gilbert with a letter saying that these were the only pair of glasses he could work with. His second pair which Dr. Gilbert had made for him made him dizzy. I think you're right that the ones the people at Ford Hospital made are too strong for me, he added. Isn't there a steel case for glasses, he asked. It would be better for him to carry when he was roughing it.

Jim finished his novel on March 15. This one had taken him 14 months to write. Even with help in the research of historical facts, the kind of books he was now writing took longer and longer.

It was a great relief to have it done at last, and he wrote jubilantly to Leigh Young, "Maybe you can imagine what that means."

He'd missed the March Conservation Commission meeting but he didn't put aside his concerns about commission business. Leigh Young had written asking why they couldn't wait longer before publicly rescinding bait fishing on trout streams, but did Young realize that trout fishing season opens May 1 and there was mighty little time to get this change into the papers? Jim replied. "I very much dislike to impress my own convictions on you," Jim said, but I have a "perfectly overwhelming sentiment against" unfair discrimination that takes bait fishing away from the farmer and small town population of our trout districts. Even rod and fly fishermen agree it's unfair.

Florida is going though the same tragic circumstances which robbed Michigan of her forest and wild life, Jim wrote Young. "Everything down here is being slaughtered almost without restraint."

"When everything is gone down here the people will wake up. Funny, isn't it, how we are compelled to be almost dead before we really realize what life is?"

They were starting for home by way of Washington on Sunday, and he'd be home by the next commission meeting.

"I will be mighty glad to get back. After all, I haven't yet found another State that equals Michigan."

The route home by way of Washington was fortunate for Jim. Wearing waders, he'd been hunting water moccasins near Englewood and a snake—or something—had bitten him on the upper thigh. It had been a pricking sensation, like that of a needle, and he'd not thought much of it then, but now it was giving him trouble and he stopped in Washington to see a doctor.

They stayed five days while a surgeon treated his wound. His leg improved and they set out again for home. Jimmy had met them in Washington, coming down from his school in Pennsylvania, and was riding home with them. Then he fell ill and they stopped again in Cleveland. Assured that Jimmy would be alright, Jim left him and Ethel there and continued on home by train. When Jimmy was better, he and his mother came on by automobile.

The April meeting of the Conservation Commission in Lansing went smoothly. Motions were made and passed unanimously. The commissioners made some appointments and approved some raises. They ordered a ban on taking fish from certain waters in Jackson County April 1 through June 15 for five years and on hunting any animal or bird in certain sections of Iosco County within the Michigan National Forest from May 1 on for five years.

Lands in several counties were designated as eligible for State Game Refuges. The commissioners passed other similar motions and recommendations and set two hearings on a ban on bait fishing. They agreed to look into several matters presented and set a season and limit on the shooting of woodcocks.

It was, all in all, a businesslike, productive and quiet meeting.

Members of the Shiawassee Conservation Club met at the clubhouse in mid-April to clean up the grounds. They worked until dark, then had supper.

Jim paid another installment on his pledge of $1,250, with another $220 still to be paid.

That spring Jim bought the land from his back property line to Oliver Street and sowed it to buckwheat in preparation for landscaping next year. He planned to have a terrace built in the side yard.

April 23 he headed north to the Lodge for several weeks.

Rumors were flying that Young, Jim and Lee Smits were about to resign from the commission. The governor denied it and said it was absurd. He had urged Young to put forth his conservation plans more rapidly, but there was no ill feeling about it. The rumors said the three were disappointed that appointments of game wardens had been turned over to Hogarth. Another rumor had Young dissatisfied that the State Legislature's House Ways and Means Committee had authorized raises for some department heads but denied one for him. Governor Green said the rumors were all wrong.

Jim was at the lodge and couldn't be reached for comment, but it was known to friends of the commissioners that all was not running as smoothly on the commission as appeared or as might be desired.

Jim came home for his great-niece Virginia's wedding May 1. He read the local papers with interest and noted that a new thing called television was the latest "child of science." It was to be like a radio with pictures.

Conservation Commission meetings were held May 4 and 5. Smits was absent, as was Bloomer. Loutit was appointed acting chairman.

The commissioners rescinded orders issued the previous year making it unlawful to take brook trout in any manner except the use of artifical flies in certain waters, and prescribing the number to be taken in one day, leaving in effect only the length, eight inches, of the catch.

They approved orders for closing a number of lakes and streams to fishing for various lengths of time, approved the dedication of certain lands for state game refuges, accepted some land in Mason County for a state park, approved some land purchases and rejected others, and adjourned for the day.

Jim presented a formal memo to the director and members that, as chairman of the Fish and Game Committee, he recommended the post of chief deputy, vacated by David R. Jones, be assumed by Col. George R. Hogarth, secretary of the commission.

Among the appointments made were those of Reuben S. Babbitt of Grayling as a warden, with a raise to $6.50 per day, recommended by Jim, and of Jim, Ernest Richardson of Roscommon, and several others as officers without compensation.

Young recommended the dismissal of John Speck as District Warden, motion made by Titus and seconded by Hill.

Baird had signed an order in May 1926 to close all streams in the state to fishing for brook trout for five years, except for rivers and streams as designated open by the Commission. Jim had investigated thoroughly, he said, and Young recommended that certain ones be opened. The motion was passed unanimously.

It seemed that rumors of disharmony among the commission members were false. Two days of meeting had produced many changes, quietly and efficiently. But Jim chafed that the commission was taking action on lesser matters and not getting down to the hard-hitting issues he felt were important.

He headed north for Roscommon and the peace of his lodge.

Chapter 30

The hills were white with juneberries as Jim drove north that May morning. His heart lifted with every mile. The smell of spring drifted in the open car windows and the dust rose in little spirals as the tires sped along the dirt roads.

Even those few days at home had him longing for the woods, that surcease from his troubles, balm to his soul. He had said it often enough, how he needed to get away into the woods.

For two weeks he would work on his new novel in the mornings, and conservation matters in the afternoons. He would talk to the men and woman and children who were the backbone of the conservation movement. They were the ones who counted, not those politicians down in Lansing. The politicians made his blood boil.

Now his mind was full of the investigation and analysis he planned to make of District II. After two weeks, he sent Young his report. If my recommendations are put into force, he said, District II will be one of the most efficiently organized in the state.

The district is a large one, he wrote, composed of four counties and is one of the worst fire hazards we have. On a whole, though, the residents were well pleased at the release of Peterson and Speck and the reinstatement of Rube Babbitt, and the district is ready to take an important step forward.

"You will recall that for a long time I have been recommending very strongly a man by the name of Mert McClure, in Roscommon, for District Warden." McClure, he said, has a splendid record, and is without doubt one of the three or four best woodsmen in the district. "HOWEVER, it has not at any time been my thought to oust a good man," and he recommended that Charles Hicking, now acting as District Warden, be given the position with McClure as his assistant. McClure, he thought, was the more valuable of the two men, but Hicking was entitled to his chance.

Hicking can be located in one part of the district, McClure in another, and the district will be well covered. Roscommon County, with two of the largest lakes in the state and many smaller ones, has only one warden; there should be two. If a second warden is appointed, I would appreciate the opportunity "to make a thorough investigation for the right man."

Hicking was a widower, he added, and "people say he is a splendid son to his old father and mother, which counts a lot with me."

But even there in the woods, from which he'd always drawn such strength and comfort, a feeling of oppression and fatigue overcame him at times.

He was back and forth often. Ethel was busy with her social affairs and trips to Flint and Lansing with the other women for shopping, swimming at the YWCA and attending plays and such.

John McDonald had left Arctic Creamery, the old Connor Ice Cream Company, for Detroit Creamery which now bought Freeman Dairy in Flint. He was made vice president and general manager and was moving to Flint. The two old friends would be closer.

Jim was not feeling well the first of June. His leg had not healed and he limped a bit.

Griffus was still complaining that Jim hadn't paid him his commission on "The Crippled Lady of Peribonka," which had still not been filmed, and Jim offered Doubleday a commission, too, if together they could sell the property. He wanted only to be rid of such troublesome matters.

In the meantime, Jim worked on a screen play for sale to Metro-Goldwyn, entitled "Freedom" and set in Borneo. He was also at work on his new novel and having trouble settling on a title. *Whip-Poor-Wills* was his first choice, *The Whip-Poor-Will* his second. He ran his pencil through this title, too, and wrote in a third one above it, *A Poet—And a Sinner.*

Ruth Martin was usually at the cabin with Jim. He had also hired a new literary assistant, Dorothea Bryant.

Bloomer and Smits were again absent at the two-day June meeting of the Conservation Commission. The members had investigated various matters, and now they voted to close the season on partridge for a year and on spikehorn deer, and to consider closing the season on squirrels and shorten the season on rabbits. A census of all fish in Michigan waters was to be made.

They voted to equip two fire stations in the Upper Peninsula with wire services so reports could be sent directly to Lansing, and asked that an investigation be made of the offer of the Hanson family to sell the state a large tract of virgin pine near Grayling for use as a state park.

For two days the commissioners made recommendations, denied or approved proposals, and appointed wardens, some without compensation, such as Earl Dutton and Ora Billman of Roscommon who had worked on Jim's lodge, and several from Owosso. They designated a number of state game refuges and approved the purchase of 10,500 acres at $3.75 per acre by the Pigeon River State Forest to enlarge the game refuge and public hunting grounds there.

Many of the actions of the Conservation Commission required enactment by the state legislature, and when the legislators failed to approve the new changes and laws the commissioners proposed, Jim called upon his fellow commissioners to use their discretionary power to override the lawmakers.

The discretionary power act gives us the only real power we have, Loutit said, "and we should use it with care." If we use it too often, he cautioned, it would certainly be repealed. "It was passed in the first place so that the commission would have power to act in cases of emergencies arising when the lawmakers are not in session. To issue these orders Mr. Curwood suggests would be abuse."

They discussed at length the right of the commission to revoke the open season on partridge without first holding an investigation, and decided at last that Jim's personal investigation was sufficient. They decided to have Young conduct a poll among sportsmen for recommendations as to closing the squirrel season, closing the season on deer, and shortening the rabbit season, all proposals Jim had made and on which he was anxious for them to take definite action.

He came away frustrated and disillusioned.

"The time is coming when the state of Michigan, north of line 20, will rival Yellowstone Park as a playground," Jim told a joint meeting of the Rotary and Exchange clubs of Cadillac in his first public speech since his appointment to the commission.

"The northern part of Michigan has a gold mine it its outdoor attractions and within a few years the residents will be wondering why they ever were discouraged because crops could not be raised," he said. The state legislature is not familiar with the problems, he said, and had "jockeyed some of the best bills and loaded them with conflicting amendments until the force of the laws were lost."

There is an increasing pressure to allow spearing of fish and for removal of other restrictions, "and the friends of wild life should do something to counteract this flood of petitions."

Michigan is "backward toward conservation," and it will take but a few seasons of open game laws to "depopulate the woods and streams..."

He'd had a new side view portrait taken and sent one now to *Bookman Magazine* for their files, if they wanted it. "I might die," he explained, "in which event it is possible you would be kind enough to use it."

Plans were going ahead for the next trip to Europe. This time they would take a place, probably in Italy, and stay the winter. He could write and Ethel could gallivant and sightsee all she wanted without dragging him along. They would find a good school for Jimmy.

Jim alternated between Roscommon and Owosso. At home the evenings were spent playing mah-jong with the Woodards, eating out, enjoying the first strawberries of the season, visiting family. Amy, never strong, worried him. He continued to have trouble with his leg. The old sore spot was aggravated when he was struck on it by a golf ball. His troublesome kidneys still plagued him. He paid the last of his last pledge on the conservation clubhouse.

Jim came home for the July meeting in Lansing. He submitted his report on muskrats, rabbits and hares, and on red, black and gray squirrels in the state. The commissioners voted to close the season on all squirrels for five years. They voted to shorten the rabbit and hare season and to close the muskrat season for two years.

Jim entered all three motions and the votes were unanimous.

The commissioners voted to close the season on deer hunting in three counties, and authorized Young to enter into a contract with Great Lakes Sand Co. to take sand and gravel off the bottom of Lake Michigan in designated places at ten cents a yard, if the company would pay for the sand and gravel it had already taken.

There was a long report on stream pollution presented by Homer Murphy, in charge of pollution control in the state.

Mert McClure was appointed assistant warden at Roscommon at a salary of $1,800 a year. They rescinded, on Jim's motion, the portion of a resolution passed by the old commission limiting the size of game refuges to eight sections of land.

The second day, July 7, began with a long report on the fish hatcheries of the state. The fish hatchery up at Sault Ste. Marie was to be used for propagation of such fish as, in Young's judgment, it was best suited for, and he could acquire a site and construct a building as he deemed necessary, upon advice of the Department's experts in fish culture.

Jim's report on the tract of pine at Grayling was entered, and his resolution concerning a uniform program of winter sports considered. The commissioners approved creation of Wilderness State Park, near the tip of the Lower Peninsula, and formalized their motions of the day before.

Jim was not satisfied with the two days' work. His fellow commissioners were "pussy-footers," he said, and were "passing the buck." They had voted for the motions he'd entered, of course, and approved his recommendation of McClure as a warden, but they were avoiding the most important issues.

He began work on a conservation article for *American Magazine* which would include Michigan's problems.

Jim held a conference at his studio with fish commissioners from New York and Michigan, and the three men discussed the merits of the propagation of muskellunge, which had been successful in New York and Wisconsin. They believed the fish would be successful in Michigan.

Jim had a strong following in St. Johns, 20 miles west of Owosso, and he gave publication rights to a series of articles he was writing on conservation to the *St. Johns Republican-News* which had always supported him and his views.

His leg was still bothering considerably and he turned down invitations to speak. The doctors couldn't seem to find a cure for the infection that persisted, and they had not been able to determine just what had bitten or stung him.

One of his conservation proposals was that the season be closed forever on spikehorn deer. The present law allowed the taking of a buck deer with horns three inches long or longer. But does were too often mistaken for spikehorns, especially by "flash hunters," those eager shooters who fire at the first flash of a deer in the woods. Jim's fellow commissioners had already told him they would oppose any such recommendation. Deer are increasing, they said, and we don't want to let them get a foothold and ruin farmers' crops. Those who are going to kill does will shoot them anyway, they said.

It was shaping up into the possibility of a bitter debate at the next meeting.

He wrote Harold Titus, a fellow writer of outdoor stories. I write an average of 500 words a day, he told Titus, and I'm lucky if I can get out a thousand words, and I work seven days a week. I urge you to build with the moving picture in mind, "that is where the money is."

Finally, he was able to go north. He wrote Lee Smits from there that he was glad he was with him on the spikehorn issue.

"But, Lee, I am growing tired—tired of fighting against the archaic ideas of the institution which calls itself a Conservation Department but which is in reality a butcher-shop." Even you, he said, who want to see wild life protected, hesitate about acting. He discussed his views on the subject of spearing fish.

"I am getting so terribly tired of it all. If we could only have a Conservation Department that could do constructive things and not eternally have in mind the barbed hook and the gun barrel.

"God knows I have spent practically all of my life next to nature, studying it and writing about it, and have gone through nearly every Conservation Department in the east and north, and they sometimes call me rabid because I stand for simple laws of clean conservation.

"...but I repeat, I am growing tired, so tired that I have got almost enough of it."

Even Green, whom he'd supported so strongly and helped get elected, doesn't understand, he said. It's costing me more than $100,000 to be on the commission, because I'm now writing only one book a year instead of two, Jim added.

"But I am so tired," he said again, "so worked out, after five months of almost constant energy expended on conservation matters, and simply to put across two or three simple things...that it does not seem that it will make much difference to me now what happens..."

When he was home again, he traded in his old car for a new seven-passenger Buick, paying $575 difference in cash, plus an extra $5.75 to get a different spare tire.

The plans for their winter in Italy were shaping up. He'd gotten a line on a villa they could rent for nine months for $1,500. His travel agent recommended they go to Tavrmina on the slope of the mountains where there was a magnificent view and which was near Greek and Roman antiquities.

The new garden and terrace were shaping up nicely, too.

Out in the shed in the back yard one day, Jim reached up on a ledge and felt something smooth and satiny. It was a snake. They weren't slimy creatures after all. He'd never be afraid of them again. "Why didn't I have the courage to touch one years ago?" he asked Ethel.

His first article in the St. Johns newspaper, "Protect the Spikehorn," appeared July 28. His next article, "Spears a Relic of Barbarism" was to appear in August. He signed his articles as chairman of the fish and game committee.

He made some changes to his will and signed it that date also.

Members of the Shiawassee Conservation Club threw their weight behind him on the spikehorn issue and sent a petition to the Conservation Commission endorsing his recommendation. The Michigan Game Congress was considering following suit, and its president wrote letters to member organizations asking them to support Jim.

Jim went to the August meeting full of hope that he could sway his fellow commissioners to his way of thinking. His leg bothered him greatly, he was running a fever and he felt very sick. But he couldn't hesitate now, not with sportsmen all behind him.

The members of the commission found Jim looking "brown, hard and keen," full of his usual vigor and enthusiastic predictions for the future of Michigan as another "Yellowstone." Only Smits had any idea that Jim was not well.

No action was taken on the spikehorn issue the first day, and fighting the fever and general feeling of ill health, Jim insisted on going back to Lansing for the second day's session.

The matter came up for discussion, and Jim, defending his ideas vigorously, got the backing of four members, but voting on his recommendation was postponed.

He went home, ill and disillusioned, and went to bed.

Chapter 31

The news that Jim was seriously ill spread rapidly. He had taken to bed on August 3, and by Friday, August 5, there was already talk that he might not live through this bout of illness. Nurses were been brought in to care for him.

On Saturday morning, Ruth went in to see him. He asked her to answer a letter for him, but it tired him to talk. He had rested better last night than the night before, but he was very weak. The doctor said his illness had been brought on by the strain of too much work and worry over a long period of time. The infection from the bite or sting, aggravated by the blow to the wound, had gained a strong hold on his system already weakened by his kidney problems and his mental and physical fatigue.

Jim had jotted down some thoughts after writing his article on how he would live to be a hundred. "Every machine weakens in some place," he had written. For him it was his kidneys. "Like a slackened suspender the resiliency is gone forever—then comes the infernal side-stepping this and that—until it becomes tiresome to a person knowing the futility of life." He should have had an operation long before. He had known that, and the consequences if he did not.

"A good strong kick by God (or nature) will bring your 'house of cards' tumbling down so thoroughly you will wonder in pain 'Where am I at'." Now there were no illusions but what he'd gotten his "kick by God."

He had wanted to write something "like Shakespeare, Goethe—Nietzsche or like Burbank—Edison...." The sadness of it was that, as he'd known when he jotted down his thoughts on what he'd done with his life, he'd "tried to please the proletariats and made money in my line —'but what a life'."

Tuesday morning he appeared to be passing the "critical" stage and the doctor held out hope that Jim would survive after all. He seemed a little easier and a bit stronger. The situation was still very grave, however. Jim had not rested well the night before.

Newspapers across the nation followed Jim's illness. Letters and messages poured into the house. Bulletins of his progress were requested by the Associated Press and other news agencies.

The house was full of quiet bustle and sober faces. Carlotta came home, but Viola, in New York, was also ill and not able to come. Ethel went about with drawn face and worried eyes.

A letter arrived from Thomas Cook & Son in Italy, answering Jim's request to find him a secretary. They had one in mind who could sepak Italian and Sicilian, and would find him a villa to rent, too. The letter was put aside.

Ruth answered Jim's correspondence as best she could, but she no longer troubled him about any of it. He was too weak.

He took a turn for the worse Tuesday night and failed to rally. He was delirious part of the time now, and sometimes in a sort of stupor. He slipped near the critical point again. The outcome had become "problematical," the doctor said. Each day inquiries as to his condition continued to pour in and messages arrived from his many well-wishers.

Jim continued to weaken on Wednesday. Two doctors from Ford Hospital in Detroit, Dr. Robert Burham, assistant to the chief of staff, and Dr. J.K. Ormond, a kidney specialist, were flown up to consult with Dr. Haviland and Dr. Hume. Their pilot couldn't find the small Hammond Airport north of town and, turning back toward the city, landed in a wheat field without mishap.

The doctors brought with them the latest technical apparatus and instruments. They gave him a mercurochrome treatment.

But the outcome, the doctors all agreed, depended largely on Jim's resistance in fighting the infection. If he can weather the next day or two, they said, there will be hope for recovery. Jim had always been a fighter and wouldn't give up, and this was largely responsible for the fact that he'd not been on the edge of death the entire time. They didn't know how tired of fighting he was.

A blood transfusion might help, the doctors said. Carlotta volunteered. She lay on a cot beside her father's bed and watched her blood pump from her veins into his. He rallied a bit, but it was only temporary. He weakened again, slipping further away. There was a slight complication during the blood transfusion, and the doctors tried to relieve it, but they stressed the seriousness of his condition. Frankly, they said, it was now very grave.

About two o'clock his kidneys ceased to function.

On Saturday, Jim's condition deteriorated further. He had been ill now for ten days. He was growing weaker and weaker, his heart action apparently failing. It was just a question of time.

All day the family sat by his bedside, waiting for the inevitable. Fred and Martha Woodard came by in the evening and found him very low. They left at ten to go home. "Poor Ethel," Martha said.

Jim had won almost all of his battles until now. There had been his struggle to get published, to be recognized as a writer, and now he was one of the highest paid and most widely read writers in the world.

People had tried to cheat him out of his money, but they'd found themselves on the losing side in court. Movie producers had stolen his material, and he'd bested them not only in court but in the trade magazines as well.

Friends had turned against him, but he'd stayed true. John Baird and Albert Stoll and Governor Groesbeck had been unequal to the task of destroying his beloved Michigan's precious natural resources, and he'd helped whip them out of office.

Even Ethel had fought him, but he had stayed firm and they'd come to an arrangement they could live with.

He had seemed to lose a few times, but in the end, things had come about his way.

He'd always won. But now he was in a fight with Death, and Death was to be the victor.

The doctors flown in so perilously from Detroit, with their modern treatments and fancy apparatus, the risky bedside blood transfusion from his valiant Carlotta, the vigils of his family, the thoughts and prayers of friends around the world—none of it was of any use at all.

The Great Arbiter was deciding this one, and the fight would be lost. Or won, depending on which way you looked at it. Hadn't he just written that death was not to be feared, that he would welcome it when the time came? And wasn't death the greatest adventure of them all? He'd had so many great adventures, and this would be the supreme one.

He'd written, oh, so long ago, about the Shiawassee River, "...and when I pass through the velvety twilight called death I am sure ...that it will be the spirit of my river which bears my soul on into the more splendid life which my faith teaches me I shall be about to enter joyfully."

And again, much later, writing about his embarking upon a life as a writer, that "nothing but death could stop me."

And now he was so tired. So very tired of it all.

At 11 p.m. on Saturday, the 13th of August, 1927, Jim Curwood died. Ethel, Carlotta and Jimmy were with him.

Family, friends, sportsmen and readers of his novels everywhere were stunned, in spite of the dire predictions that had been reported for more than a week.

"She keeps up bravely," Martha said of Ethel, taking roses from her garden to her friend on Sunday morning, "but her hands are so cold." Fred met with members of the Conservation Club to arrange a tribute to their friend who had been their staunch, supportive leader for so long.

The house was filled with friends. Martha and Ethel's other women friends arranged the flowers around the casket placed before the fireplace in the living room. Governor Green sent a tribute. A wreath of pink lilies came from Roscommon. Ethel's four brothers and families arrived from Indiana. Ray Long came from New York.

Downtown, the stores closed on Monday for Jim's funeral. Ray Long, Fred Woodard and John McDonald were among the pallbearers. Governor Green attended.

The funeral procession wound its way from the house on Williams Street, through downtown and past the theatres where so many of Jim's stories had been shown on film—closed today in his honor—and up the hill to the peaceful shaded hills of Oak Hill Cemetery where his mother and his father lay waiting.

Here James Oliver Curwood was laid to rest, in the spot he'd always known he would be, in the town he loved best.

His pen and his typewriter were stilled. His imagination would create no more stalwart heroes or dastardly villains, or beautiful but troubled heroines with long, flowing tresses.

Chapter 32
Epilogue

Jim's will was read the day after his funeral. The family gathered to hear a representative from the Detroit Trust Company tell them what Jim had planned for them all.

Ethel was to have the house, the castle and the furnishings in both, plus his personal effects. There were strings attached. If she died, or if she decided to no longer live there during her lifetime, the house would go, in turn, to Jimmy, Carlotta and Viola. As for the castle, if she didn't want it, it was to go to the City of Owosso. Jim envisioned it as a sort of memorial to him and his work.

Jimmy was to have the lodge at Roscommon.

There were three trust funds, one for each of the three children, with Ethel as a joint owner on each of them. The survivor of each trust was to take all remaining in the fund. He set aside an additional $25,000 for Jimmy, half to be paid when he turned 30, the rest when he was 40.

He left $10,000 each to Ed and Amy, and set aside $20,000 for Cora, to be paid out $300 quarterly for her care.

To his aunt Ida Griffin, his uncle Charles Griffin, his aunt Frankie Bain, his nieces Marquerite Tate and Queen Gaylord, and his cousin Golda Stretch, he left $2,500 each.

There were bequests of $5,000 each to the Dorcas Home (the orphanage) and Memorial Hospital, $750 each to Christ Church Episcopal, First Baptist, First Methodist, and St. Paul's Catholic churches and First Church of Scientist, and $1,000 to the Congregational Church.

He made provisions for grandchildren and great-grandchildren, but of course, there were none when he died.

Ethel got everything that was left.

In all, his estate totalled nearly a million dollars.

In spite of his generosity to his family and to his home town, there were some who thought he'd been mean to attach strings to Ethel's inheritance of the house and castle. But he had, in fact, left her a very wealthy woman.

Ethel became even wealthier within the next few years. Jimmy, always a hellion and growing wilder, went off on a trip around the world on a "floating university." He met a beautiful young woman from Montana, married her and brought her home to Owosso. Then he practically abandoned her to Ethel while he continued his reckless ways. His father had railed against the taverns in town many years before, but young Jimmy Curwood had not listened to his father's talk of the evils of drink.

In early May 1930, not quite three years after his father's death, Jimmy was issued his private pilot's license at Hammond Field. He was 19. Two years before, while learning to fly, he had crashed a plane at the airport. The plane had been damaged considerably, but no one was injured.

On May 8, 1930, he took two friends, Hugh Pate and Beatrice Pine, up for a spin. He had been up once that day and had a little trouble, and was advised not to go up again because of high winds and because he had been drinking. He went up anyway.

Coming in for a landing, the right wing of the plane struck a tree, shearing off some branches. The plane turned partway over and fell to the ground, nose downward but tilted slightly backward, saving the two passengers riding in the front cockpit. Jimmy, in the rear seat, suffered a broken neck and other injuries. He was taken to Memorial Hospital, to which his father had contributed so generously over the years. He died the next morning.

Ten years later, Viola, married and living in New York, died on December 6, 1940. She had no children. Viola was also somewhat of a rogue. People knew little of her other than her visits to her father.

Ethel, of course, became sole beneficiary of Jimmy's and Viola's trusts. She moved to California in the early 1940s and sold the house on Williams Street. Jimmy and Viola were both dead by then. Carlotta was married and didn't want it. Ethel turned the castle over to the city.

Along with the house went the furnishings. Without Carlotta's knowledge, Jim's personal things went, too—his manuscripts, books, pictures, business papers, correspondence, oil paintings of scenes from his books, and photographs. For 20 years these things lay in a warehouse in Lansing before Carlotta learned their whereabouts. Then she was forced to buy them back, at a sum she refused to disclose.

Ethel traveled a great deal and died in California on April 11, 1965.

This left Carlotta the sole survivor of Jim's estate. She had divorced Tony Jirus, married again, had one daughter, divorced again, and married her cousin Marguerite's widower, Ralph Tate. This marriage also ended in divorce, and she lived for many years in Florida before moving to Massachusetts to be with her daughter, Amy. Carlotta died in 1990, leaving Amy and her two sons, Kyle Curwood and Clinton James, great-grandsons of James Oliver.

The castle stood idle for many years, was used during World War II as a teen center, then was idle again until the Owosso Board of Education took it over for administrative offices, an ironical use of the writing studio of a man who had left Owosso schools before he could be told to leave. When the education offices were moved to new and larger quarters, the castle's fate remained in doubt. The city didn't really want it, and it stood idle again for several years.

The Shiawassee County Historical Society finally came to its rescue, and operates it as a museum much as Jim might have wanted. Many of the original furnishings have been found and returned to the castle. Carlotta donated many papers and pictures, movie posters and other items for display in the castle, but the bulk of his papers and things she gave to the Bentley Historical Library at the University of Michigan.

Up on the second floor of the castle's turret, Jim's typewriter sits on the old oilcloth-covered sewing machine stand his father fixed for him more than a hundred years ago. A walkway runs along the opposite side of the river, and a unique footbridge with stone towers crosses the river between the castle and one of the stone dams Jim planned so many years ago.

The castle is open now to visitors every afternoon, just as it was in the 1920s when Jim spent his mornings there doing his "literary work."

There was a bit of scandal after Jim's death. Charlotte Quinn put in a claim to the estate that Jim had gotten her pregnant, but the claim was thrown out. Charlotte had left Owosso many years before.

Three months after Jim's death, the Owosso Fair was discontinued.

As for his work, *The Plains of Abraham* was published in 1928, *The Crippled Lady of Peribonka* in 1929. Jim's autobiography was published in the United States in 1930 under the title *Son of the Forests. Green Timber*, the book he was writing at the time he died and which he had tentatively titled *A Poet—and a Sinner*, was finished by Dorothea A. Bryant, using the first several chapters Jim had completed and his notes and outline for the final chapters. Perhaps because it is so different from anything else he wrote, or because they didn't like his work being tampered with, many readers felt this book was not Jim's own work. Carlotta destroyed as many copies as she could get her hands on, claiming that "It's not my father's work."

A final book, *Falkner of the Inland Seas*, a collection of his early short stories of the lakes, was published in 1931.

Many of his short stories and articles have been reprinted in various magazines over the years, and many of his films remade—*The River's End* has been filmed at least four times—but most of them under different titles.

Bookman Magazine used the protrait he'd sent them only weeks before to illustrate the tribute written by Ray Long, entitled simply "Jim Curwood," published in the November 1927 issue.

Only two of his silent films, *Back to God's Country*, filmed in Canada's far north by Shipman-Curwood Productions and starring Nell Shipman, and *Nomads of the North*, made by James Oliver Curwood Productions with David Hartford directing, still exist.

Jim was lauded for weeks after his death in newspaper editorials and in magazines. The last articles he had written were printed with accompanying plaudits. His books were read and re-read, and for many years, *Kazan* and others of his nature books were required reading in some public schools, particularly in Canada.

Eventually, though, his fame as a writer faded, his exciting adventure stories forgotten or rejected as old-fashioned and out of date.

Even his hometown seemed to shrug and more or less forget Jim Curwood, once the national attention at his death subsided. His father's old friend and fellow sportsman, Merrick Blair, perhaps understood Jim best, if anyone could understand so complex a person. "If he had lived longer," Blair said, "the early antagonism between the boy and those who ridiculed him would have died and he would have become a much beloved citizen."

It is hard to say.

Certainly he left behind enough reminders—the nurse's home, the Elks and Masonic buildings, the hospital, the orphanage, the recipients of Welfare Fund drives, lovers of ice cream and the circus and the river, all of which benefitted from his concern and his generous financial support. Only the sportsmen remembered, and even they were somewhat late in honoring him at the clubhouse his money helped build.

And what of his conservation work? James Oliver Curwood was far-seeing and radical in his views of what should be done. It stands to reason that many people couldn't see what he saw so clearly.

At the September 1927 meeting of the Michigan Conservation Commission, his fellow commissioners passed a resolution honoring Jim and deploring "the loss of one to whom we had become affectionatly attached by association and by relation that will be treasured by us." Then they rescinded or destroyed almost all of the measures he had fought so hard—and possibly given his life—for. They revoked the ban on squirrel hunting and on shortening the season on rabbits.

"The trouble with Jim Curwood over at Lansing was that he was ten years ahead of his time in conservation ideals," the Shiawassee Sportsmen said of the commission's actions. "The politicians over there had no use for him because he had nothing to trade."

The sportsmen in Genessee County sent Leigh Young a letter berating the commission for its actions. The commissioners "didn't have the backbone to take and keep a decided stand when he was alive and facing them."

That's one thing Jim Curwood had—backbone. He took a stand and he faced his opponents, whether they were editors, movie producers, critics, or those against him in his fight to protect the forests, streams and wildlife of the state he loved best, Michigan.

The Books of James Oliver Curwood

1908 The Courage of Captain Plum
1908 The Gold Hunters
1909 The Great Lakes
1909 The Wolf Hunters
1910 The Danger Trail
1911 The Honor of the Big Snows
1911 Philip Steele of the Royal North West Mounted Police
1912 The Flower of the North
1913 Isobel
1914 Kazan
1915 God's Country and the Woman
1916 The Hunted Woman
1916 The Grizzly King
1917 Baree, Son of Kazan
1918 The Courage of Marge O'Doone
1919 Nomads of the North
1919 The River's End
1920 Back to God's Country (collection of short stories)
1920 The Valley of Silent Men
1921 God's Country–The Trail to Happiness
1921 The Golden Snare
1921 The Flaming Forest
1922 The Country Beyond
1923 The Alaskan
1924 A Gentleman of Courage
1925 The Ancient Highway
1926 Swift Lightning
1926 The Black Hunter
1928 The Plains of Abraham
1928 The Crippled Lady of Peribonka
1930 Green Timber
1930 Son of the Forests (Autobiography)
1931 Falkner of the Inland Seas (collection of short stories)